Natural Energy Boosters

Other Books by the Author

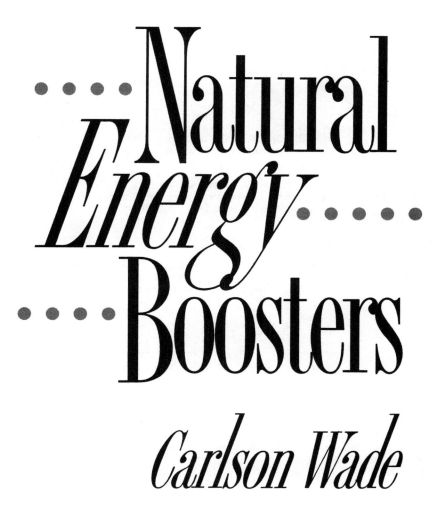

Natural Energy Boosters

Carlson Wade

PARKER PUBLISHING COMPANY
West Nyack, New York 10995

10 9 8 7 6 5

Library of Congress Cataloging-in-Publication Data

Wade, Carlson.
    Natural energy boosters / Carlson Wade.
        p. cm.
    Includes index.
    ISBN 0-13-026618-3 (case) ISBN 0-13-125215-8 (paper)
        1. Fatigue—Prevention.   2. Health. 3. Nutrition. I. Title.
RB150.F37C37   1993
613—dc20   93-25676
                                                                    CIP

ISBN 0-13-026618-3 (case)

ISBN 0-13-125215-8 (paper)

Parker Publishing Company
Career & Personal Development
West Nyack, NY 10995

Simon & Schuster

PRINTED IN THE UNITED STATES OF AMERICA

FOREWORD

Good health rarely just happens—we make it happen. We cannot choose our mothers or fathers, but we can control our eating, exercise, and living habits. Carlson Wade's latest book is an excellent treatise on what it takes to keep us healthy. He spells out the foods, the exercises, and the lifestyle changes that will keep us alive, vital, and full of energy.

People spend fortunes trying to find the beautiful spring of eternal youth. We all want to postpone old age. No cult, magic cure, or potion known to man in the past or present has succeeded in curing our people. What we have found is that nutrition and exercise can cure or prevent many of the ailments that afflict so many people as they begin to age. natural food, grown in fertile soil, free from pesticides, and eaten fresh and largely uncooked, is the food of youth.

Life, beauty, health, longevity, vigor, and youthfulness start on the dinner table, in the foods we choose to eat. There is life in live foods; there is death, old age, disease, and an early funeral in dead foods. Good red blood cannot come from junk foods. There is no health in excoriated white flour; no beauty in pie, cakes, and candies; no youthfulness in fried foods and chips; no vitality in soda crackers, pretzels, and cookies; no longevity in dead foods. In our processing of foods, we take out vital elements by the barrelful and put synthetic enricheners back in by the thimbleful.

Our diets and living habits are starting points toward changing and improving our lives. As you read this well-written and valuable health book, and incorporate its message into your daily lives, you will find an increased energy and zest for living. May you live forever or a little longer.

H.S. Holderby, M.D.
A Preventive Health Physician
73905 West Zircan Circle
Palm Desert, CA 92260

INTRODUCTION

What is energy? How can you increase its flow through your body and mind? Do you experience a mid-afternoon slump? Do you want to look younger, live longer and recharge your immune system?

NATURAL ENERGY BOOSTERS is designed to give you the answers to channel more energy into your life. Together we will take a good look at the foods you eat, the beverages you drink, your posture and level of physical activity, your mental habits, belief systems, and all important life choices. After a careful analysis of these factors, I'll give you step-by-step specific instructions for transforming a "tired all the time" feeling into a "bursting with life" state of mind. do you remember how you felt as a child with seemingly endless supplies of fresh, vibrant energy? Let's see how much of that we can recover.

The very word "fatigue" is enough to make you feel tired. Why do you become fatigued? How can you stimulate a tired body and mind and begin enjoying a more youthful lifespan? You need to identify the type of fatigue that is robbing you of the lifeforce and then create a simple daily program for supercharging your batteries for more youthful energy.

For some of you, only a few simple changes in your daily routine will help conquer fatigue. For others, more adjustments are needed. But fatigue, for whatever reason, can be overcome with the use of naturally occuring energy boosters.

No drugs, no medications, no chemicals, no potentially dangerous side effects. In their place, we will create a regimen of all natural remedies that are in harmony with your body. This book is a crystalization of the current research in nutrition, vitamin and mineral supplements, and brain chemistry. It has up-to-date discoveries that show you how you can embark on a lifetime program of vibrant living, rejuvenate your internal aging clock and boost your immune system so it becomes a fortress against infection. Additionally, I'll explain how to boost your brain power to enrich your life.

I have based this work on nearly two decades of journalistic research. It draws upon the work of physicians, biochemists, nutritionists, lab technicians, and naturopaths. Written in easy-to-understand terms, it is meant to serve as a helpful tool for all those who feel tired more often than they should.

I honestly believe that you can extend your prime years. You can add many productive years to your life, pep up your thinking, and maintain a positive joyful attitude toward life if you pay attention to your energy supply and banish its thieves forever. And I urge you to begin today.

Carlson Wade

CONTENTS

CHAPTER SIXTEEN: FOR WOMEN ONLY   223

CHAPTER SEVENTEEN: FOR MEN ONLY   237

···*One*

How to switch on your secret source of energy ... in minutes

Are you sick and tired of feeling sick and tired?

You are not alone! It's happening all around you. People from all walks of life are becoming fatigued which in turn brings on other ailments. The complaint is familiar. "I feel so tired." Or "I have no energy." In our land of plenty, it may seem unusual to find that fatigue is a common complaint. But it is.

The very word "fatigue" makes you tired! While it is true that your energy-level potentials are influenced by heredity, it is obvious that you are not enjoying your optimum level of activity for other reasons. You need to ignite your metabolism to get your energy sizzling; otherwise, fatigue will increase and short-circuit your potential for youthful vitality . . . at any age!

Fatigue: WHAT IS IT? HOW CAN IT BE WASHED AWAY?

Fatigue is like a fever—it is nonspecific in origin. It is a subjective sensation associated with different physical and emotional states or with certain social conditions.

Normal Versus Abnormal Fatigue

Of course, it is normal to get tired. Fatigue is the body's reaction to exertion that leads you to enjoy refreshing rest. But you may be plagued by undue fatigue that cuts short your participation in an average day's activities or makes you feel irritable or unpleasant.

"I'm Only Half Alive!"

Being unduly tired (fatigued) is a drain on your mental and physical capabilities. You are short-changed from the most that life has to offer. You lament that you are only half alive—or that you are an onlooker (not a participant) in the parade of life!

You are so accustomed to chronic tiredness that you hardly think of it. You manage to drag yourself around, from task to task, feeling worn out even at the start of the simplest of activities. Merely looking at a few pots to be washed is enough to leave you exhausted . . . before you have turned on the water! Are you only half alive? You *can* put more sizzle into your life with some basic adjustments that work in minutes!

Troublesome exhaustion is rarely the result of illness or depression or even just lack of sleep. It is the result of an energy-draining life-style. So you *can* revitalize your genetic programming and go from a shuffle to a sprint. How? Make these changes in your lifestyle and become recharged in no time.

1. *Banish boredom and put more sizzle in your life.* Become more active. Bring you fatigued body/mind to a social group. Get up and do something. Do some more good things for yourself. The very act of *doing* shakes away the doldrums that made you tired in the first place. Indulge in a secret passion. It will ignite your energy sparks to help you sizzle with joy.

2. *Become more physical.* Regular aerobic (oxygenation) activities will revitalize your body/mind in minutes. A 30-minute swim, a very brisk walk, doctor-approved jogging, any activity that gets you to oxygenate your tired cells will help get your pulse rate galloping. *Benefit:* You'll be feeding more oxygen-carrying hemoglobin to your red blood cells; your heart will release more blood with each beat so it works less to circulate it through your body. Physical activities will help your skeletal muscles use oxygen; your muscle cells become more fit in burning fats and fuel. Your breathing rate is balanced so you are not winded so easily. You will have more energy to expend. (Regular exercise helps you overcome stress, one of the biggest energy zappers.)

3. *Refresh yourself with a minibreak.* If your car's engine is about to conk out on the expressway, you rev it up. Suppose you're in

the middle of some tasks in the early afternoon and you feel fatigued. What to do? Take a break. Rev up yourself with a refreshing walk. Try some simple fatigue-busters: roll your head gently around for a moment or so; stretch and try to reach the ceiling or the sky; do simple body rolls. You'll have revved up your body motor! All it takes is five minutes.

4. *Plan your schedule according to your pace.* When are you more energetic? Morning, noon, later in the day? Arrange difficult tasks for those times when you're at your energy peak. Know the ticking of your biological clock. If you are more energetic at noontime, then schedule the more difficult chores at that time. You'll last longer!

5. *Avoid fatigue by avoiding sugar.* Refined sugar gives you a jolt, but you pay a penalty. Sure, a burst of sugar floods your bloodstream and prompts your body to release insulin, a hormone that gathers the sugar for storage. You feel energetic . . . for a short time. Soon, your "sugar high" becomes a "sugar low." Protect against this burst by avoiding sugar. Instead, opt for complex carbohydrates for more staying power. Complex carbohydrates are found in all grain products, fruits, vegetables, and legumes. *Tip:* Try a small amount of honey in a cup of herb tea for a more long-lasting energy boost. Honey is a concentrated sweet with an assortment of nutrients to help rev up your energy levels.

6. *Shed fatigue-causing overweight.* A heavy baggage of weight will tire you when you need to walk even a short distance. Physically carrying 20 or 30 heavy pounds will make you breathless with fatigue. Less weight—more energy!

7. *Wash away fatigue.* In particular, take a brisk shower rather than a soak in the tub. The needle-spray water (warm or comfortably cool) of a shower peps up your body and helps wash away fatigue. Falling water has a powerful energizing reaction owing to "negative ions" or molecules that have adopted an

extra electron. If you remain under the shower for an extended time, the negative ions in the air multiply to lower the levels of a brain chemical called serotonin (which makes you sleepy and tired) and make you much more energetic and cheerful. Ever notice how refreshed you feel when near a waterfall? At home you can wash away fatigue . . . in minutes.

8. *Eat a good breakfast.* During a typical night of sleep, you burn up 500 or more calories. Even if you are not hungry when you awaken, your body needs nutrients that have been depleted. These vitamins and minerals give you energy to face a brand-new day. Eat a serving of whole grain cereal moistened with low-fat milk or fruit juice with some slices of fresh fruit, a whole grain roll, bagel, or muffin with pure jam, a cup of caffeine-free beverage and you will feel natural energy almost from the start. If you skip breakfast, you face the risk of "dragging around" all morning . . . or all day.

9. *Eat a light but energizing lunch.* It's early afternoon and you face a slump. What's wrong? You probably ate a heavy lunch of animal fat and protein followed by a heavy, sweet dessert. You are the victim of what is called a "postprandial slump"— your body temperature drops, your work efficiency and mood are lowered, your eyelids are heavy, your words are slurred, you want a siesta. Avoid this drop with a light but energizing lunch: raw vegetables or salads in pita bread, a bowl of light vegetable soup, legumes in a salad, and caffeine-free beverage. You'll feel a power surge to give you day-long vitality in minutes.

10. *Avoid caffeine: it zaps your energy.* Whether in coffee, tea, soft drinks, or candies, caffeine is a time bomb that zaps your energy. Sure, caffeine sets off an insulin reaction, just as sugar does, and you have a burst of energy. But when the caffeine wears off, you become foggy, clumsy, groggy. Switch to caffeine-free products and you'll switch on your secret source of built-in energy . . . in minutes.

11. *Take B-complex vitamins for a buzz of energy.* Even if you have a marginal deficiency of B-complex vitamins, you could develop the blahs. These vitamins prompt your body to metabolize carbohydrates, fats, and proteins into fuel to give you pep and vigor. Plan your meals to include a daily variety of whole grain breads, cereals, pasta, oatmeal, peas, nuts, soybeans, potatoes, bananas, brewer's yeast, and lecithin.

12. *Change your scenery.* Even if you only get away from it all for a weekend, it is a surefire way to recharge your batteries. You need to change your routine. Physically separate yourself from your obligations. You will refresh your tired cells and tissues and open yourself to new activities. In brief, take your mind off one thing and focus it somewhere else. When you return, you are in a new perspective of seeing new things. You view your life in a new context and that is self-invigorating.

For starters, you have 12 different speedy energy boosters. Build them into your daily lifestyle and see yourself feeling revitalized, almost from the beginning.

CASE HISTORY—
Releases Energy for a Richer, More Productive Lifestyle

Joan H. not only felt tired, she looked exhausted—with a pale complexion, stooped posture, slurred speech, and a blank look. While she had responsibilities in running a household as well as a daily part-time job as a computer programmer, she always did have vitality until the last few years. And she was only 49. Would she have to give up her much-needed job? When she almost dozed off at her desk in early afternoon, Joan H. decided to see what was wrong with her energy levels.

A series if tests by her health practitioner, together with a profile of her daily activities, revealed the reason for her chronic and increasing fatigue. She had neglected her health. She was careless in her daily activities, ate heavy foods, drank too many caffeinated beverages, hardly exercised, and participated in few recreational activities. The practitioner suggested that Joan H. follow many of the preceding 12 remedies in remaking her lifestyle. It would be surprisingly easy. Better self-care from morning to evening was the prescription. Joan H. made a number of changes and within three days experienced more sustained energy. She felt more vigorous, looked more alert, had better posture, and spoke more clearly. Seeing the energy boosters at work, she easily adapted to the complete set of 12 remedies until four weeks later, she felt like a new person. She had tapped her hidden sources of energy by revitalizing her bodily systems so that she could overcome fatigue and enjoy youthful vim.

When Joan H. expressed her gratitude to her health practitioner, he added, "Your body gave you energy, with a little help from me . . . and you, too!"

THE INVISIBLE THREAT TO YOUR ENERGY

You can't always see it—but you hear it! *Noise.* It drains your energy, whether it comes from loud music, noisy sporting events, construction, vacuum cleaners, hair dryers, blenders, mixers, lawn mowers, snow blowers, stereo systems, street noises, work-related noise pollution!

You know you've been exposed to too much noise for too long when your ears begin to ring. You feel drained, even if you have done nothing. Noise has caused excessive blood pumping and an accelerated heartbeat that leaves you exhausted. Noise drains your energy!

How Much Is Too Much Noise?

Sound is measured by loudness—decibels—and by pitch—frequency. While a high-pitched sound may seem uncomfortable, loudness is the critical factor when it comes to your energy levels.

Ordinary conversation falls between 45 and 65 decibels. A busy street or loud headset might register 80 decibels. Subway trains can generate 100 decibels. *Danger:* Anything over 85 decibels can cause hearing damage and chronic fatigue. Exposure to noise over 125 decibels (for example, a jet taking off when you're standing near it) can leave you exhausted—and even cause permanent deafness. Chronic noise exposure damages the delicate hair cells of the inner ear, which cannot be repaired or replaced. You risk difficulties in communication and general fatigue and tiredness.

Beware Noise That Threatens Energy

A basic rule of thumb: if you cannot have a normal conversation, your environment is too loud and siphons away your energy. Get away from this invisible energy thief!

INSTANT PEP TONIC—IT REVITALIZES IN MINUTES

Feel tired? Want to wash away fatigue? How do you put pep back in your life? The secret is in the B-complex vitamins. This family of energizing nutrients is abundant in a food known as *brewer's yeast*, available in health food stores and many other food outlets. Brewer's yeast is a powerhouse of the B-complex nutrients which help beat tiredness and double your energy in a matter of moments. It will help you think better, function better, and resist depression or the blues. It will also give you a sparkling personality that eases feelings of tiredness.

How to Revitalize in Minutes

You can easily prepare the *Instant Pep Tonic*—one-half teaspoonful of brewer's yeast added to any fresh fruit or vegetable juice. Add a bit of honey for flavoring, if desired. Stir vigorously or process in the blender. Drink slowly.

Natural Energy Booster Benefit

The B-complex vitamins of the brewer's yeast join with the ascorbic acid (vitamin C) of the juice to stimulate activation of your sluggish enzyme systems for complete metabolization of carbohydrates. This stimulus helps increase muscular work. The *Instant Pep Tonic* promotes the onrush of many enzymes that activate metabolic responses involved in oxidation-reduction processes that help give you an abundance of energy. Nutrients in the tonic help form glucose from its storage form, glycogen, a dynamic source of energy. And the joy of the tonic is that is it quick acting.

Hints, Suggestions, Tips

Sprinkle a half-teaspoonful of brewer's yeast over whole grain cereals or add to soups or stews. Make up an amount in advance and put in a thermos container. When its time for a "coffee break," take an *Instant Pep Tonic* break instead and feel yourself pulsating with vitality.

CASE HISTORY—
"Sizzles" with Dynamic Energy in Four Days

George A. was called in by his supervisor, Fred S., who pointed to George's drop in furniture sales. George A. was told to perk up, and put more feeling in his efforts, or he might be demoted or worse, let go. Even as he listened to his supervisor, George A. felt his eyelids drooping and was overcome by an urge to sleep. He mumbled some promises.

In this situation, something unusual occurred. Fred S., himself, had once risked his livelihood (and life, too, as he kept falling asleep at the wheel while he traveled) because of recurring fatigue. But Fred had corrected this weakness in his immune system by taking the advice of a homeopathic physician who prescribed the *Instant Pep Tonic*. He wrote out the simple recipe, gave it to George A., explained how he had also been the victim of recurring tiredness, and told him to take two glasses of the tonic—one with his breakfast, another with his noon meal. The supervisor liked George A., considered him as his eventual successor, and wanted to help him as much as possible. This personal relationship did the trick.

George A. not only took the *Instant Pep Tonic* as directed, but changed his basic living methods based on the preceding 12-step revitalization program. Results? Within four days, he was not only wide awake, but sizzling with so much energy that he broke his previous sales record, was given awards and citations, and would soon be a supervisor when the present one moved elsewhere. And all this because of a surge in natural energy, thanks to the quick-acting *Instant Pep Tonic*.

Breathe Easy and Energize Yourself Quickly

"Another common, often overlooked cause of fatigue is simply breathing wrong," says Dr. Jack Soltanoff, a chiropractor-nutritionist practicing in West Hurley, New York. "Many of my patients who seek help are diagnosed as having chronic hyperventilation syndrome (HVS), which results from poor breathing patterns."

Fatigue-Causing Problem

HVS patients breathe shallowly and rapidly, leading to hyperventilation—the excessive loss of carbon dioxide. Dr. Soltanoff says, "Hyperventilation causes fatigue because the loss of carbon dioxide affects the blood's hemoglobin, making it less able to carry oxygen throughout the body. So even though you're breathing quickly, you're getting less air." Symptoms also include tingling, coldness, or numbness in the fingers, anxiety, and frequent sighing or yawning. "That's because you hold your breath to make up for the carbon dioxide lost in hyperventilating."

How to Correct Hyperventilation

First, Dr. Soltanoff suggests that you correct your posture. "Keep your tummy firmly tucked in when you stand up straight. You'll relax your diaphragm muscles and improve their movement during breathing. And try not to tense your muscles excessively."

Test Your Breathing

From a sitting or standing position, put one hand on your chest, one hand on your abdomen. As you breathe, both hands should rise with each breath. Either one or the other does not rise? Then you are probably taking shallow, rapid breaths and hyperventilating.

Natural Energy Booster

As you are reading this, correct your posture. Breathe in and out . . . fully. In and out . . . in and out. "If you breathe from your nose and keep your mouth closed, you will not hyperventilate—your nasal passages are too narrow. Repeat this easy exercise for a few moments whenever you feel tired or stressed. You'll soon refresh yourself and help energize your sluggish mind and body," says Dr. Soltanoff. "It's a natural energy booster I prescribe to my patients who are sick and tired of feeling sick and tired."

With this assortment of suggestions, you can wake up your tired body and enjoy the surge of youthful energy . . . at any age!

HIGHLIGHTS

1. Recurring fatigue can be eased and eliminated with one or more of the 12 natural energy-boosting programs outlined. Some work in minutes. Others will help revitalize your body and mind within a day or so. Start right now!

2. Joan H. was able to tap her hidden source of energy and release a powerhouse of youthful vitality in a matter of days, with the set of 12 natural energy boosters.

3. Be wary of noise—it is an energy robber.

4. The *Instant Pep Tonic* is brimming with nutrients that are specifically targeted to boost your energy. One or two glasses daily will help you wake up and live!

5. George A. saved himself from debilitating fatigue with the *Instant Pep Tonic*. It helped him sizzle with dynamic energy in only four days.

6. Dr. Jack Soltanoff shows how to breathe your way to new energy. There is a right and wrong way to breathing. See the difference in a minute.

Two

How to feed your brain to energize your lifestyle

Are you getting enough of the right nutrients to nourish your brain and keep you feeling alert and energetic? If you have difficulties in remembering names, dates, and places, your brain may be in need of certain nutrients found in everyday foods to help you sharpen your thinking abilities and enjoy a more energetic lifestyle.

Your thinking, your memory strength, and your intellect depend upon a well-nourished mind. Brain fatigue may well deplete your ability to think young and to act young. As you read this, your brain is changing biologically. It is filing away pieces of information as memory. Your brain is able to store knowledge but only if it is given the proper nutrients to protect against fatigue and so-called aging. And these nutrients are easily available in a variety of foods. You *can* feed your brain to energize your mind and body!

CHOLINE—STAR BRAIN FOOD

Can you remember the first words you said this morning? What did you have for dinner yesterday? Who was the last person you telephoned? If your think your memory needs some stimulation, try nutrition. The star nutrient is *choline,* a member of the B-complex family. It can enhance memory and revitalize your gray matter so you feel energetic all over.

The choline connection discovery was made by Richard J. Wurtman, M.D., neuroscientist of the Massachusetts Institute of Technology, Cambridge, Massachusetts. He found that choline is able to help treat such diverse conditions as a disabling disease called tardive dyskinesia, manic-depressive illness, and the common form of progressive senility known as Alzheimer's disease.

"In no sense here are we treating nutritional disease," says Dr. Wurtman. "We are simply taking advantage of a curiosity of the brain to treat nonnutritional diseases."

What Is Choline?

A B-complex member, choline is one of the few substances that is able to penetrate the so-called blood-brain barrier, which normally protects the brain against variations in the daily diet. When choline does so, it passes directly into the brain cells.

How Does Choline Energize the Brain?

This nutrient stimulates certain brain cells to produce acetylcholine, a central nervous system neurotransmitter that acts on other nerve cells and muscles and organs throughout the body. There is much evidence linking cells that use acetylcholine to the formation of memory. It is choline that helps feed and energize your brain in this manner.

Where Is Choline Found?

Present in many foods, choline is especially abundant in egg yolks, meat, and fish. But these foods are also high in fat and cholesterol, not to mention calories, which overburden your cells. Another excellent source is *lecithin*—a food made from soybeans or sunflower seeds, available as granules to be sprinkled over salads and cereals or added to muffins, puddings, and wherever the imagination leads. In the brain, lecithin will be transformed into acetylcholine, a vital compound for the transmission of messages from one nerve to another. *Superenergizing Benefit:* Lecithin acts as a stimulus to your memory and thinking ability. It revitalizes your brain and energizes your body, too!

Tasty Daily Brain-Energizing Food

Lecithin is a food that you can enjoy without limit. The usual recommended dose as a supplement to energize your brain is one or two tablespoons a day. You may eat it directly from the spoon—just chew it up like any other food—or, if you prefer, mix it with fruit or vegetable juice, using a blender. Although it does not dissolve readily, the granules do begin to disintegrate at once and will become part of your beverage in a minute or two. It is great with cereals, hot or cold. Try it with yogurt, too. In gravies and sauces, it gives a smoother and more stable result. It improves the workability of batter and baking mixture, and thus improves the quality of the finished product. Cooking does not cause any loss of nutritional value.

Simple Energizing Program

Plan to use about two tablespoons of lecithin daily in any of the tasty methods mentioned. You will feel your thinking become all the sharper, your memory much more vivid, and your overall energy capacity much more youthful than before. This is the power of choline!

Choline Improves Memory and Brain Energy

Robert H. Garrison, Jr., a registered pharmacist in San Diego, California, and author of *The Nutrition Desk Reference*, cheers choline as a remarkable brain energy food. "Choline is produced in the body and supplied in the diet as a component of lecithin (phosphatidylcholine). It is a constituent of acetylcholine, the neurotransmitter that is reduced in Alzheimer's disease.

"Studies testing the theory that dietary administration of choline increases acetylcholine levels and slows the progression of memory loss in Alzheimer's patients produced contradictory results.

"Supplementation with choline or purified soya lecithin (containing 90 percent phosphatidycholine) on a few occasions has improved brain function in patients with mild memory loss. . . . If choline or lecithin are useful in the treatment of Alzheimer's disease, they probably are most helpful in the early stages of short-term memory loss."

TRYPTOPHAN—FOOD FOR YOUR MIND

Tryptophan is an amino acid (protein by-product) that influences the neurotransmitter serotonin. Once tryptophan reaches the brain, it acts as a precursor: it signals the brain to make more of certain brain chemicals. Tryptophan is unique among amino acids in how it is affected by carbohydrates. Eating carbohydrates stimulates your body to secrete insulin, which in turn, prompts amino acids in the blood to be taken up into muscle. Tryptophan, however, is unaffected by insulin; it remains in the blood and is free to cross into the brain with little or no competition. *Bonus:* Tryptophan helps buffer the mental and physical effects of stress (an energy drainer) so you can think better and more clearly.

Food Sources of Tryptophan

Corn, brown rice, legumes, and most dairy products contain tryptophan. *Tip:* It is available in supplements, to be taken with the guidance of your health practitioner. Be careful, though, as tryptophan can cause sleepiness, which could explain contented drowsiness after a snack of milk and cookies. (Remember, it is the precursor to serotonin, which makes you very relaxed.) A little bit of tryptophan is all that is needed to refresh and regenerate your brain cells so you feel and think better.

TYROSINE—BRAIN STIMULANT

This amino acid increases the production of dopamine and norepinephrine, which buffer the effects of stress. You need these biological compounds (known as catecholamines) to regulate blood pressure, heart rate, muscle tone, brain metabolism, and nervous system function.

Tyrosin shields you from the brain shock of sudden, extreme stress. In this manner, your brain is able to function without the assault of external shock waves.

In reported situations, those people who took tyrosine performed better at mental tasks, had a significant edge in alertness or quick response. Furthermore, those who took this brain stimulant were less anxious or tense and felt their thinking to be much more youthful and clear.

Food Sources of Tyrosine

Common sources are meat, fish, and dairy products (but these may have too much fat or cholesterol that slow brain function). More favored sources are whole grains, soybeans, and legumes. Supplements are also available, to be taken with advice from your health practitioner.

Protect against brain fatigue. Revitalize your lifestyle with these important nutrients. They are food for thought!

CASE HISTORY—
Boosts Brain Power and Thinks Young Again

Oscar N. made increasing errors when teaching his junior high school class. His pupils scored poorly on tests and made many errors in their work. Oscar N.'s superintendent worried about this drop in performance enough to monitor a typical teaching session. That was when he observed that Oscar N. had difficulties in answering questions; he confused names and dates and would give wrong interpretations and answers. He fumbled his words. Something was amiss.

The superintendent suggested that Oscar N. be examined by a neurologist who also was aware of nutritional importance in basic health. Tests showed that Oscar N. was extremely deficient in choline and was starting to have very low levels of both tryptophan and tyrosine. The neurologist recommended a food program that emphasized these important nutrients. He also suggested that Oscar take four tablespoons of lecithin granules in a variety of ways, every single day. This soybean derivative was a powerhouse of these three nutrients that would penetrate the brain's blood barrier and start the release of neurotransmitters needed for better function.

Results? In ten days, Oscar N. experienced such a boost in brain power, he was as alert as a youngster (he was only 52) and spoke clearly and lucidly. His memory was so sharp, he could deliver names, dates, and places with rapid-fire answers. He had used foods to energize his brain . . . and his body, too!

Morning Brain Tonic

In a glass of fruit juice, add one tablespoon of lecithin granules. Add a bit of maple syrup or honey for flavor. Crush a tryptophan and tyrosine supplement capsule. Add to the tonic. Process in a blender for two minutes. Drink slowly.

Brain Energizing Benefit

The choline from the lecithin combines with the other two nutrients to be zipped up with the vitamin C of the fruit juice and the concentrated carbohydrates of the maple syrup or honey. In this potent package, the nutrients penetrate the brain's blood barrier in a matter of moments to encourage the release of those neurotransmitters that revitalize your thinking ability. The *Morning Brain Tonic* works swiftly and gently at the same time to sweep away sluggishness and give you a natural surge of energy that lasts well into early afternoon . . . and then some.

Boost your mental energies for an important meeting or any other activity with the *Morning Brain Tonic*. (And if you feel the need for a "brain lift" at any other time of the day, take the tonic again! While it works powerfully in the morning, it acts as a welcome booster at other times, too.)

Herbs to Help Energize Your Brain

Herbs will help pep up your body as well as your mind so you can not only feel better but think better (the two functions go together).

Here are some herbs that, traditionally, have been used to act as natural energy boosters for your brain.

Sage.   Herbalists have long believed that sage (meaning wisdom) could improve the vitality of the brain, enhance memory, and boost intelligence. This aromatic herb is flavorful as a tea, or as a brew, as recommended by your herbal pharmacist.

Rosemary.   In ancient Greece, students wore rosemary garlands to boost their powers of memory or recall. In *Hamlet*, Ophelia gives Hamlet a sprig, saying, "There's rosemary . . . for remembrance." Rosemary tea will help sweep away the cobwebs from your thoughts and help you understand daily matters with more clarity.

Ginkgo.   One of the oldest surviving herbs on earth, ginkgo reportedly is able to improve the blood flow to the brain, which simultaneously boosts memory and mental functioning. Ginkgo was recognized as being "youthful for the mind" in China's first great herbal text, the *Pen Tsao Ching* (The Classic of Herbs), attributed to legendary emperor/sage Shen Nung.

Ginseng.   The root of an ivylike groundcover, it is recognized as being the ultimate mind energizer—it enhances memory, boosts learning ability, and protects against assaults of stress. Ginseng has a fleshy, multibranded root. With a bit of imagination, some roots look like the human form, with limblike branches suggesting arms and legs. Ancient Chinese herbalists called the plant "man root" or *jen shen*, which became "ginseng." Shen Nung described ginseng as "enlightening the mind and increasing wisdom . . . continuous use leads to longevity." Herbalists have long recommended its use to energize the body and mind, to protect against so-called old age, lethargy, mental weakness. It is called the "root of immortality," which could be an exaggeration but certainly worth including as a natural energy booster.

In particular, ginseng is able to alert the immune system. It stimulates the manufacture of white blood cells (macrophages and natural killer cells) that detoxify dangerous microorganisms. Ginseng prompts the production of interferon, the natural virus-fighting substance, and creates detoxification that might otherwise cause fatigue and premature aging.

Wake up your sluggish metabolism with ginseng, available as a tea, among other forms to be used with the guidance of your herbal practitioner.

CASE HISTORY—
"Magic Tea" Boosts Speedy Day-Long Energy

Always active, Martha J. felt her energy slipping through her fingers, a little at a time, until it took her "forever" to get up in the morning; it was even more difficult to perform her usual household activities. She did part-time work at a local lodge, but her constant fatigue threatened even this small task. Was this what it meant to be old? she wondered, at the age of 56.

One day she forced herself to remain at the lodge after her work to listen to a herbal practitioner talk to the members. He explained how herbs have been used for thousands of years to help stimulate the body's natural healing processes . . . and in today's world with concern over safety of medicines, usage of herbs was becoming even more widespread.

After the lecture, Martha J. approached the herbalist and asked if anything could be done for her chronic tiredness. He immediately recommended she obtain herbal teas—sage, ginkgo, and ginseng. "Drink one cup of each tea daily, with a bit of lemon juice and honey, for a tasty treat. Give it two weeks . . . maybe less, maybe more . . . and see how it boosts your energy," was his advice.

Martha J. followed his suggestions. She enjoyed the three different teas and waited for results in two weeks. They happened in four days. She felt a heaviness lifted from her shoulders. Her thinking was sharp and clear. Her circulation had improved. Her energy was so upbeat, she awakened earlier than usual, did much more work than before, and even went to late-night parties with lodge members. Thanks to the power of herbal teas, her energy had been boosted . . . body and mind! Her age 56? She felt (and acted) like age 36!

Natural Ways to Boost Fuel for Thought

James F. Balch, M.D., of Greenfield, Indiana, author of *Prescription for Nutritional Healing,* offers advice for improving your memory and enhancing your energy potential.

"The B vitamins play an important role in maintaining memory, especially choline and B6 (pyridoxine). The amino acids are also very important. A diet that is nutritionally deficient and high in processed foods, junk foods, and fried foods may cause poor memory and concentration. A hormone imbalance may also cause memory loss. The brain could also be affected by allergies to certain foods."

Recommended Herbs

Dr. Balch recommends anise, blue cohosh, ginkgo, bilboa extract, ginseng, rosemary, and bee pollen for memory improvement.

Seven Steps to Better Memory

Dr. Balch offers these recommendations as natural means of improving memory and the brain power, too:

1. Consume the following foods often: whole grains, tofu, farm eggs, legumes, wheat germ, soybeans, fish, brewer's yeast, nuts, millet, brown rice, and raw foods.

2. Avoid dairy and wheat products for one month. If there is no memory improvement, slowly add these foods back to your diet.

3. Do not consume refined sugars—these "turn off" your brain!

4. An all-carbohydrate meal will adversely affect your memory. For a better memory, combine complex carbohydrates with

foods comprised of 10 percent protein and 10 percent essential fats.

5. Practice holding your breath for 30 seconds every hour for 30 days. This improves mental alertness.

6. Exercise is very important. Walking is an excellent form of brain exercise.

7. Keep yourself in an environment that makes you use your brain. Don't let boredom, restlessness, or depression take hold. Always keep doing things that are satisfying and stimulating to the mind.

How to Energize Your Memory Power

"What's that name again!" Or "Was that appointment for Tuesday or Thursday!" Then again, "I'm so sorry to be late for lunch. I completely forgot we had an appointment this afternoon."

Memory lapses! Forgetfulness! In today's activity-filled lifestyle, it is not unusual to forget a few basics such as the name of someone you met a short while ago or a few figures given to you an hour ago. But if you forget an important business or social appointment, you could be headed for embarrassment and trouble, too.

Science tells us that as the human brain evolved, there was less need for early man or woman to remember so much to survive, yet the modern brain has extra memory capacity that can be pressed into service with certain tricks of enhancement.

The following set of memory energizers stimulates an enzyme to manufacture acetylcholine, that important neurotransmitter that carries messages between neurons or brain cells.

Neurotransmitters are abundant in your hippocampus, a small cluster of brain cells involved in memory. Your goal is to energize or jog your production of neurotransmitter chemicals so you can think more clearly and remember much better.

With the use of these associative helps, such as making a rhyme for a person's name, an imprint is made in the brain. It energizes neurotransmitter function to give your hippocampus more memory recall. (Remember? You just read that!)

A set of memory joggers to give you better recall is offered by Erwin DiCyan, Ph.D., a Brooklyn, New York, psychotherapist who has helped many patients develop better memory power ranging from faces to entire pages and books. "Remember, you never lose the memory of something you learn. The problem lies in retrieving it."

Dr. DiCyan offers these memory joggers:

1. *Understand and repeat.* Make sure you thoroughly understand the topic or event you need to remember. Then repeat or review, saying out loud or even to yourself what you have just learned. *Example:* When introduced to someone, tack on the name to the "How do you do?" greeting. As often as possible, repeat the name during the conversation. You will better remember the name for future meetings.

2. *Use the association trick.* To remember something you have just learned, associate it with another item. Purchasing apples, bananas, and eggplant becomes, "Abe." Remembering Evelyn Zimmer becomes "EZ" or "easy." This "linkage" helps you recall names, dates, events, purchases, and so on.

3. *Use familiar rhymes.* Remember "Thirty days hath September"? It helped you remember how many days in the 12 months of the year. Use the same memory trick in current situations. *Examples:* Do you move the clock ahead for spring for daylight savings time? The rhyme, "Spring forward, fall back," energizes your memory. Make a simple rhyme and keep repeating until it can always be called into action.

4. *Make a word out of numbers.* Most telephone numbers or street addresses can be made into a word, much easier to remember than figures. *Example:* 487-2263 spells "husband." Make two words, if need be. Keep repeating it to help you remember the word-created number set.

5. *Correct your posture and boost your memory.* Can't think straight! Your posture may be putting a crimp on the blood supply to your brain. Basically, your brain requires up to 30 times more blood than other organs. But allowing your upper body to sag can create kinks in your spine that squeeze the two arteries passing through the spinal column to the brain, depriving adequate blood. What happens? Fuzzy thinking and forgetfulness, especially in the middle years. To improve memory and energize your brain, visualize a quiet getaway where you can think more clearly. Breathe deeply to give yourself energized awareness.

6. *Keep track of everyday objects.* Keys and glasses have an uncanny way of getting lost if you're not organized. Establish a place for them—a front hall, table, a desktop—and return them to the same place every time. Try giving your brain an extra boost by saying out loud, "Okay, keys, you're in my purse." Silly, but effective.

7. *Find your car in a big parking lot.* Distinguishing your car by attaching a red flag or styrofoam colored ball to the antenna is the easiest. Try to park in the same place every time you go to this lot. Look for a landmark nearby (but not another car; it may be gone when you return), describe the landmark out loud to use your eyes and ears for recall. You can also write down the aisle number.

8. *Find something you stored for safekeeping.* Did you hide your good jewelry from potential burglars before leaving on vacation and then forget where it is? Retrace your steps on the day you hid it. Call up the sounds, the weather, the smells. What else happened while looking for a place? Try focusing on the time you hid the jewelry as well as on the room and you are more likely to find it.

9. *Remember to turn off lights or the oven.* Define a sequence of the same activities each time you leave the house. Make it a

pattern. "Check the lights, the kitchen, pick up your keys, grab an umbrella" is a typical scenario to run through. *Tip:* A checklist posted by the door also helps if you need a visual reminder.

10. *Practice recalling facts from what you have read.* Do not read this book (or anything else) with TV or music or the radio playing. Avoid distractions. Don't try to read if your mind keeps wandering to something else. If you find yourself drifting, take time to concentrate on this distraction, get rid of it, then return to your reading. Make notes to remember important points.

Energize Your Brain

An alert memory, says Dr. DiCyan, may be your key to success. You've scored when you meet someone and can say, "Did you enjoy your five-day weekend vacation at the Hideaway Resort in the town of Hillcrest off the northern coast?" Wait . . . did you remember to greet the person by name? That would have made it perfect!

How to Energize Through Breathing

At least 60 minutes of vigorous aerobic exercise performed five times a week should help improve memory, reaction time, and reasoning ability. *Benefit:* Exercise sends more oxygen to the brain, enabling it to function with more energy. Try to schedule some form of aerobic activity (brisk walking, leisurely jogging, cycling, or swimming) for at least 60 minutes, five times a week. Be sure to check with your health practitioner before starting any exercise program.

FEED ENERGY TO YOUR BRAIN

The B-complex vitamins are vital in feeding energy to your brain. The role is extensive. These vitamins are coenzymes or catalysts, in many of the body's more important functions, particularly in the process of oxidation (burning of food into fuel or energy). This means that the B-complex vitamins are needed to supply your brain with its energy source: glucose. If deprived of glucose, your brain functions weakly. Tiredness, mood swings, fatigue, depression, and poor memory are only some of the symptoms.

With the B-complex vitamins, you actually feed energy to your brain so it is able to help you enjoy a more youthful lifestyle at any age.

Food sources include lecithin, such as whole grain and enriched breads and cereals, pasta, oatmeal, peas, dark green vegetables, mushrooms, brewer's yeast, soybeans, walnuts, bananas, and potatoes, as well as meats, milk, eggs, seafood.

It can be tasty to feed energy boosters to your brain! Refreshing, too!

Your brain is amazing. It weighs slightly more than 3 pounds and has about 100 billion nerve cells. Yet it conducts your life with every breath you take and with every bit of food you eat. With the use of natural energy boosters, you can enjoy a more vigorous life. Think about it!

HIGHLIGHTS

1. Choline is a brain food that can revitalize your thinking powers and energize your mind.

2. Lecithin is a tasty natural food that will energize your brain quickly. Take it in a variety of different ways.

3. Tryptophan is an amino acid that becomes food for your mind. Works speedily.

4. You can stimulate your sluggish brain with tyrosine, an amazing nutrient.

5. Oscar N. was able to boost brain power and safeguard his teaching job with the use of various mind foods.

6. You can wake up to a day of energy with the *Morning Brain Tonic*.

7. Herbs may be used to help energize your brain.

8. Martha J. used a "magic tea" (made of herbs) that gave her energy in a short time when she thought she was "getting old."

9. You can improve memory and brain power by following one doctor's set of seven steps that are quick to show results.

10. A psychotherapist offers ten suggestions to improve your memory and ease forgetfulness.

11. Aerobic fitness activities (as simple as brisk walking) can oxygenate your brain and help you think more youthfully.

12. Energizing B-complex vitamins send a stream of energy to your brain to make you feel glad and youthful all over!

Three

Hope and help
for chronic
fatigue syndrome

You feel deep-down dog-tired. Your partner says it's all in your head. You say it's in your head, your neck, your arms, your back, your legs. You're tired down to your toes. You're tired all the time. Something is draining your energy. A common complaint . . . often diagnosed as chronic fatigue syndrome. ("Syndrome" means a group of symptoms that occur together but can result from different causes.)

We all get tired; most of us, at times, have felt depressed. But the enigma known as chronic fatigue syndrome (CFS) is not the ups and downs we experience in everyday life, or even the temporary persistence of such feelings in response to exceptional physical or emotional stress. CFS is characterized as—a fatigue that comes on suddenly and is relentless, causing debilitating tiredness. It does not go away with a few good nights of sleep. Instead, it steals your energy over weeks and months and years.

WHAT IS CFS?

A complex illness characterized by incapacitating fatigue (experienced as exhaustion and extremely poor stamina), neurological problems, low-grade fevers, sore throats, headaches, dizziness, aching joints, difficulty in concentrating, memory lapses: these symptoms wax and wane but are often severely debilitating and may last for months or years.

Who Is at High Risk?

While all segments of the population are at risk, the most likely victims are women between the ages of 22 and 44.

Why Does It Happen?

Causes include emotional stress, hormonal derangements to immunological disorders, and various infections. CFS may represent a response to a viral illness that is associated with dysfunction of the immune system. The possible virus may be traced to many infections such as herpes, allergies, respiratory distress, and viruses yet to be discovered.

How Does It Begin?

The onset is often sudden but not alarming because many of its symptoms—headache, sore throat, low-grade fever, fatigue and weakness, tender lymph glands, muscle and joint aches, and inability to concentrate—mimic those of the flu. But whereas flu symptoms usually go away in a few days or weeks, CFS symptoms persist or recur frequently for more than six months.

CFS often begins after an acute infectious illness such as the flu, bronchitis, hepatitis, or gastrointestinal illness. For some, it follows a bout of mononucleosis, the "kissing disease" that temporarily saps the energy of younger people. CFS develops more gradually and seemingly with no apparent cause. In some situations, it begins during a stressful time, such as a career change, family problems, minor or major disruptions.

While many CFS-prone people say they feel depressed, it is not clear whether the depression caused CFS or developed later when patients are sick and tired of being tired. CFS victims are more likely to have allergies, and their immune systems may not produce the normal amount of substances needed to regulate the body's response to illness.

Looking For the Cause

A recurrence of the Epstein-Barr virus, which causes infectious mononucleosis and, after recovery, results in a lifelong (although usually latent) infection is a possible cause of CFS. It is theorized that the Epstein-Barr virus or other viruses slumbering in the body somehow are awakened to cause the disorder.

Is It Mononucleosis?

Also known as "mono" or "the kissing disease," nearly all cases are caused by the Epstein-Barr virus. Almost anyone at any age can get mononucleosis, although most documented cases involve persons between the ages of 15 and 30. No sex difference is established, but it seems to occur slightly more often in men than in women. The virus that causes most cases of mononucleosis infects certain salivary gland cells. Hence its nickname "the kissing disease." *Caution:* Sharing drinking glasses or beverage cans may also spread the disease.

Mononucleosis Symptoms

Tiredness, weakness, a general complaint of "not feeling well," headache, fatigue, chilliness, puffy eyelids, and a loss of appetite are all symptoms. Later, a familiar trio of symptoms appear: fever, sore throat, and swollen lymph glands, especially at the side and back of the neck, but also under the arm and groin. A fever of 101°F. to 105°F. lasts for approximately five days and sometimes intermittently for one to three weeks. The swollen lymph glands, varying in size from a bean to a small egg, are tender and firm. Swelling should gradually disappear over a few days or weeks. Difficulty in swallowing may accompany these symptoms.

It is believed that some cases of CFS are traced to Epstein-Barr virus and mononucleosis and as a means of helping to ease symptoms and promote a return of energy, basic improvements are suggested.

How to Ease Virus-Caused Fatigue

Avoid strenuous exercise. There is the possibility of damaging your spleen. (This internal organ is located high on the left side of the stomach, just underneath the diaphragm. It filters worn-out red blood cells and other foreign bodies from the bloodstream.) Other activity should be limited only by symptoms and how you feel.

There is no drug treatment for mononucleosis. Rest, plenty of fluids to guard against dehydration, and a well-balanced diet are recommended. Salt gargles are soothing for sore throats. Most cases should subside quickly with adequate rest.

It appears that there is not one cause for chronic fatigue syndrome, but rather a number of different factors that can trigger a similar set of symptoms.

To protect yourself against CFS, whether from Epstein-Barr syndrome or mononucleosis, you need to strengthen you body's immune system to minimize fatigue from any source.

NATURAL ENERGY BOOSTERS TO FREE YOURSELF FROM CHRONIC FATIGUE

While there is no proven cure for CFS and its related virus-causing problems, there are natural energy boosters that help overcome the symptoms and restore more vitality and well-being.

James F. Balch, M.D., of Greenfield, Indiana, and author of *Prescription for Natural Healing,* offers these home remedies:

1. *Herbs.* Combine or alternate the teas brewed from certain herbs—burdock root, dandelion, echinacia, goldenseal, and pau d'arco—and drink four to six cups daily.

2. *Digestive Help.* Make sure that you drink plenty of water—eight glasses a day—and juices that add fiber to your diet so that your bowels move daily.

3. *Foods to Avoid.* Shun fried foods, junk foods, and processed foods; eliminate stimulants including coffee, tea, and soft drinks; and avoid sugar and white flour products such as bread and spaghetti.

4. *Foods to Include.* Because a well-balanced diet contains 50 percent raw foods and fresh "live" juices, be sure that your diet

consists mostly of fruits, vegetables, whole grains, seeds, raw nuts, skinless turkey, and deep-water fish. These quality foods supply nutrients that ultimately renew energy and build immunity. Do *not* eat shellfish.

5. *Green Drink.* Take chlorophyll in tablet form or obtain the liquid of vegetables, such as a "green drink" from leafy greens, wheatgrass. Plenty of rest and a proper diet are very important. Take a protein supplement from a vegetable source—or a good vegetable protein drink for between meals.

6. *Avoid Aspirin.* Limit your use of aspirin, which may bring on Reye's syndrome, which occurs after a viral infection, most often the flu or chickenpox; symptoms are confusion, nausea, weakness, double vision, speech impairment, hearing loss, fatigue.

Dr. Balch adds, "Make sure you do not overexert yourself with heavy exercising." Do a small amount of exercise daily, even if only brief walks or stretching. Overexertion could worsen symptoms and may prolong the course of the illness. But most energy experts believe you should not stay in bed too long since this can be emotionally and physically devastating. Ration your limited energy . . . but make use of it!

CASE HISTORY—
"It's Not All in My Head!"

After going to different doctors, Noreen K. was all the more determined to find some healing for her recurring tiredness. Granted that chronic fatigue syndrome is a complicated illness, it does require a thorough medical workup, which this store supervisor did not receive. She complained of feeling tired, getting up exhausted, going home before quitting time, being unable to do simple sales, feeling depressed, and perhaps the worst, snapping at customers and co-workers. She felt she was falling apart.

Noreen K. dragged herself through her simple tasks, feeling a heavy weight on her shoulders, watching the clock to be able to go home and flop into bed. Then came restless sleep. She awakened more tired than when she went to bed!

She felt increasing depression, a common symptom of chronic fatigue. She went to a specialist in immune medicine who know of this condition since his wife had experienced it only recently. The doctor put Noreen K. through various tests (important for an exact diagnosis of CFS), which included immune studies (such as blood tests that looked at antibodies) and a general metabolic examination. So it was that she was diagnosed as having chronic fatigue syndrome.

Noreen K. complained, "It's all I can do to drive to the shopping mall, fill a small bag with groceries, and make it back home. I find it a tremendous effort to shop for anything else. Housework? I always could do it . . . but now it's neglected. Worse—I can't think clearly and feel all confused. Yet others said it was my imagination! Can you believe that?"

The immunologist told her the first good news she had heard since the problem began. "It is not all in your head! It may be caused by a virus. We'll help rebuild your immune system to supercharge your body with energy—to 'chase out' the offenders in your system."

Noreen K. was given a lifestyle improvement program—herbal teas, lots of water daily, inner cleansing with more fiber, foods to avoid, foods to include, and the important green drink. (See the preceding six-step energy-boosting plan upon which Noreen K.'s recovery was based.) To avoid overexertion, she was told to ask for part-time duties on her job for about two weeks. She needed to keep active, but within limits, namely, measured doses of taking-it-easy to ease some symptoms. On this program, it took close to three weeks before she felt an easing of her chronic tiredness. Her depression lifted, her temperament was brighter, and she became more cordial and pleasant to coworkers and friends. She soon resumed full-time work. She could soon do normal shopping and spring cleaning (although it was early winter). Her immunologist confirmed that this basic six-step plan had revitalized her defense system. She had been able to "knock out" the viral infection and was now bristling with energy. "I feel like telling everyone—it's *not* all in my head!" proclaimed the vibrant Noreen K.

CHASE FATIGUE WITH ZINC

Feel rundown? Always tired? Difficulty in coping? Think zinc! It is vital for energy boosting. Zinc is a trace mineral that promotes a healthy immune system and protects against fatigue—chronic or otherwise. Here are some of the ways:

- Zinc helps form insulin, which keeps your energy levels strong and persistent.
- Zinc synthesizes protein and metabolizes carbohydrates to revitalize your body and mind.
- Zinc helps you absorb many vitamins, especially the B-complex group, that you need for energy of body and mind.
- Zinc is involved in rebuilding cellular membranes, even genetic coding, so that you have greater resistance to the virus or other causative factors that bring on fatigue. You also need sufficient intake and absorption of zinc to maintain the proper concentrations of vitamin E in your blood to further enhance your immune system to free yourself from chronic fatigue.

Food Sources of Zinc

Zinc is found in legumes, whole grains, seafood, brewer's yeast, lima beans, mushrooms, pecans, pumpkin seeds, soy lecithin, soybeans, sunflower seeds.

Zinc Supplements: A Little Goes a Long Way

Daily intake of *less* than 100 milligrams will enhance your immune system response. *Careful:* Taking more than 100 milligrams can depress your immune system, so seek advice from your health practitioner on the amount you need.

CASE HISTORY—
Zinc Today, Fatigue-Free Tomorrow!

As his energy kept slipping through his fingers, Fred M. refused to believe that he was "getting old." He was in his middle fifties and had always displayed much energy as an active family man, automobile salesman, volunteer fireman in his hometown. So why was he "losing his touch"? Why was he falling asleep immediately after dinner? Why were mornings difficult when previously he would bounce out of bed with amazing vigor?

Fred M. had a thorough examination by his nutrition-minded family physician. The diagnosis was a weakened immune system; additionally, a viral infection with flulike symptoms refused to let go. He was becoming exhausted with the lingering illness.

Immediately, the physician put Fred M. on a less physical program . . . but with some activity. He then advised him to improve his nutrition: avoid fried foods; prepare meals with more whole grains, fruits, and vegetables; and drink lots of water for internal detoxification of the clinging virus. Then he recommended 50 milligrams daily of zinc . . . since tests showed that, with his chronic fatigue, he was seriously deficient in this mineral.

Fred M. followed the guidelines . . . but it was the zinc supplement that overturned the constant fatigue within a matter of weeks. He was able to bounce back with more vigor than before—proudly exclaiming that he had zapped his fatigue with zinc! (Actually, the doctor prescribed a diet containing foods high in zinc, too, so this was doubly helpful, in addition to the supplement.) He soon worked full time, joined a fitness class, and became an active member of his family and community. Zinc had made him new!

INHALE SCENTS AND SUPERCHARGE YOUR BODY AND MIND . . . IN MINUTES

It's a new scientific discovery as a natural energy booster—it's called aromatherapy!

Certain aromas will sharpen your thinking, ease weariness, revitalize your body. Scents, perfumes, aromas that you inhale can supercharge your body and your mind, too. You can help "breathe away fatigue" in a matter of minutes.

Scents Influence Your Mind, Mood, Body, Health

Charles Wysocki, Ph.D., an olfactory scientist at the Monell Chemical Senses Center, Philadelphia, Pennsylvania, explains that "an odor is first detected by the olfactory epithelium, a receptor sheet of cells located in the nose. This starts a chain of events that leads to an information flow to the olfactory bulb and the limbic system of the brain, which plays a key role in regulating body functions and the emotions.

"Smell," points out Dr. Wysocki, "is the only sensory system to project directly into the limbic system, making it perhaps your most basic, primitive sense. The study of scent is definitely on the increase. We've learned a lot, but we're a long way from fully understanding smell. We're still on a great adventure."

ENERGY BOOSTERS WITH REFRESHING SCENTS

A group of scientists presented their aromatherapy findings at the annual meeting of the American Association for the Advancement of Science to suggest that you can "recharge your body batteries," by taking a good whiff of certain scents.

Increased Vigor

William Dember, Ph.D., and Joel Warm, Ph.D., at the University of Cincinnati, tell of giving test subjects a whiff of peppermint or muguet (lily of the valley) through oxygen masks. Dr. Dember says that those receiving the fragrances performed 25 percent better than did those given only whiffs of pure air. (A replication study conducted by Raja Parasuraman, Ph.D., at Catholic University, Washington, D.C., achieved the same findings using only peppermint.)

How Scents Heal Fatigue

Dr. Dember explains, "Maybe what fragrance is doing is raising the level of physiological arousal." Another possibility as that "there's some sort of pharmacologic effect on the centers of the brain that affect alertness, something chemically special." It is believed that certain scents alert important chemical messengers in the brain, called neurotransmitters, that help overcome fatigue, chronic or occasional. Dr. Dember has much hope for scents as a means of increasing energy. "Truck drivers, even passenger car drivers, who need to keep alert while traveling long distances, could find it helpful."

More Energy in the Worksite

In a reported experiment to the American Association for the Advancement of Science, Japan's largest businesses use a computerized technique to deliver scents through air-conditioning ducts. Scents, say the Japanese, reduce stress and also boost energy and efficiency among workers.

In one study, 13 key-punch operators were monitored eight hours a day for a month. When the worksite was scented with lavender, errors per hour dropped 21 percent. When jasmine was introduced, errors dropped by 33 percent. When stimulating lemon was introduced, errors dropped by 54 percent.

Why Scents Are Energizing

Junichi Tagi, vice president of Shimizu's subsidiary, S. Technology Center America, Inc., in Boston, Massachusetts, says "These key-punch operators reported feeling better than they did without them." The fragrances were selected using the principles of aromatherapy, an ancient form of herbal medicine. It is believed that essential oils, the distilled essences of flowers, herbs, and plants, will revive the body and mind. These scientists and aromatherapists further believe that oils such as lavender and chamomile are relaxing, lemon and jasmine are stimulating, and pine and eucalyptus are invigorating.

Enjoy a Pine Forest

If you can! A mixture of molecules in pine helps make you feel invigorated. If you cannot make it to such a forest, then breathe in pine fragrances from a bottle.

Are "Sick Buildings" Making You Sick and Tired?

It's probable. Sealed in airtight buildings, you inhale smog molecules, carpet, paint, and other chemical odors. You inhale a soup of man-made chemicals in such compressed buildings. *Problem:* Your nose detects chemical molecules and feeds tiredness to your brain centers to make you feel tired and groggy. *Solution:* Seek more ventilation. Take frequent "fresh air breaks" by going outside for a walk in a park or cleaner air region. Carry small vials or bottles with perfumes and take occasional whiffs.

How to Cope While You Heal Fatigue

Having chronic fatigue can make you feel overwhelmed, out of control . . . like you are walking on an emotional tightrope. There are days when you may have a little energy for a while, and days when you cannot even pull yourself out of bed. There are days when you can be optimistic in spite of your limitations, and days when you are so depressed, you feel nothing can help. You need to stop wasting energy on feelings of anger, helplessness, frustration, and guilt—energy that could be used more productively.

For example, prioritize your life. When you have low energy, do what is urgent and forget everything else. If you don't feel like doing housework, don't do it. Do not push yourself. Ask for help. Let family members pitch in to do some shopping, cooking, cleaning.

Confined to bed? Keep your mind busy. Read uplifting books and magazines. Watch funny movies on a VCR. Try a low-energy hobby such as stamp collecting, knitting, fun-filled puzzles, or any-thing that keeps your mind busy when your body is weak.

If you find it too difficult to do gardening, switch to caring for some houseplants. Make your surroundings as pleasant and com-fortable as possible.

Get out as often as possible, even if it's just lying outside on a lawn chair. If you are too fatigued to go to a movie theater, but would enjoy some company, ask some friends over to watch television. *Important:* Socializing balances the feeling of isolation.

Anticipate problems and their solutions. Whenever you plan an activity, discuss potential problems. Contingency plans provide alternatives if problems arise. Rehearse what you would do if . . the car broke down on the highway . . . overwhelming fatigue hits while you are shopping . . . you missed connections while traveling.

Taking risks can be stressful, but careful planning and prepara-tion will reduce stress and make activities more enjoyable.

Listen to Your Body

Balance rest and activity. You are usually the best judge of when to stop and when to keep pushing. Always stop before you feel ex-hausted. Accept your limitations! If you are having a lot of really bad days, eliminate unnecessary tasks and, as suggested, delegate the others.

Pamper yourself. Listen to music. Light some scented candles. Take a perfumed bath. Read a stimulating book. Have reasonable expectations for yourself and for others.

Keep Your Sense of Humor

What's happening to you is not very funny, but looking for the bright side can make getting through difficult times more bearable. Humor is energizing! Family and friends hurt, too, when they see your difficulties. Try joking. It breaks the tension, makes you feel better. If you are so fatigued you spill something and make a mess, laugh it off by saying, "I learned this from my children." If you are embar-rassed because your intolerance to cold requires a lot of heavy clothes, make a joke by saying, "I'm trying to set a new fashion trend." Laughter can be a great natural energy booster! It's fun, too!

Hints, Tips, Suggestions

The good news is the CFS may not worsen over time, but appears to plateau and gradually improve. You may regain a satisfactory level of activity by regulating your lifestyle. This means sleeping at regular hours, eating properly, and learning to pace yourself and budget energy reserves.

Do not drop out of work completely (which may worsen the depression) but work on a part-time schedule or at home. Never push yourself to the point of collapse. Allow extra time to get things done. Meals should have adequate amounts of nutrients. You may feel better if you cut out sugar and keep fat to a minimum. Focus on learning to cope with chronic fatigue, and you've got the best initial energizer available.

Always sick and tired? Stop feeling sorry for yourself. It's not all in your head. It's CFS—and it can be overcome with natural energy boosters. Only you can make it happen!

HIGHLIGHTS

1. Chronic Fatigue Syndrome (CFS) is a total body exhaustion that can mimic flu symptoms but is longer lasting, unless healing methods are promptly brought into use. There is a relationship to mononucleosis and the Epstein-Barr virus disorders.
2. Follow the natural energy boosters as outlined by a physician to help free yourself from chronic fatigue.
3. Noreen K. insisted that fatigue was not all in her head and followed a self-renewal program that healed the disorder in a short time.
4. Zinc is a powerful mineral that fights fatigue quickly.
5. Fred M. used zinc to zap fatigue and become rejuvenated and energetic.

6. Inhaling certain fragrances—aromatherapy—can make you alert in body and mind.

7. A set of hints and suggestions help you cope with fatigue and speed up healing while you self-energize.

Four

Wake up
your tired
blood

Tired for no visible reason? Distracted and unable to think clearly? Irritable? Upset because you have difficulty in handling routine tasks? Chilly—even though others around you are warm?

If you've had any of these complaints on and off for weeks, you could have so-called "tired blood." It may lead to anemia. Nutritionally deficient blood can sap your energy, drain your emotions, and depress your immune system so you are at risk for serious illness. And it all begins with a feeling of tiredness that weakens you and makes you lethargic or . . . lazy!

IRON: NATURAL ENERGY BOOSTER

Dietary shortages of iron represent a most widespread nutritional deficiency. Familiarly known as "tired blood," the condition can bring on anemia with worsening of exhaustion. Iron is an important energy-boosting mineral needed to make healthy blood. It combines with protein in the foods you eat to form hemoglobin, a substance in the blood that carries oxygen to all of your body tissues, giving you a feeling of energy and youthfulness.

Women and Need for Iron

An adult woman's physiological need for iron is about 1.8 milligrams daily (the range is 1.2 to 2.0 milligrams). This amount will replace losses from menstruation and from normal bodily functions. Although an adult body contains only 4 to 5 grams of iron, this mineral is essential to every living cell. About 70 percent of this iron is in hemoglobin. (*Globin* is a protein and *heme* contains the iron in red blood cells.) Women need this iron to help protect against fatigue and the risk of anemia.

Danger: What Happens If Iron Is Deficient?

A small deficiency can sometimes exist for months or years before the fatigue symptoms are detected. When the iron stores are depleted and you do not take in enough iron from foods to meet your body's needs, the amount of hemoglobin produced drops; the red blood cells become small and pale. This is iron-deficiency anemia. If not corrected, such symptoms as easy fatigue, weakness, pallor, and shortness of breath may appear.

The physical working capacity becomes sharply reduced; there may be a lowered attention span and learning ability. You feel weak, constantly tired, or emotionally upset, and experience recurring fatigue. You face the risk of energy-zapping anemia . . . your blood cells are starved for oxygen!

Healthy Blood = Super Energy

The adult body contains approximately 5 to 6 quarts of blood. Each day, your heart pumps some 13,000 quarts to supply your body's cells with essential nutrients, energy, and oxygen. Your blood's red cells, which are its most abundant, transport oxygen. Your blood's white cells combat harmful microorganisms and other foreign matter. The platelets help the blood to clot. The cell-free plasma carries energizing nutrients, waste products, antibodies, hormones, and coagulation factors. So you see that the loss or serious depletion of any of these blood components is a risk to your health—and a serious drop in energy.

To enrich your bloodstream and boost your energy, several vital nutrients are needed on a daily basis.

IRON FOR MORE VITALITY

Iron is necessary for the functioning of all your body cells. Iron becomes part of hemoglobin, the red coloring matter in the blood, to carry oxygen from your lungs to your cells to help burn food for energy.

Iron, Anemia, Energy

An iron shortage that reduces the hemoglobin in the blood cells and reduces the blood's oxygen-carrying ability can lead to anemia, with its characteristic feelings of tiredness, irritability, poor attention span, pale complexion, breathlessness on exertion, brittle nails; prolonged iron deficiency saps energy, lowers resistance to infection.

How TO GET MORE ENERGY-PRODUCING IRON IN YOUR DIET

Dr. Brian L. G. Morgan of the Institute of Human Nutrition at the Columbia University College of Physicians and Surgeons of New York City, and author of *Nutrition Prescription,* has these suggestions:

- Consume a food high in iron. There are two kinds of iron in food source: *heme* iron in meat and *nonheme* iron in plant foods.
- For better absorption, increase your intake of vitamin C (foods such as citrus fruits, tomatoes, broccoli, cabbage, and bananas, for example) when eating foods that contain iron.
- Avoid caffeine products or those containing tannin (commercial tea) because they reduce your body's ability to absorb iron in the foods you eat.
- Take 300 milligrams of ferrous sulfate or ferrous gluconate supplements three times a day with meals and preferably with a rich source of vitamin C for better absorption.
- Do not take calcium or zinc supplements or antacids when you are taking iron supplements, since these decrease absorption.
- Foods rich in *phosphate* (almonds, whole grain cereals, cheese, nuts) *phytate* (wheat germ, wheat breads, cereals, nuts) or *oxalate* (coffee, tea, berries, whole wheat bread, rhubarb, spinach, cocoa) should be avoided when taking iron supplements.

Dr. Morgan also suggests, "In preparing food, steam your vegetables and cook your foods in iron pots whenever possible. Because iron can be leached from vegetables if they are cooked in large amounts of water, it is preferable to steam them. Also, the acids in foods being prepared in the kitchen leach iron from iron pots and pans, which then becomes available as dietary iron.

Food Sources of Iron

Vegetable sources of iron include whole grain cereals (especially if iron fortified; read the label), oatmeal, prune juice, dried apricots, blackstrap molasses, cooked lima beans, cooked kidney beans, cooked lentils, tofu, cooked peas, wheat germ. Animal sources include beef liver, chuck roast beef, ground beef, turkey, but these are high in fat, calories, and cholesterol so you may want to emphasize meatless sources. Make a compromise: occasionally have meat (choose lean varieties), then fill your iron needs with iron-rich plant foods.

Folic Acid Boosts Energy

A little-known nutrient, folic acid is involved in the production of red blood cells. A deficiency could lead to varying degrees of anemia and a feeling of tiredness, lethargy, and general weakness. Basically, your red blood cells, which carry the oxygen around your body, have a normal life span of 120 days; some cells must be replaced every day. A deficiency in folic acid could result in a reduction of old cells.

Food Sources of Folic Acid

All green vegetables are rich in folic acid (also known as folacin). Its name is taken from the Latin *folium*, meaning "leaf." Good sources are broccoli, cooked beets, chick peas (garbanzos), oranges, asparagus, romaine lettuce, kidney beans, banana, lentils, carrots, cauliflower, cantaloupe, and brussels sprouts. *Simple Folic Acid Plan:* Enjoy at least one raw fruit or vegetable every day. Cooking? Avoid copper utensils because this mineral destroys folic acid in cooking. Use stainless steel or glass pots.

Vitamin B12 Enriches the Bloodstream

Vitamin B12 is an essential for normal blood formation. Lack of this vitamin causes nerve tissue deterioration, which leads to a sore back, numbness and tingling in the feet, and the risk of pernicious or serious anemia. Early-warning signs include listlessness, fatigue (especially on exertion), palpitations, and lightheadedness. Vitamin B12 is needed to put new life into your aging blood cells.

Food Sources of Vitamin B12

A potent source is beef liver, but if you are concerned about the fat and cholesterol, alternative selections include salmon, sardines, and cheddar cheese. You may want to try a food supplement of B12 (with the approval of your health practitioner) to provide the body with this blood-building vitamin, if you prefer to avoid meat.

With these three basic nutrients, you can help enrich your bloodstream and feel more alive and energetic.

CASE HISTORY—
Boosts Resistance, Strengthens Immune System, Feels Younger with Energetic Bloodstream

Helen Y. felt herself growing weaker. Her complexion was sickish, her breathing was labored, she felt herself growing cold even when under the warm sun. She wore a sweater almost all the time. Her hands were so cold, she was embarrassed to shake hands with others. Even in the middle of the summer, Helen Y. had to sleep with warm socks and a woolen hat!

Catching colds and developing allergies made her weaker and weaker. Her immune system was depressed. She felt gloomy because of this constant tiredness. A visiting relative who was a practicing gynecologist suggested she "wake up" her "tired blood." Helen Y. was told to increase her intake of iron, folic acid, and vitamin B12 through everyday foods.

Simple Program

Breakfast includes iron-fortified oatmeal or cereal; lunch includes cooked beans with other foods; dinner includes cooked peas, lentils, and sun-dried apricots. Lean cuts of meat were optional.

Helen Y. could not believe it was so easy to eat her way to a younger bloodstream. She quickly nourished her cells with the three vital energy-boosting nutrients. Within four days, she was more energetic and active. Her hands and feet felt "as warm as sunshine." She had a stronger immune system. No more sniffles, allergies. She was a powerhouse of vitality. Simple foods had put new life into her "tired blood."

POWER-PACKED ENERGY DRINK

Add two tablespoons of blackstrap molasses to one glass of fresh fruit juice. Add chunks of sun-dried apricots and some pitted prunes. Process in blender for two minutes. Drink slowly.

Energy Booster Benefit

The iron in the molasses combines with the vitamin C of the fruit juice together with the folic acid of the apricots and prunes to speedily enter your bloodstream and nourish your cells. Oxygen speeds throughout your body, providing youthful warmth and a feeling of vitality. *Tip:* Crush a vitamin B supplement (dosage determined by your health practitioner) and add to the *Power-Packed Energy Drink.*

OXYGEN, BRAIN, IRON, ENERGY

Patrick Quillin, Ph.D., R.D., of southern California and author of *Healing Nutrients,* has this connection between energy and nutrition:

"The brain is an incredibly thirsty oxygen sponge. Although representing only about 5 percent of an adult's body weight, the brain uses up nearly 25 percent of the body's oxygen supply. After only a few minutes without oxygen, the brain quickly begins to deteriorate. Red blood cells deliver this vital oxygen supply to the brain. If the blood supply is low (anemia), changes in emotions or intellect result."

Food for Your Brain

Here we see the importance of the red blood cell–building nutrients. Dr. Quillin explains, "The brain demands a continuous flow of oxygen. Oxygen is delivered via red blood cells, which are built directly from the nutrients iron, copper, zinc, vitamin B6, protein, folacin, and vitamin B12. Although many people are given iron supplements for anemia, iron alone will not build red blood cells." You need this package of nutrients from food to help nourish your brain and energize your life.

Ten WAYS TO BEAT FATIGUE WITH AN "IRON FIST"

You know you have "tired blood" when you are constantly troubled with fatigue, feel light-headed, complain of sluggish thinking abilities. You lack energy because your blood lacks enough oxygen-carrying red cells. When your tissues and organs are malnourished or starved for oxygen, your entire body starts to weaken. You are always as worn out as your cells!

You need to provide sufficient iron together with the other nutrients that manufacture new red blood cells packed with hemoglobin, the red cell protein that transports the energizing oxygen.

"But I Eat Healthy Foods!"

I hope that you do. Suppose your breakfast is shredded wheat in low-fat milk, a slice of toast, a cup of coffee. Your lunch is a salad with low-fat cheese, some grapes, and iced tea. Your evening meal has some seafood, carrots and peas, rice, tea, and dessert. Is that healthy? Except for a few items (coffee, tea, dessert—if a pastry or

sugary confection), it has much going for it. Low in fat and cholesterol, high in fiber, calcium. So what is wrong? It is very low in iron!

Eating Habits Are Changing . . . for the Better and Worse

You omit red meats to reduce fats and cholesterol, but this cuts out
iron, copper, vitamin B12, zinc, to name a few blood-building energizers. Also, you need to balance the *combination* of foods to avoid
interaction with iron or copper to decrease the amount your body
absorbs. So while you are wise to adjust your eating programs for
low-fat, low-cholesterol, you need to make wiser changes so you will
be able to nourish your bloodstream no matter what changes you
make.

Here's the good news. You can beat your fatigue with an "iron
fist" that need not include the familiar beef and liver and organ
meats. Make some modifications. You *do* have choices. Here they are.

1. *Eating meat? Keep it lean.* Iron is not restricted to the fat of
   meat. Select smaller portions of lean, red meat for suitable iron
   and other nutrients. You will have the blood energizers without
   too much fat. Try poultry and fish, good iron sources, and
   usually lower in saturated fat than meat. *Tip:* You need not eat
   meat every day. One or two small portion a week should be
   enough.

2. *Combine lean meat with vegetables and grains.* Here is the
   energizing trick: *nonheme* iron found in plant foods is better
   absorbed with a small portion of meat and grains eaten at the
   same time. For example, have a very small portion of meat
   (poultry or fish, is desired) together with vegetables (beans,
   broccoli, lima beans, potato, squash, etc.) and some grains
   (Cream of Wheat, wheat germ, cooked noodles or spaghetti,
   any fortified breakfast cereal.)

3. *Be careful with calcium.* Dairy products may slightly block iron
   absorption because of a high calcium and phosphate content.
   Of course, you do want to continue with calcium-rich foods, but
   it is wise not to combine an iron-rich meal with too many

calcium or dairy foods. *Tip:* Do *not* take a calcium supplement with an iron supplement together. *Reason:* The calcium binds with the iron. *Tip:* Take them at different times of the day, perhaps eight hours apart.

4. *Consider meatless sources of iron.* Yes, you can obtain nonheme iron from plant products; while not as thoroughly absorbed as iron from meat, it can be an alternative source if you shun meat. Good sources are dried apricots, navy beans, broccoli, brussels sprouts, dates, lentils, lima beans, sun-dried peaches, peas, potatoes, prunes, raisins, squash, and tofu.

5. *Take vitamin C + iron foods to boost energy.* Vitamin C tends to promote better absorption of nonheme iron in fruits, vegetables, and fortified grains. This is good news if you want to avoid meat. A glass of orange juice with your cereal will more than double the amount of iron your body absorbs. (Now you understand why this combination in the morning gives you energy!) *Important:* This blood energizing takes place *only* if you eat the vitamin C food together with the iron food *at the same time.*

6. *Learn these fiber do's and don'ts.* Dietary fiber is important to control cholesterol overload and promote inner cleansing, but try not to have too much of a good thing. Certain fibers, as in bran, latch onto nonheme iron and push it speedily through the digestive system; the iron has little chance to nourish your blood cells. This could be a problem if you are on a high-fiber program. *Tip:* Have adequate amounts of fiber, but don't go overboard. Your daily fiber intake may be about 30 grams for a safe threshold.

7. *Avoid coffee and tea.* Can't avoid them? Make a change and do *not* drink with your meals. The caffeine and tannins in these beverages encircle iron, grab hold of it, make it less available. If you have a cup of coffee or tea with a high-iron meal, more than half of that iron cannot be absorbed and is "washed out" of your

body. Switch to coffee substitutes made from grains or herbal teas. Or, at least, wait several hours after a meal so iron can be absorbed before you indulge in these "no no" beverages.

8. *Use iron cookware.* When acidic foods such as tomato sauce are cooked in iron pans, some of the iron leaches into the food, providing an additional iron source. For example, a typical spaghetti sauce simmering in an iron pot for about 20 years will have its iron content increased up to ten times. Okay, the pot provides nonheme iron, but it is valuable in its own way in enriching your bloodstream.

9. *Choose iron-fortified foods.* Always popular are the enriched or iron-fortified breakfast cereals. But you need a variety of foods so be sure to read labels. *Tip:* If a product is fortified with vitamin C as well, it means the iron is all the better absorbed. This is your double whammy for superenergy!

10. *Plan to use supplements.* Discuss potencies with your health practitioner. You may find it difficult to meet your iron (along with other blood nutrients) from daily foods. Everyone skips meals on occasions, goes off a prepared diet, travels, and is unable to stick to a food plan. Supplements are helpful. *Tip:* If the supplement has iron and other minerals, take it with some orange juice because its vitamin C will promote top absorption.

You can superenergize your body and mind with the important blood-building vitamins and minerals with this easy and tasty ten-step plan. You will feel results almost from the first day.

Hints, Tips, Suggestions

- Dried peas and beans are good sources of iron and protein and should be enjoyed regularly.
- Lima beans, green peas, dark-green leafy vegetables such as kale, collards, and turnip greens are good sources of blood-building nutrients. Have them often.

- Sun-dried fruits used as a breakfast fruit, as dessert, or as a snack will increase iron in your bloodstream.
- Substituting blackstrap molasses for sugar in baked beans, gingerbread, and puddings will add to the flavor as well as the iron content of these foods.
- You have a big selection of iron-fortified foods: whole grain flour, bread, rolls, cereals, brown rice, cornmeal, macaroni, noodles. Be sure to read labels!

With these guidelines, you can see how easy and tasty (and energizing!!) if is to feed vitamins and minerals into your bloodstream.

CASE HISTORY—
Recharges with Sizzling Energy in Four Days

As an interior decorator, Janet G. was expected to be bursting with energy and enthusiasm. It was all part of her profession to stimulate sales of artistic decorations. She had to do considerable traveling, and this, no doubt, made it difficult to follow a healthful eating program.

Janet G. found herself feeling heavy, prematurely tired (yawning at 11:00 a.m. right in front of a client!), wanting to take more and more frequent naps . . . that became longer and longer in duration.

She might have ruined her career had it not been for an astute hematologist (specialist in blood disorders) who wanted her to decorate his new office. He saw that she wore a heavy sweater and dress, even though it was warm. Her hands were very cold. He shuddered when they shook! He observed her lethargy and lackadaisical attitude. It was as if she didn't care—yet he knew she loved decorating and this was not her personality!

He put her through a series of tests and discovered that her level of hemoglobin was very low because of a poor selection of foods, especially those high in iron and copper and zinc and the aforementioned nutrients. This was a cause of her fatigue, lack of stamina, and poor physical and professional performance. He outlined a simple plan to help energize her bloodstream and overcome the fatigue that was threatening her lifestyle: small portions of meat together with fruits and vegetables for better absorption. Janet G. was told to select packaged foods that were iron fortified. "Read the label," she was directed. He introduced her to the preceding set of ten steps to knock out her fatigue and self-energize with an "iron fist." He added, "A vitamin-mineral fist is more like it."

Janet G. followed the program . . . almost from the start, her red blood cells became so energized, she was wide awake all day long, disdained naps, discarded her heavy clothes, and was warm and vibrant. She received a bonus because of her youthful zealousness in creating a beautiful office for the doctor. And Janet G. became a ver in "iron power" for superenergy! She felt remade in ʳs!

ERGY PUNCH

add a half teaspoon of brewer's yeast (for vitamins several pitted prunes, chunks of sun-dried apricots, ɔured almost to the brim. Add a crushed vitamin B12 in blender for two minutes. Sprinkle with sun-dried ed. Then enjoy!

nefits

ıd mineral of the grains and fruits combine with the vitamin C of the juice and become absorbed with the vitamin B12 to exhilarate the oxygen carrying power of your bloodstream, to improve the level of hemoglobin, and to give you an almost "instant" surge of energy. A bonus is that in this combination, the energy is long lasting, for many hours. It's a great pickup! It lasts and lasts and lasts. (The raisins are also power-packed with vitamins and minerals; chew slowly to release these blood-building nutrients that will oxygenate your system and give you a feeling of being remade . . . in body and mind. (They go together.)

Do you feel like something the proverbial cat dragged in? And then dragged out again? You can revive-regenerate-remake yourself with a richer bloodstream. You have a variety of natural energy boosters to wake up your tired blood. Do it now!

HIGHLIGHTS

1. Iron is the star mineral in providing a superenergy booster. Read how you can enrich your bloodstream with iron if taken in certain ways that are compatible with your metabolism.

2. Protect yourself against anemia with the suggestions given for mineral improvement in your diet.

3. Be alert to the energy powers of lesser-known vitamins and minerals including folic acid, B12.

4. Helen Y. was able to use nutrition to energize her bloodstream and became all the younger in her approach to daily living.

5. Try the *Power-Packed Energy Drink* for "instant vitality." You can even put it in a thermos and take it along to work or on travels and enjoy a small amount for a speedy pickup.

6. Nourish your brain with iron-carrying oxygen and enjoy super energy very quickly. Try the "brain foods" described.

7. You can beat fatigue with an "iron fist" with the ten suggestions. Easy to follow, quick to show energetic results.

8. Janet G. supercharged herself with energy after following this ten-step plan as recommended by her client, a hematologist.

9. The *Superenergy Punch* packs a wallop in terms of energy! And it's meatless, too!

...Five

Mood foods –
they make you mad,
sad, or glad

You're in the mood. Or *not* in the mood. You feel upset, unhappy, or energetic. These are mood swings. They go up and down and in other directions. You can set your moods on the right course with the right foods that add, instead of deplete, energy.

Physical exhaustion is a "healthy tired" feeling. Mental exhaustion wears you out. Why do you constantly feel fatigued? Why do you tire so easily? You may be wearing yourself out because of the wrong foods. Can you feed yourself high-octane energy to make you feel cheerful?

You *can* gain control of your moods with a nutritional program that puts sizzle into your energy resources.

Can You Enjoy Speedy Mind Alertness?

Judith Wurtman, Ph.D., research scientist in the Department of Brain and Cognitive Science at the Massachusetts Institute of Technology, in Cambridge, Massachusetts, and author of *Managing Your Mind and Mood Through Food,* offers this thumbnail "instant energy" plan:

"Protein increases your alertness. Carbohydrates make you sleepy. Fat dulls your ability to perform physically and mentally. Ups and downs, the mental energy or lack of it, are the results of changes in your brain chemistry."

Cells, Neurotransmitters, Food

What happens is that messages are passed from cell to cell in the brain by electric impulses and by chemicals called *neurotransmitters.* Three of the chemicals—dopamine, norepinephrine, and serotonin—are manufactured by your brain from the food you eat.

Dopamine and *norepinephrine* are alertness chemicals. When they are activated, you are motivated, more energetic, and attentive. You respond with vigor more speedily to stimuli.

Serotonin is a calming chemical. When it flows, feelings of stress and tension are lessened, and you have brain energy so you can concentrate more easily. Serotonin also slows reaction time and, Dr. Wurtman explains, "depending on the time of day, it may make you feel sluggish or sleepy."

If you are in need of an energetic mind, eating only three or four ounces of protein will send forth a supercharging of dopamine and norepinephrine to help you think better.

From "Tired" to "Tiger" in Five Minutes

A half-cup of any protein food (lean meat, fish, egg whites, low-fat cheese, peas, beans, nuts) with a tiny amount of fat (one-quarter teaspoon of vegetable oil) will give you a "quick shift" into a more alert state. This "energy snack in a cup" is a powerhouse of energy in minutes after eating.

Beware of "Sad Fat"

Go easy on gloom-causing fat. Dr. Wurtman cautions, "It slows absorption into your system and slows mental processes so your mind is also dulled. Doubling your intake will not make you twice as alert. Neither will doubling your intake of carbohydrates make you twice as mellow." But cutting down on fat will boost your energy and help you feel more alert and cheerful.

Power Menu Plan for Mental Alertness

To send your fatigue into remission, build your food plan around the menu as suggested by Dr. Wurtman:

Breakfast: Protein and carbohydrates with fruit.

Lunch: Low in carbohydrates, low in fat and calories, high in protein, free of alcohol.

Dinner: It depends on your plans after dinner. To be alert, eat sparingly; eat protein, either before or along with carbohydrates. In other words, do not start dinner by eating a roll with butter. If you want to be relaxed, eat lots of carbohydrates such as a big plate of pasta.

WHY DOES PROTEIN HAVE THE IMPORTANT "ENERGY FACTOR"?

Protein contains tyrosine, one of the ingredients of the "energizing" chemicals. It is only minimally concentrated in cerebrospinal fluid but does pack a wallop in terms of giving you a long-lasting energy jolt! As an intracellular protein, it is primarily concentrated in brain tubulin (small cylindrical hollow structures). Rapid metabolism is the key to the protein's energy factor in helping you banish fatigue of the body and mind in a matter of moments.

In brief, tyrosine is an essential amino acid that readily passes the blood-brain barrier. Once in the brain, it is a stimulant for the neurotransmitter of dopamine, norepinephrine, and epinephrine. These neurotransmitters are an important part of your body's sympathetic nervous system; with adequate tyrosine from foods, your brain is given a speedy boost in energy!

SIMPLE TRICKS TO BOOST ENERGY

Protein maximizes your brain's production of alertness-boosting transmitters and controls the relaxing serotonin production. A nice balance. How to achieve the best of both possible worlds? That is, to be energetic when you want to and relaxed when you need to? Based on Dr. Wurtman's research, here is your simple plan:

1. Within three hours of awakening, eat something—skim milk yogurt and fresh fruit, a high-fiber cereal, whole grain muffin.

Caution: Skipping breakfast lowers energy levels; you're more likely to overeat at lunch, leaving you sluggish in the afternoon.

2. Say "no" to high-fat lunches such as a roll with butter or any fatty food. Say "yes" to broiled fish or chicken without skin instead of a marbled steak. *Caution:* Avoid alcohol because it can sap your energy for much of the afternoon. Try skim milk (high protein/low fat) or plain seltzer with a spritz of lemon or lime juice.

3. Finish lunch about two hours before an afternoon task. "That allows you enough time so that you won't be in the middle of digesting your food and you won't be hungry," says Dr. Wurtman. *Caution:* Avoid business lunches, since shop talk can be a drain on your energy reserves while eating and afterward.

4. In the evening, follow the same plan of a high-protein/low-fat menu. If you later want to relax, try high carbohydrates. *Caution:* Avoid alcohol because it will interfere with your need for mental-physical energy.

What About Energy Snacks?

"Eating a candy bar may give you an energy lift, but it will be followed by a deep low as the body begins to digest the candy's high-fat protein," says Dr. Wurtman.

What's an energy-seeking person to do? Try a whole grain muffin with sugar-free jam, graham crackers, plain popcorn, or whole grain cereal. "These naturally sweet/starchy snacks can restore mental energy, as well as put you back into a focused state of mind."

The Seesaw Tug of War with Caffeine

Caffeine has a reputation for being an afternoon pick-me-up. Caffeine metabolizes slowly. Therefore, a second cup of coffee at 10:30

A.M. will not give you energy; it will cause fluctuations and a drop in your energy.

Caution: Caffeine and carbohydrates work synergistically to pull you out of a mental slump—the carbohydrates help you settle down and focus, the caffeine pushes your mental energy up a few notches. Again, you have this up-down, up-down pattern that gives you shotgun energy to be followed by the deflation of a punctured balloon!

Steer clear of caffeine; switch to natural beverages as an energizing substitute.

Sleep Better at Night

You need a good night's sleep to have energy the next day. Avoid sleeping disorders by skipping your midafternoon coffee break. Eat mostly carbohydrates after 4:00 p.m. Dr. Wurtman explains, "Carbohydrates alone—*not* consumed with protein—spurs the brain's production of serotonin and calms you down." Good carbohydrate sources include whole grain breads and cereals, pasta, brown rice, legumes, and potatoes.

CASE HISTORY—
Improves Mood, Becomes Cheerful, Feels Superenergetic with Simple Nutritional Changes

School administrator Eugene B. was always known for having a cheerful personality. But some changes made him gloomy. He had long spells of pessimism, had chronic anxiety, displayed hostility toward those on the school board, and then to members of his family.

Was he becoming neurotic? Eugene B. faced loss of his job (he snapped at coworkers and management) and discord in his home life. Something was wrong. A physical examination showed nutritional imbalance. The internist was aware of mood foods and asked about Eugene B.'s eating plan. He would eat fatty foods, sugary foods, and cared little about wholesome or more natural foods. He also had a strong coffee habit as well as downing soft drinks from a local vending machine. (Many of these soft drinks are high in caffeine as well as sugar—double trouble for energy levels.) He complained of increasing tiredness.

Eugene B. was put on a simple four-step plan as outlined earlier. He was eased off his unhealthy foods as slowly given the low-fat, high-protein foods. His temperament underwent a remarkable transformation. He became his familiar self: cheerful, greeting everyone by first name, had more energy, and was soon alert, cordial, and youthfully vigorous. He had used "mood foods" to alert the brain chemicals of dopamine and norepinephrine to change his mood from sad to glad!

Seventeen Sparks to Start Your Energy Sizzling

Fatigue often brings on neuromuscular aches as well as emotional disorders. To quicken your step, to go from a shuffle to a sprint, to put your body and mind in high gear and wash away fatigue, try these speedy energizing remedies.

1. *Keep yourself active.* Energy stimulates energy. Do not allow yourself to surrender to malaise or monotony. When you feel sluggish, get up and start to do something. Push yourself. Even if it is just a hobby, this initial energy spark will ignite into total body-mind invigoration. Harold H. Bloomfield, M.D., author of *The Holistic Way to Health and Happiness*, tells us, "Love is energy; being creative is energy; health is energy. The more good things you do for yourself, the more energetic you're going to be." Just *doing* can stimulate you to shake off the doldrums that brought on that initial tiredness.

2. *Get regular exercise.* An oxygenation or aerobic workout stimulates your pulse rate to gallop. You'll feel primed for action. Exercise sends more oxygen-bearing hemoglobin into your red blood cells. Your heart pumps more blood with each beat,

easing its work to circulate the blood throughout your body. Exercise gives your skeletal muscles more vigor for oxygen uptake. Your muscle cells are able to metabolize oxygen more efficiently. Your breathing rate stabilizes and you are not winded so easily. With exercise, your entire body and mind work with efficiency and energy. Many studies show that daily exercise overcomes stress, one of life's most dangerous energy thieves!

3. *Refresh with a minibreak.* It's midafternoon and you feel in a slump. For many people, this fatigue symptom occurs earlier and can last all day. Shake off the doldrums. "We all come with different energy levels," says Charles Kuntzleman, Ph.D., author of *Maximum Personal Energy.* "Some people have God-given high-level energy even though they do everything wrong, just as some people are born beautiful and some are born average." Dr. Kuntzleman suggests you ease tension by shrugging your shoulders, rolling your head. "Better yet, do a lap around the work site, the building, or the block." It helps rev up your senses and you return with superenergy.

4. *Pace yourself.* Plan ahead. Schedule difficult tasks for times when you know you'll have an energy peak. Don't tackle serious matters after a day's work or the clock strikes 9:00 p.m. or beyond. If you are a morning lark or a night owl, then plan to do your tasks during these high-energy biological clock times. Listen to the ticking, and when the energy alarm goes off, go to it!

5. *Sugar is an energy thief.* Yes, sugar boosts energy, but a slow-down follows soon afterward. When sugar floods your blood-stream, the signal is for your body to release insulin, which gathers sugar for storage. Your former "sugar high" becomes a "sugar low." Avoid sugar; instead, select complex carbohydrates for slow release into your bloodstream. Switch—from a "short burst" to "staying power" . . . at work or at home or anywhere else.

6. *Shed unwanted pounds.* Obesity is an exhausting load you carry around the clock. Physically carrying 30 to 40 extra pounds will make you more fatigued. Obesity can wear you out psychologically. It affects your perception of yourself, making you self-conscious, which is energy draining. You're constantly mentally defending yourself: "Hey, I'm O.K. My waistline's just a little big." Who do you think you're fooling! Get rid of the energy-draining excess weight and energize as a big burden is lifted from your body and mind.

7. *Yoga is a key to energy release.* Join a yoga class. Actually, yoga is not an energy source. Rather, it releases the energy locked within by melting away the blockage of pent-up tension. Yoga practitioners note that tension is blocked energy trying to break free. With yoga, you do away with tension and energy pours forth.

8. *A simple shower is a powerful energy booster.* It matters not whether hot, cold, or tepid. It has to feel good. Stand under a needle-spray shower and feel yourself reviving. When you turn on a shower, the air starts to change. It becomes filled with "good" *negative ions.* As noted in the first chapter of this book, negative ions are molecules with an extra electron. Higher concentrations of negative ions in the air will reduce levels of serotonin so that you feel more energetic and cheerful. Ever notice how good you feel near a sparkling waterfall? The surrounding air is supercharged with negative ions because of the water exchange. Do the same thing at home by standing under a brisk shower for 15 or so minutes. A terrific pick-me-up! And a great way to ease muscular aches and pains. It's the basis for healing hydrotherapy.

9. *Munching nuts can be an "upper."* Feel fatigued, sluggish, worn out? You may have what is called "the mineral blues." Your muscle cells may be deficient in potassium and magnesium. Water soluble, these minerals are easily lost through evaporation, perspiration. *Caution:* If your supply of these minerals

drops below normal, the mildest deficiency drags you down in fatigue. *Remedy:* For a snack, munch assorted nuts (salt-free and fat-free, preferably untreated with chemicals) for a speedy "upper."

10. *What about vitamin C?* It's a great way to help you increase blood-nourishing dietary iron and give you youthful energy. This nutrient acts as a "pep pill" if your body reserves are low. If you have chronic low energy, it could be from a need for this vitamin found in citrus fruits and their juices as well as most fresh fruits and vegetables.

11. *A good breakfast is energizing.* Even if you are not hungry at the sound of the alarm clock, a night's sleep has drained your body of those very nutrients you need to produce energy. "If you don't eat breakfast," cautions Max M. Novich, M.D., coauthor of *The High Energy Diet for Dynamic Living,* "you're likely to 'drag along' all morning." A good breakfast with protein and complex carbohydrates is a "must" for energy in the day ahead.

12. *A light lunch gives extended energy.* You're facing a mountain of work (so it seems in your fatigued mind's eye) and it's only 2:00 p.m. Why the slump? Think back? Did you have a heavy lunch? Was it especially high in fats and refined carbohydrates? If so, you are the victim of "postprandial dip" in which your body temperature, blood sugar, emotions, and work efficiency have dropped. An afternoon siesta is helpful. But not many can do this. Avoid the slump with a lighter lunch—low (very low!) in fats, high in complex carbohydrates (vegetables, grains, legumes)—with an emphasis on salads.

13. *How's your social life?* When you last spoke to someone, did you become an "ear" for a chronic complainer? Each complaint drills into your subconscious and you feel yourself drained out, cell by cell. Listening to naysayers or prophets of gloom will exhaust your own energy sources. Granted, you cannot avoid these complainers, but you can keep them to a

minimum in your social life. Instead, mix with upbeat people, those with energy, those with hope, love, and laughter. It will rub off on you. People who love, have fun, and enjoy life will give you good feelings about yourself and boost your energy levels.

14. *There is a safe time for coffee.* Yes, coffee whips up your emotions in the morning, but its caffeine is a time bomb. It prompts insulin to shoot out (just as sugar does), to have you spinning on all wheels for an hour of manic energy. When it's over, your low blood sugar leaves you exhausted. *Caution:* A cup of morning coffee interferes with you circadian rhythms, your internal alarm clock that, throughout the day, raises and lowers your temperature, blood pressure, and so on. It causes myriad body chemicals to turn on and off, to make you feel energetic or clumsy, sharp or foggy. *Remedy:* If you must have caffeine beverages, do so at British tea time, between 3:30 p.m. and 5:00 p.m. By the time the letdown comes, you will be ready for an energizing dinner.

15. *The B-complex vitamins give you a buzz.* The slightest deficiency of any of the B-complex vitamin group could give you a serious case of the blahs. These vitamins act as a family group to metabolize proteins, carbohydrates, vitamins, and fats into energizing fuel. Without them, you're out of steam! Try sprinkling wheat germ, whole grain cereal, or chunks of natural bread on low-fat cottage cheese for a tasty treat to boost your energy. A combo of wheat germ with chunks of fresh fruit will help give you energy, too. Fuel vitality with whole grains and their B-complex power.

16. *Set yourself a goal.* Something to live for . . . something to look forward to. It's called *hope.* Anticipation of a good thing ahead is a terrific energy booster to roust you out of the doldrums. If you work all day, the expectation of a happy event at night is enough to supercharge you with vitality. That sense of excite-

ment is like an "amphetamine response," says Michael R. Liebowitz, M.D., in *The Chemistry of Love.* "When we are looking forward to things, especially when pursuing a valued goal, we liven up, have more energy, and concentrate better." What is your goal? Start planning! It's a great energy booster.

17. *Take a break.* A vacation, if only for a few days, is a surefire way to recharge your batteries. A change of scenery is as refreshing as a jolt of bottled energy—if it could be so packaged. The reason is simple. Getting away from it all gets you out of your routine. Put some distance between yourself and whatever you're working at. You'll feel refreshed in a matter of minutes. In addition to separating yourself physically from your problems, you're opening up yourself to other things. Essentially you're taking your mind off one thing and putting it on something else. When you return, you'll see things with a new perspective. You begin to see your life in a new context and that becomes a natural energy booster. Take a loving interest in life . . . and you will create new energy!

There you have a set of 17 natural energy boosters. Make use of them and feel yourself revitalized in a matter of minutes.

CASE HISTORY—
Becomes a Powerhouse of Energy After Being "Dragged Down"

As a textile consultant, Nina T. was always on the alert. She had to keep aware of trends in decorating and fashions. She was always visiting department stores and devising ways to boost sales in textiles. She also functioned as a designer for some of the larger fabric companies. She, herself, looked like a fashion model and she was in her late fifties. At the same time, Nina T. had to manage a household, taking care of two school-age children and a demanding husband.

She had always been responsive to their needs, but in the last few months, these obligations started to drain her energy.

What was wrong? She became careless in her eating methods and her life-style. She become more of a workaholic. She would eat "fast foods" that were largely sugary-salted-fatty "easy to prepare" processed meals . . . and this caused such a depletion of her energy-producing nutrients, she started to feel "dragged down."

She neglected her home; everything was in disarray. She performed the basic necessities and even these started to be avoided. Nina T. felt her words becoming sluggish before it was noontime. Small wonder. In an effort to negotiate with store buyers, she often skipped breakfast. Worse, she would gulp down coffee with a pastry that gave her a momentary lift and then a deep flop. Her energy levels had a seesaw motion. She could hardly make it through midafternoon.

Her family felt the distress. They had to prepare their own meals (not the greatest!) or do some housework. What was wrong with Nina T.?

When she admitted the increasing fatigue to a department store buyer, her colleague suggested she visit the store's registered nurse who was also a registered dietitian. Nina T. had a thorough diagnosis and the nurse-dietitian said she needed to revitalize her nutrition and lifestyle programs.

Nina T. was told to follow a program of low-fat but high-protein foods with complex carbohydrates. *Taboo* was anything with sugar or refined carbohydrates or processed foods. She could also snack on nuts whenever she needed a lift. A wholesome breakfast and filling (but fat-free) lunch and the same for dinner.

There was still more. Nina T. needed to schedule fun and games to refresh her mind; in so doing, she would unleash her energy potential for a more productive and happier life.

This strategy worked! In two weeks, she had won the battle over stress and fatigue. She was rewarded with physical and mental energy to be her best. Nina T. was again a powerhouse of energy. Her home life sparkled. Her work was efficient. Her family was loving again. All together—she was supercharged with vitality again!

Active Body + Active Mind = Natural Energy Boosters

You feel recurring aches in different parts of your body. A stubborn letdown feeling gives you a case of the blahs. You want to send these negative feelings into remission and enjoy energetic health. You can do it with more activity.

Beware Being Sedentary

The sedentary body must work harder because your heart and lungs are less efficient: poor circulation deprives various body tissues of oxygen; muscles may deteriorate.

If you are too sedentary, your body burns fewer calories. Pounds pile up. You feel sluggish.

Remedy: Regular aerobic exercise fights fatigue by reversing this cycle. It increases the flow of oxygen throughout your body. And oxygen is the "gas" that gets your motors moving.

With an active body, oxygenation clears away the cobwebs from your mind and body and gives you refreshing energy. If you have gone through some sluggish or sedentary living, start to revive with a 20-minute walk. If comfortable, walk up several flights of stairs instead of using the elevator. Or try doing a dozen jumping jacks! In a matter of moments, you'll rev up your body engine and feel a burst of energy from head to toe. Do it now!

Feed yourself a cheerful mood. The right foods can help you feel glad all over—and that includes more vitality. Banish fatigue by supercharging your body and mind with energy-boosting foods—and the love of life!

HIGHLIGHTS

1. A proper balance of protein and carbohydrates can help you feel alert and in a happier frame of mind, not to mention improve your energy.

2. Try the *Power Menu Plan for Mental Alertness*. Protein does have the important "energy factor" that works in minutes.

3. A simple eating plan as outlined by a scientist will help soothe your mood and boost your energy at the same time. Tasty, too.

4. Eugene B. brightened his mood and enjoyed superenergy with some simple nutritional changes.

5. A variety of 17 different remedies will help brighten your attitude and put your body and mind in high gear. Washes away fatigue, too.

6. Nina T. was saved from moody blues and became a power-house of energy with easy changes in her eating and living routine.

7. Oxygenate your body and activate your mind to chase away gloom and feel vibrant and vigorous again.

Do you have the low-sugar blues?

CASE HISTORY—
Blue Moods Threatened to Wreck His Life

William C. was looked up to as a good example in his community. A happily married man and father of three children, he was a rising success in his travel business. He was a member of the local chamber of commerce. He greeted everyone with a warm handshake and a smile. Then something started going wrong.

He had bouts of insomnia. He would wake up, unable to go back to sleep. He snapped at his youngsters and was sharp with his wife. At work, he was abrupt with his coworkers and customers. He had visible signs of trembling; he became forgetful. He would stagger as he went from his computer to the next desk, yet he was a nondrinker. He would squint at large type on papers when his vision had always been good. His words were slurred. He was in the midst of mental confusion and antisocial behavior. His family life and business could be threatened by this disassociative behavior and lack of concentration, not to mention his mood swings—sometimes gentle, other times hurtful!

Something was happening to William C. and the mystery had to be solved before these blue moods could destroy his very existence.

A medical client suggested a thorough physical examination. Grouchy but aware he had a problem, William C. consented. Yet aside from the routine finding that he was "tired," little could be found to pinpoint the cause of his recurring fatigue and mental exhaustion. (He was frequently found sleeping in the storeroom in the middle of the day!) Finally, an endocrinologist and specialist in blood sugar diagnosed the possible cause: hypoglycemia.

Other doctors could not find it. No surprise since hypoglycemia is elusive, unfamiliar, and frequently pooh-poohed by doctors as "all in your mind." The fatigue *is* in your mind and in your body and in your bloodstream too. This is what the endocrinologist (hormone specialist) told William C. Immediately, he was put on a nutritional recovery plan. Within four weeks, after several glucose tolerance tests (GTT, described shortly), he was balanced again.

He had the familiar smooth temperament. He slept at night. Was energetic in the daytime. Trembling vanished. He was alert, with a clear mind, good vision, in complete control. His family life and business were saved because his blood sugar had been balanced. Life became sweet again!

Hypoglycemia—What Is It?

The word *hypoglycemia* literally means "below-normal blood sugar": *hypo*, "below or under"; *glycemia*, "sugar in the bloodstream."

It's an elusive disorder, puzzling and controversial, but for millions of victims, it causes physical and emotional fatigue. If unchecked, it can be devastating. This specter is hypoglycemia.

Typical Symptoms

Depression, dizzy spells, headaches, undue fatigue and exhaustion, drowsiness, muscular aches, leg cramps, insomnia, nervousness, irritability, poor coordination, anxiety, attacks of weakness and light-headedness with or without fainting, lack of concentration, staggering, rapid heart action—all these are typical symptoms.

The affected person feels tired much of the time, fatigued without obvious cause, tired on awakening, often too tired to function effectively in domestic, occupational, or family activities. It could be hypoglycemia.

What Is Blood Sugar?

The sugar in your blood is glucose. This glucose is measured by how many milligrams are found in 100 milliliters (approximately

3 1/2 ounces) of your blood. Normal blood sugar is between 70 and 120 milligrams per 100 milliliters of blood before meals. After meals, it may reach 140 for a short time, but it soon settles down toward the premeal level. Anyone with blood sugar below 65 milligrams is suspected of having low blood sugar or hypoglycemia.

Why Do You Need Glucose?

Glucose is the fuel your body burns for energy and heat. It is an essential nutrient for your brain, for your body to run, just as your car needs fuel to run. Glucose is used by every cell in your body for this energy.

If your blood sugar level is declining, your brain reacts. Emotional distress is typical. Physical reactions are also evident. Recurring aches ranging from arthritis to backache can be the penalty because a glucose deficiency is bending your mind!

Your brain, perhaps more than any other organ, demands glucose. While some organs (liver and pancreas, for example) store glucose and burn reserves, if the supply drops below normal, or can use alternative substances for fuel in an emergency, the brain is a glucose glutton! It must have glucose continuously—a steady, second-after-second supply. You could say your brain lives on glucose. Without it, you lose control of many vital functions of mind and body.

Is Your Brain Protesting a Glucose Shortage?

Low blood sugar manifests itself in exhaustion, headaches, temper outbursts, irritability, sleeping problems, indecisiveness, nervousness, mood swings, eating disorders, nightmares, and suicidal tendencies. *Danger:* When blood sugar levels drop too low, your brain triggers an anxiety or panic attack—sweaty palms, heavy breathing, speedy pulse, dry mouth. Your brain is crying for help—answer this plea and your fatigue may well be erased so you enjoy better energy—of brain and body!

Glucose Tolerance Test

This test measures the amount of sugar (glucose) in your blood at specific intervals. It is known as a five-hour, seven-sample glucose tolerance test, given after a doctor has taken a complete medical examination and history and studied your symptoms.

The test is usually begun in the morning after you have fasted (had nothing to eat) for 10 to 12 hours. A sample of blood is drawn from your arm. Then you are given a glucose solution to drink. In half an hour, blood will again be drawn and a urine sample requested. (In the case of diabetes, sugar may show up in the urine.) After that, blood and urine samples will be taken on the hour for the next 5 or 6 hours. Your physical and emotional symptoms are also noted.

During the GTT, no tobacco, chewing gum, food, or drink, except water, is allowed. Normal nonstrenuous physical activity is permitted.

A normal fasting blood sugar is usually between 80 and 120 milligrams. Following a meal, the blood sugar level may rise to around 140 milligrams. A reading of 170 or higher is considered abnormal, and further medical testing for diabetes is desirable.

When to Take the Test?

There appears to be a special value in "afternoon" testing. It may be used either in place of the morning test or as a checkup after a period of treatment (usually six months). When the morning test is borderline or equivocal, hypoglycemia may show up with the afternoon test that is done four or five hours after a normal breakfast and normal activities. This seems to be especially true where there is a family history of diabetes.

The reason for an afternoon test may be that the adrenal glands have rested and recovered somewhat during the night but will be depleted by 3:00 or 4:00 P.M. It is a sign of our times that afternoon tests are difficult to arrange because of the inconvenience to laboratory personnel if the tests are not completed by "quitting time." However, if symptoms indicate hypoglycemia and the "morning" test is not clear cut, you should specify an afternoon test.

Are You a Tired Victim of Seesaw Blood Sugar?

You may be energetic one minute and fatigued the next. It is not how low your blood sugar goes but *how fast you go to the low*. Your sugar may drop rapidly from 180 to 90 milligrams over a one-hour period and possibly trigger more problems than if it would slowly drop from 110 to 50 milligrams over a two- to three-hour period.

Another important energy factor is how long your blood sugar remains below your fasting level. If it returns to your fasting level in an hour, you may not notice it. On the other hand, if the sugar dropped to 65 milligrams and remains there for a few hours, your symptoms may be more severe. From this it becomes apparent there are no set numbers to be used to diagnose hypoglycemia. You need a steady supply of glucose to avoid hypoglycemia.

Why You Should Avoid Refined Sugar

Sweets and starches from overly processed and presweetened foods will dump an overload of sugar into your system with the roar of a roller coaster. You get an initial rush as blood sugar levels shoot to a high crest. Your pancreas tries to cope with the sugar overdose by pouring forth extra insulin, a hormone that withdraws sugar from the blood. Suddenly, you plummet downward on this sugar roller coaster. You have a sudden and shocking drop in blood sugar.

The first remedy is to avoid refined sugars and starches.

Protein Helps Control Blood Sugar

Your symptoms will be eased with the use of protein. This nutrient is metabolized into sugar at a slow, steady rate so your pancreas doesn't have to cope with the shock of excessive sugar.

Which Protein?

Animal protein includes lean meats, seafood, eggs, dairy products. Meatless sources include peas, beans, nuts, whole grains, pasta, brown rice, corn, millet, barley, lentils, soy milk, tofu, texturized vegetable protein.

Careful: Overconsumption of animal protein can cause a severe calcium-magnesium deficiency. *Reason:* Meat contains 22 times more phosphorus than calcium. Since these two elements are needed in about equal amounts, this excess of phosphorus cannot be properly digested with extra calcium. *Danger:* Osteoporosis, osteoarthritis, dental disorders, and calcium deficiency–related problems.

Suggestion: Meatless proteins should be considered for their high biological protein value in helping to control seesaw blood sugar levels.

Six STEPS TO CONTROL HYPOGLYCEMIA AND BOOST ENERGY

Stuart Berger, M.D., a New York City specialist in nutritional medicine and author of *How to Be Your Own Nutritionist,* agrees that hypoglycemia can be an exacerbating factor in asthma, allergies, arthritis, ulcers, and recurring fatigue.

Whatever the cause of sugar imbalance, the result is the same. Dr. Berger describes what happens in your body. "First, the blood sugar skyrockets. Then your pancreas—your body's sugar thermostat—sounds the alarm, telling its insulin-producing cells to get on the job. This hormone spills into your bloodstream and mops up the excess sugar, storing it in the liver. After this chemical crisis, your blood sugar falls even lower than it was before . . . and you have fatigue.

Your plan to control this energy thief is an eating program that smooths out the peaks and valleys of the sugar-insulin hypoglycemia cycle.

Dr. Berger offers six steps to energy boosting that he recommends to his patients.

Step One. Adopt a diet higher in protein, lower in carbohydrates with a moderate amount of fat. "For the optimal hypoglycemic diet, organize your daily intake with 15 percent of your calories in protein, because this is the most time-released of any energy source, 20 percent in dietary fat, 10 percent in simple carbohydrates (fresh fruit), and 55 percent in complex carbohydrates (vegetables and whole grains).

Step Two. Eat slow-absorbing carbohydrates rather than fast-absorbing ones as this slows down the "sugar rush" that triggers a powerful insulin overreaction. All carbohydrates are not created equal when it comes to how fast they break down. *Example:* Stanford University studies show that the body's insulin release in response to carbohydrates rice and corn is lower than that of potatoes and gelatin. Dr. Berger suggests that you balance your diet to include carbohydrates (whole grains, fruits, and vegetables), which break down their sugar energy in a more orderly time-release fashion.

Step Three. Graze, do not stuff. Space your meals into smaller, less elaborate ones instead of big sit-down affairs. Eat to satisfy hunger but not to get stuffed. Spread meals out through the day to ease strain on your system and to produce steady energy.

Step Four. Say "no" to junk food—anything that is highly refined, sugary, and artificial. Hyperconcentrated sugar found in sticky-sweet confections shocks your pancreatic insulin-producing cells into a red alert. You could worsen your current health problems or trigger new ones because of this sugar antagonism. Resist junk food and you may resist and recover from hypoglycemic symptoms.

Step Five. Eliminate caffeine (coffee, tea, chocolate products, cocoa, many soft drinks, certain over-the-counter medications), alcohol, and tobacco. These are artificial stimulants that trigger blood sugar fluctuations. Hypoglycemia coupled with a stimulant strains your physiological organs and systems, such as adrenal glands, stomach, and neurological and cardiovascular networks. Avoid "instant" stimulants; be kind to your systems and you will help shield yourself against hypoglycemia.

Step Six. Shed unnecessary pounds. If you more than 20 percent over ideal body weight, you are at higher risk of sugar disorders of all kinds such as hypoglycemia and diabetes.

Quick Energy Boost for Low Blood Sugar: Brewer's Yeast

In *Hypoglycemia: A Better Approach*, nutritionist-author Dr. Paavo Airola tells us: "Brewer's yeast is one of the best foods for the hypoglycemic. In addition to supplying a wealth of nutrients, it is one of the few excellent sources of chromium. If you are not getting enough chromium, you are subject to impaired glucose tolerance. Chromium deficiency can also have an unfavorable effect on the victims of blood sugar. Brewer's yeast also contains the glucose tolerance factor, which makes the chromium more available to the body."

Dr. Airola tells of a physician who "found that by giving brewer's yeast to patients who had disorders in glucose tolerance, he was able to stabilize their blood sugar levels within a month. He also found that brewer's yeast could prevent attacks of low blood sugar."

How to Take Brewer's Yeast

Dr. Airola suggests, "One tablespoon of brewer's yeast powder mixed in half a glass of freshly made or canned pineapple juice, or freshly squeezed grapefruit juice, can be taken two or three times a day, preferably one hour before meals. Taking brewer's yeast in this manner will totally eliminate the problem of gas."

Include Calcium at the Same Time

Dr. Airola advises, "When taking yeast, always take one tablet (200 milligrams) of calcium supplement with it. Yeast is rich in phosphorus and low in calcium. An addition of calcium will achieve a better mineral balance and improve the utilization and metabolism of all the yeast's minerals. Even taking the yeast with some form of calcium-rich sour milk such as yogurt, kefir, acidophilus, and buttermilk can be helpful."

Caution: Never eat yeast intended for baking. It may multiply in your intestines and will actually devour your body's own B vitamin reserves.

Morning PEP-UP DRINK

Because many people have hypoglycemic symptoms in the morning after a night's restful decline of blood sugar, Dr. Airola feels this special *Morning Pep-up Drink* will give a steady rise and stabilized level of glucose to give you long-lasting energy.

1 cup kefir, yogurt, or other soured milk
1/2 small banana or equivalent of other fresh fruit
1 teaspoon dry skim milk
1 teaspoon brewer's yeast powder
1 teaspoon sesame, chia, or flax seeds

Place all ingredients in a blender. Run on high until seeds are liquefied. Drink slowly or eat with a spoon.

Within moments, your glucose levels are stabilized and you feel more energy that lasts and lasts and lasts.

How CEREALS OVERCOME HYPOGLYCEMIA—QUICKLY

Endocrinologists agree it is imperative for the maintenance of even, sustained sugar levels in the blood that the assimilation of carbohydrates be as slow as possible. Dr. Airola tells us that "cooked cereals such as buckwheat or millet or whole grain breads digest much more slowly than raw cereals, releasing sugar into the bloodstream gradually and at a slower pace. This is extremely important in the preventive as well as therapeutic diet for hypoglycemia.

"When you eat a bowl of buckwheat cereal, oatmeal, a five-grain cereal or millet cereal for breakfast or lunch, along with a dab of butter or a tablespoon of vegetable oil and a glass of fresh milk, such a meal will remain in your stomach for many hours—half a day!—slowly releasing high-quality proteins, fatty acids and gradually converted starches (sugars) into your bloodstream."

BREAKFAST ENERGY FOOD

Dr. Airola explains that with breakfast cereal, you can give yourself a steady supply of energy-boosting complex carbohydrates. Here's how to start off the day with energy.

> 1 cup hulled millet
> 3 cups water
> 1/2 teaspoon honey (optional, since it's a concentrated sweet)
> 1/2 cup powdered skim milk

Place millet in a pan of water mixed with powdered skim milk and heat mixture to boiling point. Simmer for ten minutes, stirring occasionally, to prevent sticking and burning. Remove from the heat and let stand for a half hour or more. Serve with nonfat milk, vegetable oil, a bit of butter, or homemade applesauce.

Vegetables Stabilize Blood Sugar

Dr. Airola considers vegetables to be "excellent health-promoting as well as medicinal and should form an important part of the hypoglycemic diet." He adds that most vegetables have special sugar-regulating factors that help promote energy. Enjoy vegetables with natural herbs and spices. You "will help improve your health as well as turn vegetable dishes into delectable gourmet foods."

Two Important Energy-Producing Vegetables

Jerusalem artichokes and string beans contain *insulin,* which is converted into fructose in the body, says Dr. Airola. Fructose is a form of fruit sugar that is well tolerated by the body without unfavorably affecting blood sugar levels. He suggests eating raw Jerusalem artichokes in salads. String beans are best steamed.

CASE HISTORY—
From "Droopy" to "Dynamic" with High-Energy Foods

Helping her husband in his car rental business had never been much of a burden for Marge S.O. She liked getting out of the house for several hours daily, negotiating with customers, meeting new people. She had always been able to balance work and home. Then something went wrong. She became tired after only a half hour in the office. She felt jittery. She would be short-tempered, which certainly was unwise for the business. At social affairs, she would slump in a chair, feeling her eyelids heavier and heavier. She was becoming "droopy."

A registered dietitian who frequently rented a car to go to outlying districts to see patients, noted Marge S.O.'s constantly recurring fatigue. She suggested a glucose tolerance test and an eating history as well.

In her grouchy condition, Marge S.O. was stubborn and refused, insisting nothing was wrong with her. But the dietitian persisted and all but "dragged" her off to the doctor who was knowledgeable in the field of hypoglycemia. The test confirmed suspicions. Her blood sugar was on a seesaw curve. She admitted to drinking loads of soft drinks (sugar and caffeine), eating sweets (sugar), skipping meals (dangerous for blood sugar swerves), and disregarding important needs for protein and valuable complex carbohydrates.

Immediately, Marge S.O. was put on a complex carbohydrate program with moderate protein, but no sweets or caffeine in any form.

Because she was in a serious hypoglycemia state, the doctor recommended that Marge S.O. prepare about 16 ounces of the *Morning Pep-up Drink* and have half in the morning at home and the other half at work, brought along in a thermos. No more skipped meals. More vegetable protein and complex carbohydrates.

Still she found mornings and the 10:00 o'clock slump difficult. The doctor told her to start off the day with the *Breakfast Energy Food*. This did the trick. Within three weeks, Marge S.O. was again a bundle of joy instead of a bundle of nerves. She went from "droopy" to "dynamic" and was a delight to live and work with. And she loved herself better, too!

Simple Guidelines for Energy Balance

James F. Balch, M.D., of Greenfield, Indiana, and author of *Prescription for Nutritional Healing*, offers these steps:

1. Include vegetables, brown rice, Jerusalem artichokes, seeds, grains, nuts, yogurt, raw cheese, cottage cheese, and kefir milk in your diet.

2. Remove sugar, refined and processed foods such as instant rice and potatoes, white flour, soft drinks, alcohol, and salt from your diet. Avoid sweet fruits and juices such as grape and prune (mix with 50 percent water if used). Avoid macaroni, noodles, gravies, hominy, white rice, yams, and corn. Eat beans and baked potatoes twice a week.

3. Do not go without food. Instead, eat six to eight small meals throughout the day. Some hypoglycemics find that eating a small snack before bedtime helps. In addition, rotate your diet, as food allergies are often linked to hypoglycemia and can aggravate both conditions, making the symptoms more pronounced.

4. Stabilize blood sugar swings with a high-fiber diet. During a low-blood-sugar reaction, combine fiber with protein food (i.e., bran or rice crackers with raw cheese or almond butter). Instead of eating applesauce, choose a whole apple. The fiber in the

apple will inhibit fluctuations in blood sugar. Add a glass of fruit juice for a rapid rise in blood sugar. Fiber alone (found in popcorn, oat bran, rice bran, crackers, and guar gum) will slow down a hypoglycemic reaction. Spirulina tablets (a microalgae plant food, it reportedly is a powerhouse of nutrients, available in health stores) taken between meals will further stabilize blood sugar because of its high-protein content.

5. Eliminate caffeine, alcohol, and smoking, all of which result in profound swings (i.e., instability) of blood sugar.

Hints, tips, suggestions

*   Limit milk to less than two cups daily. Lactose (milk sugar) triggers the release of insulin in the same way as sucrose (white table sugar).
*   Avoid caffeine because it tends to cause a hypoglycemic reaction with seesaw energy.
*   Avoid alcohol, which prevents the liver from producing glucose when blood glucose levels go down below normal. If you drink alcohol, you only worsen the hypoglycemic reaction.
*   Space meals evenly throughout the day to balance blood glucose levels. You may have three balanced meals that are alternated with three small snacks to level the blood glucose further.
*   Guard against unrelieved stress and anxiety, as these can touch off an adrenaline discharge. You experience symptoms identical to those associated with low blood sugar.

You need not endure fatigue, unhappiness, drowsiness, nervousness, and other physical and emotional symptoms. You can enjoy natural energy when you sweeten your personality and balance your blood sugar. Life becomes energetic and beautiful, too!

HIGHLIGHTS

1. William C. was almost defeated with his blue moods until he was diagnosed as having low blood sugar. A set of nutritional corrections gave him natural energy and a cheerful personality.

2. Discover if your tired feeling is traced to hypoglycemia via a glucose tolerance test. It can be a lifesaver!

3. Avoid refined foods, increase modest amounts of protein, and balance your blood sugar for more energy.

4. A six-step plan outlined by a physician will help free you from the grip of fatigue and bounce back with more pep.

5. Brewer's yeast is the basis of a doctor-recommended *Morning Pep-up Drink* to supercharge your body and mind for day-long vigor.

6. Cereals, as in the easy-to-prepare *Breakfast Energy Food,* will revitalize your source of energy.

7. Marge S.O. went from "droopy" to "dynamic" with high-energy foods. You can too.

8. Follow the simple guidelines to balance your blood sugar and energy potential.

•••*Seven*

Pep up your thyroid for thyroid for super energy

Feel sluggish? tired in the morning? fatigued in the afternoon? all dragged out in the evening? It could be the fault of a malnourished or lazy thyroid.

One of the most puzzling human endocrine glands is your thyroid, which controls the metabolism of body energy. In other words, it regulates the rate of speed at which you live and the amount of "food fuel" you need to keep your mechanism operating.

So important is the energy influence exerted by the thyroid upon your entire body, including your endocrine glands, that once every hour your entire volume of blood passes through this gland to become energized with its secretions.

Hidden Powerhouse of Energy

The thyroid gland, about 2 inches long and 1/4 inch wide, butterfly shaped, is in your neck, its two wings wrapped around the windpipe just below the Adam's apple. The thyroid weighs less than an ounce, but it has a dynamic impact on your levels of energy.

Think of it as your body's regulator. It functions by releasing hormones, the more important of which is the iodine-containing hormone *thyroxine*. This hormone helps regulate your heartbeat, body temperature, the energy rate at which you burn calories, and the speed at which food moves through your digestive tract.

If your thyroid is well nourished, it is able to dole out a proper amount of hormone to keep these processes humming with energy. But something may go wrong. A deficiency of nutrients causes problems. Your thyroid may turn overactive and pump out too much hormone or underactive and pump out too little. Either way, the unhealthy hormone levels can cause reactions upon your metabolism and your energy levels. In particular, you may have an underactive thyroid, commonly called *hypothyroidism.*

Lazy? Chilly? Always Tired?

It could very well be caused by hypothyroidism. Your body processes are slowing down. For some unknown reasons, this sluggishness overwhelmingly afflicts women, especially those between ages 35 and 60. Women develop this lazy thyroid four times more often than men!

Symptoms of Lazy Thyroid

Fatigue heads the list followed by poor appetite, overweight, muscle weakness, dry and scaly skin, hair loss, recurrent infections, slow speech, digestive upset, and constipation. Intolerance to cold is very frequent, especially while others feel hot. Your morning tiredness is also accompanied by palpitation of the heart, extreme exhaustion after the slightest exertion, headaches, and emotional depression.

Listen to your body's preliminary warning signal! You could be caught up in the grip of hypothyroidism and need nutritional help before you succumb to serious fatigue, among other disorders.

Quick Self-test for Thyroid Energy

To test yourself for an underactive thyroid, keep a thermometer by your bed one night. Upon awakening next morning, place the thermometer under your arm. Let it remain for 15 minutes. Keep absolutely quiet. Any motion can disturb your temperature reading. If the reading is 97.6°F. or lower, you may have an underactive thyroid. Keep a log. Take the readings for one week. If the figures are below 97.6°F. over a period of time, see your health practitioner.

Thyroid and Your Personality

Your basic personality is influenced by the thyroid hormone thyroxine. Mood changes may swerve from total exhaustion to sudden outbursts, alternated with periods of hilarity and depression. Nourish your thyroid so it can release a *balanced* hormone supply to help you enjoy a pleasant and energetic personality.

IODINE—THE MINERAL THAT FEEDS YOUR THYROID

Organic iodine is the most important mineral for the thyroid's production of thyroxin. So essential to your energy is this hormone that a few milligrams of iodine often means the difference between youthful energy and chronic fatigue, not to mention emotional disorders. Your thyroid needs energizing iodine!

Where to Find Iodine

Good sources include vegetables, seafood, lean meats, kelp (seaweed available as a powder or in tablet form or else in small sheets that are chewy good), and some dairy products. In particular iodine is found in saltwater fish, asparagus, dulse (another form of seaweed that is available dried, granulated, or ground into powder to be used as a condiment or for flavoring), white deep-water fish, garlic, lima beans, mushrooms, sesame seeds, soybeans, summer squash, Swiss chard, and turnip greens.

Avoid These Negative Thyroid Foods

Certain foods block the absorption of iodine into the thyroid gland when eaten raw in large quantities, namely, brussels sprouts, cabbage, cauliflower, kale, spinach, and turnips. Yes, these are good foods, but if you have thyroid difficulties, it is best to eat them cooked. Of course, with sufficient iodine over a period of time, your thyroid should be adequately nourished so that these foods may be eaten, in small amounts, if desired.

Be Careful of Chemicals in Water

Fluoride and chlorine will block iodine receptors in the thyroid gland, reducing iodine-containing hormone production. Drink bottled spring water that is free of these chemicals if you are prone to fatigue-causing hypothyroidism.

CASE HISTORY—
"Why Am I Always So Tired?"

Having raised three children, Noreen L. always had an abundant supply of energy. She was able to manage a household, help her husband when needed in his wholesale business, participate in local activities, and enjoy life. Yet, when she reached her late forties, she started to feel increasing fatigue. She was irritable when she was always known for being cheerful; she complained that she was exhausted even when waking up in the morning after a deep sleep; she detected heart palpitations. Even in the midst of a warm climate, Noreen L. felt chilly, often shivering when others wore summer clothes. Her energy drain made her lethargic. She was called "lazy" in jest but it made her feel hurt since she had always been lively and youthful.

Noreen L. went from one doctor to the next, always complaining, "Why am I always so tired?" Answers ranged from "it's all in your head" to "you need a change of scenery" to "get enough rest." Yet she still felt weaker and weaker.

She might have become a semi-invalid if she had not read a book by a natural health researcher on the problem of a sluggish thyroid. The advice was to have a thorough endocrine gland checkup and determine if the tiredness was caused by lack of thyroxin. She sought help from a recommended gland specialist, and tests confirmed her suspicions: her thyroid was malnourished, deficient in iodine, among other nutrients.

Immediately, Noreen L. was given a list of iodine-containing foods and told to take one-half teaspoon of kelp or dulse (a powerhouse of iodine) daily as a seasoning. At the end of nine days, she perked up. She felt energetic. Familiar smiles returned to her face. Her heart beat steadily. Her energy made her feel warm and no longer so chilly even in hot climates. And how could anybody call her "lazy" when she took a part-time job, participated in a volunteer organization, and soon announced she was going for a second honeymoon with her husband?

With natural iodine from everyday foods, she had stabilized her mischievous thyroid and became "made over" with energy boosters.

Garlic: Food for Your Thyroid

Depending upon the soil in which it is grown, garlic is believed to have the highest iodine content of any land-grown plant. It may often have four times as much iodine as onions, which also have a high content of this energy booster. Use garlic daily as a flavoring, and you should experience revitalization of your glands for more energy.

How to Energize Your Thyroid for More Vitality

If you are concerned about a sluggish thyroid (and you should be!), you can energize your gland with these simple programs. They also help improve your general health, too! A neat package!

Avoid Overweight

A sluggish thyroid means a slower metabolic rate, which means obesity! Check your weight regularly. Any gain that refuses to go away indicates your thyroid may be at fault. While nourishing your thyroid, also control your weight!

Eat Enough Fiber Daily

A sluggish thyroid brings many body functions to a grinding lethargy. This includes a "lazy intestine." *Meaning:* Problems of constipation. Protect yourself with adequate amounts of fiber each day. These include the familiar bran, whole grains, raw vegetables, fiber-rich cereals, prunes, figs, almonds, and walnuts. Become "regular" as you nourish your thyroid with fiber as well as iodine foods.

Iron + Folic Acid = Energetic Thyroid

Lesser known is the need for these two nutrients: iron and folic acid. Many folks with a sluggish thyroid show deficiencies of these nutrients that work with iodine to energize your gland and body, too. Good sources of both are brewer's yeast, broccoli, and orange juice. Supplements are available to be used with the guidance of your health practitioner.

Keep Cholesterol Under Control

Folks with hypothyroidism to also tend to have above-average blood cholesterol readings and, hence, an increased risk for coronary artery illness as well as stroke. Minimize the amount of animal fat in your diet: keep eaten cholesterol under 300 milligrams daily.

Herbs to Feed Your Thyroid

Considered "natural medicines," some herbs have the concentrated power to revitalize your thyroid with an abundant source of iodine and other nutrients to take up the slack of malnourishment. The most effective herbs are the following:

Bayberry. Improves metabolism and helps rev up a sluggish circulation while nourishing your thyroid.

Black Cohosh. Helps balance hormonal flow so that nutrients are able to nourish the thyroid and boost energy potential.

Goldenseal. Alerts and energizes your glandular system and helps to balance thyroxin secretion owing to the presence of two constituents—*berberine* and *hydrastine.*

These herbs are available at any herbal pharmacy or health store. A small amount daily (flavorful as a tea) will go a long way toward providing a natural energy booster for your thyroid.

Case History—
Grouchy, Sleepy, Irritable—Health on Decline

What was happening to Elizabeth U.? She had always been bright as sunshine. But she was becoming a gloomy dark cloud—threatening and forbidding, erupting into a violent storm upon the slightest provocation.

Her family was worried. Elizabeth U. was not only grouchy, but she was always shuffling around, looking sleepy, becoming irritable if questioned about her obvious health decline.

She had recurring and increasing fatigue; her speech was slow, her words were slurred, her temper was short. As a sales manager, she would snap at coworkers and (worse) snap at customers! Her supervisor, Hank D., had to do something to protect the business and his long-time friend.

Hank D. had encountered a similar situation with a family member and speculated that Elizabeth U. could be troubled with a malfunctioning thyroid. He insisted upon a thorough examination and emphasized tests for an iodine deficiency.

The laboratory results confirmed these suspicions: Elizabeth U. had experienced a decline in iodine as well as several other nutrients, and her thyroid was malfunctioning. At once, she was given an iodine-boosting nutritional program that included those foods containing the mineral required. She was also instructed to drink goldenseal tea daily—one or two cups. Within a short time, Elizabeth U. started to cheer up. She was alert, cooperative, always smiling, a personality as bright as sunshine! She was as beloved as before as soon as her thyroid was nourished with iodine and she was energetic again.

Someone remarked, "Now you're the old Elizabeth U. we always loved." She corrected with a smile, "I'm the *new* and younger Elizabeth U., thanks to a healthy thyroid!"

Never Underestimate the Energy-Boosting Power of Your Thyroid

It may be small, but this oft-puzzling gland holds the key to health and vitality of your body and mind. Feed your thyroid properly, and you will become supercharged with energy and power . . . quickly!

Highlights

1. Meet your thyroid, a hidden source of energy.
2. Note the symptoms of malnourishment and heed early warnings while you have time.
3. Iodine is food for your thyroid and the source of energy and youthful warmth.
4. Noreen L. was always tired until she discovered simple ways to wake up her sleepy thyroid.
5. Check out additional energizing steps to improve your thyroid for more vitality.
6. Simple herbal teas help nourish your thyroid.
7. Elizabeth U. was made "younger" and more vital when her thyroid was properly nourished.

Eight

How to detoxify your body (and mind) of seven energy thieves

Just as some foods give energy, other foods steal energy. These same so-called "foods" cause toxic clogging of your body and mind. You feel fatigued and "dragged down" because of this overload of wastes. The continual assault on your health by an array of toxic substances will do more than drain away energy and make you feel tired before your time. The effects can be as debilitating as severe headaches, insomnia, depression, and chronic illness.

But there is good news. With a series of detoxification programs, you can free yourself from the grip of addiction to these energy thieves and enjoy a more energy-filled life-style. You can expel the toxins from your body with the use of nutritional remedies and living adjustments.

Energy Thief #1—Alcohol

Call it a "recreational drug" that may give you a brief lift but is followed by a serious letdown, even collapse. Not much of recreation, is it?

Even in moderate amounts, alcohol increases the risk of certain health problems. There is the danger of developing breast cancer and colon cancer. Alcohol increases the risk of developing a serious stroke, a ruptured blood vessel in the brain. Alcohol contains calories that gives you a brief lift of energy and then a subsequent drop. If you have a weight problem, alcohol can add to it. Women should be wary of alcohol more than men. Women typically have a higher percentage of body fat and less body water than men do. Since alcohol dissolves much more readily in water than fat, the difference in body composition means that when alcohol enters a woman's body, it becomes more concentrated and, therefore, has a more potent reaction, than the same amount of alcohol would in a man's body.

These empty calories can impair mental faculties and drain away much-needed energy. To detoxify your system of alcohol, recognize that it is a potent drug with energy-draining dangers and that avoidance is the best path.

Nutritional Help to Detoxify Alcohol

You will help detoxify by starting on a program of nutritional help. It is reported that taking 500 milligrams each daily of: vitamin B3 (niacin) and vitamin C will help eliminate toxic wastes and ease the drinking urge. To help minimize withdrawal symptoms, you will be helped by taking 0.5 grams of evening primrose oil four times daily. These nutrients are available at most health stores as well as pharmacies.

Easing the Urge to Drink

Make some changes in your routine. Keep away from drinking chums, bars, parties. Never feel you owe excuses to anyone. "No thanks, I'm not drinking," is all you have to say and let it stand. An alternative is to order seltzer with a slice of lemon or lime and sip slowly. If you habitually had a drink at 5 o'clock, then get out of your house, take a walk, go for a drive, visit a shopping mall, try a film. Gradually, as you detoxify, you'll feel an easing of the urge and the symptoms. Your biggest reward will be a return of energy and less fatigue with a clear mind. You'll have overcome the energy thief of alcohol.

ENERGY THIEF #2—CAFFEINE

Is your day filled with sips of coffee or tea? How about soda pop? Millions of people "must" start the day with a caffeinated beverage as a "wake-up" jolt. But the effect is temporary. It saps your energy and you become deflated as a punctured balloon!

Caffeine Drains Energy

After the initial perk to your cardiovascular system, caffeine works on your muscles. There is a burst of energy that drains you so that you have a "tired, worn-out" feeling . . . and this can happen within a matter of hours. Caffeine is also believed to deposit toxic wastes on certain brain receptors, blocking your thinking processes, depressing your mental centers.

What Are the Toxic Effects of Caffeine?

As with all drugs, the effects vary depending on the amount taken and the individual. If you drink two cups of coffee (150–300 milligrams of caffeine), the effects begin in 15–30 minutes. Your metabolism, body temperature, and blood pressure may increase. Other toxic effects include increased urine production, higher blood sugar levels, hand tremors, decreased appetite, and a loss of coordination. *Caution:* Since it is a diuretic, caffeine also increases urine flow, which causes dehydration and drains out your energy, too.

Caffeine Content of Beverages and Foods

Item	Milligrams Caffeine	
	Average	Range
Coffee (5-oz. cup)		
Brewed, drip method	115	60–180
Brewed, percolator	80	40–170
Instant	65	30–120
Decaffeinated, brewed	3	2–5
Decaffeinated, instant	2	1–5
Tea (5-oz. cup)		
Brewed, major U.S. brands	40	20–90
Brewed, imported brands	60	25–110
Instant	30	25–50
Iced (12-oz. glass)	70	67–76
Cocoa beverage (5-oz. cup)	4	2–20
Chocolate milk beverage (8 oz.)	5	2–7
Milk chocolate (1 oz.)	6	1–15
Dark chocolate, semisweet (1 oz.)	20	5–35
Baker's chocolate (1 oz.)	26	26
Chocolate-flavored syrup (1 oz.)	4	4

Source: FDA, Food Additive Chemistry Evaluation Branch, based on evaluations of existing literature on caffeine levels.

Caffeine Content of Soft Drinks

Brand	Milligrams Caffeine (12-oz. serving)
Sugar-Free Mr. PIBB	58.8
Mountain Dew	54.0
Mello Yello	52.8
TAB	46.8
Coca-Cola	45.6
Diet Coke	45.6
Shasta Cola	44.4
Shasta Cherry Cola	44.4
Shasta Diet Cola	44.4
Mr. PIBB	40.8
Dr Pepper	39.6
Sugar-Free Dr Pepper	39.6
Big Red	38.4
Sugar-Free Big Red	38.4
Pepsi-Cola	38.4
Aspen	36.0
Diet Pepsi	36.0
Pepsi Light	36.0
RC Cola	36.0
Diet Rite	36.0
Kick	31.2
Canada Dry Jamaica Cola	30.0
Canada Dry Diet Cola	1.2

Source: Institute of Food Technologists (IFT), based on data from National Soft Drink Association, Washington, D.C. IFT also reports that there are at least 68 flavors and varieties of soft drinks produced by 12 leading bottlers that have no caffeine.

Caffeine Content of Drugs

Caffeine is an ingredient in more than 1,000 nonprescription drug products as well as numerous prescription drugs. Most often it is used in weight-control remedies, alertness or stay-awake tablets, headache and pain relief remedies, cold products, and diuretics. When caffeine is an ingredient, it is listed on the product label. Some examples of caffeine-containing drugs are:

Prescription Drugs	Milligrams caffeine
Cafergot (for migraine headache)	100
Fiorinal (for tension headache)	40
Soma Compound (pain relief, muscle relaxant)	32
Darvon Compound (pain relief)	32.4

Nonprescription Drugs

Weight-Control Aids

Dex-A-Diet II	200
Dexatrim, Dexatrim Extra Strength	200
Dietac capsules	200
Maximum Strength Appedrine	100
Prolamine	140

Alertness Tablets

Nodoz	100
Vivarin	200

Analgesic/Pain Relief Tablets

Anacin, Maximum-Strength Anacin	32
Excedrin	65
Midol	32.4
Vanquish	33

Diuretics

Aqua-Ban	100
Maximum-Strength Aqua-Ban Plus	200
Permathene H2 Off	200

Cold/Allergy Remedies

Coryban-D capsules	30

Triaminicin tablets	30
Dristan Decongestant tablets,	
Dristan A-F Decongestant tablets	16.2
Duradyne-Forte	30

Source: FDA's National Center for Drugs and Biologics.

The Major Sources of Caffeine

While coffee is the chief source of caffeine, soft drinks, tea, drugs, and chocolate also contain significant amounts of this addictive drug. Still, you can be selective as there are differences among brands and types of soft drinks, just as brewing times and methods of preparation make a big difference in the caffeine potency of coffee.

You need to kick the caffeine habit. Otherwise, it could wipe out your energy. Try this detoxification program.

1. If you "must" have coffee, drink instant coffee or instant or brewed decaffeinated coffee. You'll have less caffeine.

2. Drink a combination of half regular and half decaffeinated coffee.

3. As you taper off, switch to decaffeinated tea or caffeine-free herbal teas.

4. Brew tea for less time. A one-minute brewing, versus three-minute brewing, can cut caffeine in half.

5. Read soft drink labels carefully. A "cola" drink may contain some caffeine. A 12-ounce cola averages about 40 milligrams of caffeine. Check noncola beverages for any added caffeine.

6. Be alert to medications. One dose of an over-the-counter pain relief capsule can contain as much caffeine as is found in one or two cups of coffee. Cold tablets, allergy or headache relievers, weight-control products, and diuretics often contain caffeine.

Some prescription drugs contain caffeine, so discuss this with your physician.

7. Taper off gradually. You'll have fewer withdrawal symptoms than if you quit cold turkey.

8. Change your mug for a smaller one; measure a level, not heaping, teaspoon of coffee; sip slowly or with a spoon; dilute with more hot water or low-fat milk.

9. Switch to decaffeinated beverages, even though the beans have been sprayed with pesticides and the caffeine may have been removed by chemical solvents of questionable safety, and slowly taper off these substances.

10. Look for coffee substitutes made from roasted barley, rye, chicory, and shredded beetroots. Also use herbal teas made from plants, available in most health food stores and supermarkets. Rotate brands and flavors for variety.

CASE HISTORY—
Detoxifies the Caffeine Energy Thief and Is Rewarded with Supervitality

Granted that Philip R. had a lot of responsibilities as a construction foreman, but he always felt more energy when drinking a few cups of coffee at the start of the day. Then he began to drink more coffee while on the job—and would even munch a few chocolate candy bars for "snacks" and "pickups."

Problem: His energy swerve zoomed up— and then plunged! He found himself slumping on the job, unable to keep his eyes open, feeling jittery, developing trembles. Sure, the caffeine was an energy booster—but Philip R. paid the penalty in a slump. His body was becoming overloaded with toxic caffeine. He needed to kick the habit or his job (it required alertness of body and mind) would be in jeopardy.

A company nurse listened to his problem of fatigue, asked about his eating methods, and quickly recognized the thief of energy—caffeine. She told Philip R. to switch to coffee substitutes, to give up caffeine-containing chocolate, and to enjoy fresh fruit slices for a better pickup. Yes, he was going to have withdrawal symptoms, but he was so drained of energy, he had to nip this chief without delays or face total collapse.

He managed to make the adjustment in a short while. Since his job was at risk, he had the incentive to quit caffeine cold turkey. Before long, he had detoxified his system and was able to stay alert, feel vigorous, and have more mental energy. He had caught the energy thief and banished him from his body . . . and mind!

Energy thief #3—Fatty calories

Fats are a source of energy, but they act as a risky energy thief, also. A double-edged sword! Too much can drain your energy. *Danger:* Fats choke tissues by coating them with toxic wastes and deprive them of oxygen. Fats coat a fatty film around red blood cells and blood platelets, causing them to stick together. This toxemia reduces the cellular ability to transport oxygen; the fatty calories choke your capillaries (small blood vessels). Such blockage causes fatigue; there is a reduction of the amount of oxygen fatigue available to your cells.

Fats steal energy by setting off *ketosis*. That is, blood sugar is burned off speedily, forcing your body to go to your fat reserves for energy. Fatty acids taken from the fat reserves do not burn efficiently. Instead, they produce acid metabolites called ketones. This outpouring of ketones will prompt ketosis. *Risk:* Your metabolism causes sugar unrest. Your brain is starved by a deficiency of glucose (the only source of food for your brain). Ketones are acidic and change your blood pH (acid-alkaline balance). A highly acid blood makes it difficult for body-brain energy to function. You suffer unrelieved fatigue because of this imbalance. In some cases, you may have irregular heartbeats.

Fatty Calorie Detoxification Program

Keep intake of fats to a minimum. Remember that a meal high in fats will make you feel tired and lessen your ability to think properly because the tissues are not receiving enough oxygen. To detoxify fat:

1. Go easy with animal fats. More complex carbohydrates are needed to supply a constant flow of energy and warmth.

2. Choose low-fat foods. Use moderate amounts of polyunsaturated and monounsaturated fats. Reduce saturated fats such as butter and palm and coconut oils.

3. Avoid foods with hidden fats such as chips, doughnuts, cookies, snack crackers, cakes, pies, fried foods, and some processed and convenience foods.

4. Eat less added fats such as salad dressing, margarine, butter, mayonnaise, and gravy.

5. Try low-fat cooking methods such as broiling, steaming, roasting, baking, microwaving, grilling, stir-frying, and braising. Of course, these cooking methods are low fat only if you don't add fat while preparing! Be sure to baste or marinate with low-fat sauces.

Get the fat out! Your cells will be detoxified, and you will sparkle with youthful energy!

ENERGY THIEF #4—OVERWEIGHT

Your extra poundage drains away much of your energy. So you go on a diet—you skip meals. You may wait until afternoon to eat. After going 20 hours or more without food, you are so hungry, you will eat more than you should. You are exhausted—low blood sugar because of lack of food. If you try coffee and a pastry "to give yourself a lift" you are on a roller coaster. You zoom up . . . then zoom down. You crash! You have sacrificed your energy to your overweight. But you want to lose weight, right? Try these detoxification steps that help melt pounds (fat, too) and give you energy.

1. Set realistic weight-loss goals. About one pound lost per week is realistic. This rate promotes long-term detoxification of body fat, not just water weight that can be regained quickly.

2. Boost intake of fiber foods to help you feel full.

3. Drink at least six glasses of liquids daily. Include bottled spring water and herbal teas. They are fat-free fillers.

4. Put less food on your plate. Chew slowly. Limit animal fat. Use "good" fat (unsaturated fatty acids) such as olive oil and nuts in moderation. A little bit goes a long way.

5. Eat three meals a daily. *Never* skip breakfast!

6. You must snack? Try celery and carrot sticks or low-fat cottage cheese topped with fruit slices, crackers topped with sesame butter, unsalted and unbuttered popcorn, an assortment of chunks of fresh fruits and vegetables.

7. Exercise—as simple but effective as walking—helps burn up fatty calories and detoxify wastes so you lose weight all the more effectively. Exercise also gives you an emotional lift. Plan at least 60 minutes daily. It's a great energy booster. And so easy, too!

8. Increase intake of complex carbohydrates that offer protein: tofu, lentils, plain baked potatoes (avoid toppings), sesame seeds, beans, brown rice, and whole grains offer the nutrients that help to detoxify and energize and cause appetite satisfaction with weight loss. What more could you want?

ENERGY THIEF #5—SALT

Common table salt (sodium chloride) is the enemy of energy. In high concentrations, it changes the delicate fluid and mineral balance of your body. Excessive salt causes fluid build-up and high hydrostatis pressure in the cells. This may lead to cardiovascular problems. Salt chokes the bloodstream so that the blood cannot circulate properly. Your blood is responsible for bringing nutrients and oxygen to all body cells. Your blood also transports metabolic toxic waste for elimination by your body. A problem here is that water increase in the tissues makes this cleansing process more difficult. You feel this in drained-out energy!

Sodium-sensitive people are susceptible to high blood pressure, a condition that can cause fatigue because of an unusual process. For example, when your blood pressure rises, your body assumes that you need rest to help bring down the pressure. Therefore, certain receptors send signals to make you feel tired. You rest. Your blood pressure drops. But you upset this process with salt intake, and it causes reactions that give you some energy and some fatigue. Salt can be a killer thief of life . . . and energy!

How Much Salt Do You Need?

The National Research Council recommends no more than 2,400 milligrams of sodium a day for the average adult. One teaspoon of table salt contains 2,325 milligrams of sodium. And you can get this amount from most foods so you can eliminate salt from the shaker and enjoy good health.

How to Detoxify the Salt Habit

Try some of these hints:

1. Read food labels. Specific claims such as "low in sodium" must show the sodium content on the label.

2. Start with moderate changes. Cut back on your taste for salt gradually. You weren't born with a preference for salt; it can be "unlearned." Gradually reduce the amount of salt in your favorite recipes until you've got it down to half or even less.

3. Cut back or cut out salt used in cooking rice, noodles, pasta, or hot cereals.

4. Try adding new herbs and spices instead of salt to foods or the water you cook them in.

5. Put herbs and spices in your salt shaker and use as a healthful substitute.

6. Be wary of canned and frozen foods; many contain salt. Read the label. Switch to natural, wholesome fresh foods as much as possible.

7. Eating out? Choose foods without sauces. If you prefer a sauce, ask for it "on the side" so you can control the amount you use.

8. Unsalted nuts and seeds (caraway, poppy, sesame) add flavor and crunch to broiled fish (classic combination: almonds on filet of sole) and stir-fried vegetables (sesame seeds and broccoli).

9. Sprinkle grated lemon or orange peel over broiled chicken or baked squash. Grate all the peel from the fruit; use the amount desired and freeze the leftovers.

10. Add a bit of honey, herbs, and mild vinegar (like rice vinegar) to a tossed green salad.

Kick the salt habit and you'll feel superenergy in body and mind. And improved health, too!

ENERGY THIEF #6—SUGAR

Also known as sucrose, this energy thief is metabolized into glucose and fructose to provide energy. In the form of glucose, it enters your bloodstream speedily, then calls upon insulin to enter your cells. But sugar in refined form can be destructive to your energy and can bring on varying levels of hypoglycemia. That is, excessive insulin is released, forcing an overwhelming amount of glucose into the cells. This brings down blood glucose into the cells, which in turn, brings down blood glucose levels to such a depth, you feel fatigue, depression, even dizziness.

Too much insulin (because of sugar overload) causes brain cells to absorb more than the required amount of electrolytes (blood-circulating ions) and to swell with water. Fatigue is only one of the symptoms exhibited because of this sugar-insulin reaction.

The remedy appears to be a diet low in refined carbohydrates, namely, sugar—not only from the shaker but in foods. You can detoxify this energy thief with these methods:

1. Always read package labels. Sugar may be listed as sucrose, glucose, turbinado, dextrose, fructose, corn syrup, corn sweetener, or natural sweetener. The closer sugar is to the top of the listing, the greater its content. Avoid such products!

2. Use fruit juices, unsweetened herbal tea, seltzer with a slice of lemon, vegetable juice as a substitute. A mixture of seltzer and undiluted frozen fruit juice makes a delicious low-sugar "natural" soft drink.

3. Reduce sweet desserts and use only if you cannot control the urge, but in small amounts.

4. Select fresh fruits or those canned in their own juices or in water.

5. Ready-to-eat cereals without sugar should be selected. Hot cereals are less likely to contain sugar but be sure to read labels. Sweeten cereal with fresh fruit slices.

6. Reduce sugar in recipes. As your sweet tooth adjusts, reduce to one-half, one-fourth, and as little as possible. *Tip:* Use apple juice concentrate in place of sugar in recipes.

It is important to remember that while honey has nutrients, it is a concentrated sweet and can create "sugar problems." Use a small amount of honey, if you must. Since it is so concentrated, a little goes a long way. The same applies to blackstrap molasses.

You want a constant flow of energy and you can enjoy it with complex carbohydrates and moderate protein in contrast to the brief "rush" from refined sugar.

Energy thief #7—smoking

You know smoking is deadly! It also drains away your energy. Tobacco smoke contains nicotine, carbon monoxide, carcinogens, and irritant substances. As these toxic invaders settle in the body, they act as energy thieves. Carbon monoxide, when combined with your hemoglobin, blocks oxygen from being transported through the body, thereby bringing on feelings of fatigue, and depression, too.

Sidestream smoking can often have the same effect. Even if you are a nonsmoker, breathing in these toxic fumes from someone else can steal your energy, not to mention health.

To help you uproot and cast out this energy thief, try these remedies:

1. The urge lasts about three minutes. Yes, it is difficult to resist, but try it! Do not sit and wait while you have the craving. Instead, do exercises, take a walk, anything to get your mind off the compulsion to light up and drain your energy.

2. Cut down usage. Postpone lighting for five minutes the first day, six minutes the second day, and continue adding a minute a day. While waiting to light up, do something enjoyable and distracting.

3. Join a support group if you find it is helpful.

4. There will be distress as you undergo detoxification during the first five or six days. Some feeling of irritability, depression, headaches, or sleep disturbances will further drain energy. But you will soon be rewarded with inner cleansing and a feeling of revitalization once the toxic wastes are eliminated. In a short time, you will feel new surges of energy.

5. Make a dietary change—ingest less animal protein since these foods (meat, fish, eggs, poultry) make acidic urine at a time when you are already washing out acid wastes. Switch to fruits (except cranberries, plums, prunes), vegetables, nuts, and seeds, which create a more alkaline environment. *Benefit:* It is believed that alkaline foods take longer to flush nicotine out of your system. This means the nicotine is *slower* to be washed out and your craving is decreased. Many have found that a vegetarian or meatless diet helps make the detoxification all the easier.

Free yourself from the grip of tobacco and you will be rewarded with health and better energy . . . and your life, too!

CASE HISTORY—
Overcomes Addictions, Enjoys Health, Better Energy

That after-dinner drink (along with a lot of beers during the day), the heavy food laced with salt and sugar, the nonstop coffee, and habitual smoking turned Raymond O'N. into a nervous wreck. He tried to blame it upon his high-pressure job as a credit manager for a large financial institution. Granted, he had many deadlines, negotiations, obligations, and endless conferences. But his toxic habits were taking their toll on his health.

When he kept falling asleep at meetings, when he felt his energy slipping away, leaving him exhausted even after a night of sleep (which was not always satisfying), he decided to see an internist.

Tests confirmed that he was abusing his body with toxic overload through bad habits.

Raymond O'N. was put on a special program. Get rid of the bad habits. Not easy to cut them out at one time, but unless he did it, his blood cells would actually snuff out his life because of clogging wastes.

He eased up on his drinking and smoking, omitted salt and sugar, and managed to go down to one or two cups of coffee daily. (He said he wanted to cling to something!) In four weeks, he bounced back with new vigor and energy. No, it was not easy. Withdrawal symptoms were painful. He almost collapsed at times. He "slipped" and would take a taboo smoke or drink but only on occasion so the danger was brief. Before long, he said he felt "made over" into a new body and mind—he had overcome the addictions and healthy energy was the well-deserved reward.

Protect yourself against toxic threats to your energy. Expel the toxins from your body and you will enjoy youthful vitality and be fatigue-free forever!

Highlights

1. There are seven basic energy thieves you need to nip in the bud to prevent toxic overload, the cause of much fatigue.

2. Philip R. detoxified the caffeine thief of energy and was rewarded with new vitality.

3. Raymond O'N. was about ready to give up because of his constant sleepiness and fatigue, but thanks to the help of an internist, he made some changes and detoxified his bad habits. He was rewarded with healthy energy!

4. Free yourself of alcohol, fatty calories, overweight, salt, sugar, and smoking, and you will free yourself of many life-threatening ailments. Only *you* can do it!

Nine

Refresh yourself with sleep – without pills

You wake up and the world seems new. You slip out of bed with a smile on your face and a spring in your step. You're alert, refreshed, energetic. The reason: a good night's sleep. At any age and every stage of life, the better you sleep, the better energy you have, the better you enjoy life.

Unfortunately, not all mornings begin brightly. All too often, just prying your eyes open can take considerable effort. Your body feels achy and drained. You're edgy, irritable, foggy. The problem: not getting the restful sleep you needed.

WHAT IS A GOOD NIGHT'S SLEEP?

Many people would reply by saying a minimum of eight hours of rest. But the answer does not depend solely on how many hours you log in bed. Night after night, you need deep, uninterrupted sleep in a bed that provides adequate comfort, support, and space. What matters most of all is how you feel in the morning. If you wake up full of renewed energy, you've had a good night's sleep.

There is no one formula for how much sleep is enough for you. Instead, you are an individual. You have an innate sleep "appetite" that is as much a part of your genetic programming as hair color, height, fingerprints. But a rule of thumb would be from five to ten hours; the average is seven and a half.

How Much Sleep Do You Need for More Energy?

To figure out your sleep needs, keep your wake-up time the same every morning and vary your bedtime. Are you groggy after six hours of shuteye? Does an extra hour give you more energy? What about an extra two hours? Since too much time in bed can make some people feel sluggish, don't assume that more is always better. Listen to your body's signals, and adjust your schedule to suit them.

Your Needs Undergo Changes

Sleep needs change with age. The older you are, the less total sleep time you may need. A newborn may spend 18 hours asleep. From infancy to adulthood, sleep decreases by more than half. Throughout the middle decades of life, 7 or 8 hours of sleep generally are needed to provide adequate rest. For older folks, 6 hours may suffice to produce next-day energy.

Bad Nights/Bad Days

What happens when you don't get the rest you need? Fatigue! Weariness brings on irritability and depression. You mope instead of cope; you snap at others, complain about anything and everything. While everyone around you may be laughing, you're yawning. Bad moods are only some of the consequences of bad nights. Without refreshing sleep, you cannot perform at your peak. Even half an hour less sleep than usual can drain your energy and impair the way you feel and function the next day. Sleep is vital for energy of body and mind.

IMPORTANT TIPS FOR RESTFUL SLEEP

Your dinner should be eaten about five hours before going to bed. A full stomach is not too comfortable and does not provide restful sleeping. On the other hand, if you go to bed hungry, you toss and turn. Strike the happy medium and have a comfortable meal that is given about five hours to digest before you turn in.

You may benefit from a soothing combination of nutrients: (a) 1,000 milligrams of magnesium early in the morning will help to soothe your nerves, muscles, and heart; (b) 1,000 milligrams of calcium about an hour before bedtime helps to regulate muscle contraction, soothe nerve transmission, make you feel tranquil.

These minerals are available as supplements to be used with the guidance of your health practitioner. In this combination, taken at the times suggested, you help your body and mind welcome inviting sleep. *Bonus:* The magnesium-calcium program gives you natural refreshing sleep so that you awaken with youthful energy!

CASE HISTORY—
Insomniac Becomes Nervous Wreck with Drugs, Pills

Was insomnia something that Barbara P. had to live with? She often said, "I want to live without this tossing and turning." She was a bundle of nerves; she would lie awake for hours, staring at the ceiling, wishing sleep would come. While she had many responsibilities as an administrator with the school system, she did not really take her concerns to bed with her. No matter what she did, sleep was always out of reach.

Desperate, she took prescription drugs and pills. While they gave her "instant sleep," she awakened groggy, more nervous than if she stayed awake in frustration all night. She could not depend on drugs. How would she overcome the insistent insomnia that was making her a nervous wreck with bouts of fatigue throughout the day?

She heard a teacher tell of having been advised to try the magnesium-calcium program to correct her own insomnia-caused fatigue. It was so simple, Barbara P. doubted its effectiveness. The other teacher said, "It's certainly better and more natural than a drug. And it worked!" Desperate, she tried the remedy. She would take 1,000 milligrams of magnesium shortly before noon. Then she would take 1,000 milligrams of calcium one hour before bedtime. This combination spaced so that each one would metabolize individually for greater effectiveness was exactly what Barbara P. needed. Gone was her insomnia. Gone was her doubt.

The troubled administrator was soon able to enjoy a night of refreshing sleep—without any drugs or pills. She awakened with a clear mind and energetic body. Life was now full of joy—and energy—thanks to the magnesium-calcium combination that gave her restful sleep and energetic days!

How to Adjust Your Circadian Rhythm and Sleep Better

Circadian (daily) rhythms are natural biological functions that influence your sleep and energy cycles. Circadian rhythms are coordinated by an inherent timing mechanism known as a biological clock. Most people's clocks are synchronized to the sun's 24-hour cycle—sunrise means waking and working; sundown brings dinner and sleep. The master timekeeper in your body helps synchronize you with such outside cycles as day and night. Like orchestra conductors, they coordinate hundreds of functions inside your body. You react to complex inner rhythms of rising and falling tides of hormones, immune cells, electrolytes, and amino acids.

Is Your Work Shift at Fault?

Charmane I. Eastman, Ph.D., associate professor of psychology, and director of Rush Medical Center's Biological Rhythms Research Laboratory in Chicago, Illinois, tells us, "Most night shift workers go home to sleep during the day when their bodies want to be awake, and they have to work at night when their bodies want to sleep.

"The circadian rhythm of body temperature is a marker for your clocks. Body temperature rises and falls in cycles parallel to alertness and performance efficiency. When body temperature is high (generally during the day), alertness and performance peak, but sleep is difficult. A lower temperature (generally during the night) promotes sleep, but hinders alertness and performance."

Your work shift could be responsible for sleep difficulties. If you can't change your work arrangement, you may need to adjust your body clock so that sleep is more inviting.

How TO RESET YOUR BIOLOGICAL CLOCK

Charles P. Pollak, M.D., acting director of the Institute of Chronobiology, New York Hospital-Cornell Medical Center, White Plains, New York, explains that "chronobiology is the field of science that explores the many bodily changes governed by the hours and seasons."

Delayed Sleep Phase Syndrome—a Form of Insomnia

Left to itself, your body tends to run on a slightly longer schedule than 24 hours—a 25-hour cycle. Some mechanism continually resets your biological clock so that you should be able to go to sleep at the same time as the night before and agree to wake up at a certain time. *Problem:* Conflict between natural biological rhythms and adjustments required by life's demands may be responsible for a type of insomnia called *delayed sleep phase insomnia*.

Dr. Pollak explains, "People with this condition are consistently unable to fall asleep at the desired time. They tend to be 'night owls' and often feel most productive late at night. Once asleep, they virtually need explosives to get them up for work in the 9-to-5 world. If they fall asleep at 3:00 A.M. and are forced to rise at 7:00 A.M., the problem remains. Exhaustion will not reset the biological clock."

Remedy: Dr. Pollak has come to the rescue with a treatment approach that calls for going to sleep progressively *later*. On the first night, instead of 3:00 A.M., hold off until 6:00 A.M. You get the normal amount of sleep, waking up at perhaps 1:00 P.M. The next night sleeping and waking are put off yet another three hours. This is continued until the desired bedtime is reached.

"Once your inner clock is on the same schedule as 'outer time' and living requirements, you should stick to it, since regularity is critical to maintaining the time frame."

Are YOU AN OWL OR A LARK?

An "owl" is said to be an evening person. A "lark" is a morning person. Measurements of circadian rhythms in evening persons show heart rates peaking between 5:00 and 6:30 p.m. The heart rates in morning persons peak between 1:00 and 2:00 p.m.

It's in Your Glands

Owls start the day more slowly, produce more level amounts of the hormone adrenaline, and are able to improve performance through the day and into early evening. Larks release more adrenaline during the morning hours, followed by lesser levels of performance as the day moves on. *Tip:* Know your own situation and start to adjust to your glands for better sleep and more energy.

Simple Self-test for Energy

When do you perform best? Evenings or mornings? If you are locked into a workday that may not be suited to your daily peaks and valleys, try to adjust the timing of your tasks so that they best coordinate with your abilities at the different times of days.

Can you work best around 8:00 A.M. and thereabouts? Schedule activities for those hours. Or do you work best around 4:00 P.M. and thereafter? Plan your activities for those hours.

You could even keep a diary for one week. Rate your alertness, mood, irritability, and performance. Recognize your "high" and "low" hours. Then try to adjust accordingly so you have energy when it is needed and can go to sleep when needed, too.

Be Careful of Sleeping Pills

Isn't it easier to take a drug for troubled sleep? You could pay the penalty, says Peter Hauri, M.D., director of the Mayo Clinic Insomnia Program in Rochester, Minnesota. "Sleeping pills are self-limiting in their long-term effectiveness. You need a nondrug approach in the long run. Drug companies have nothing to gain by comparing their products to the nondrug approaches. So there have been almost no sound direct comparisons of sleeping pills and nondrug approaches." If you have short-term insomnia (it lasts up to three weeks or so), try sleep hygiene: examine habits that interfere with slumber, for example, drinking beverages with caffeine too close to bedtime.

Chronic insomniacs (those whose sleep problems last longer than a month, and sometimes for years) who are most tempted to turn to sleeping pills "should be very careful with sleep medications. If you take them in the long term, they don't help you any more and you do even worse for a time if you stop. If you were sleeping just four hours a night with the pills, you may sleep only a half hour for a week or so after you stop the pills. So you find yourself staying on them just to avoid the withdrawal. For chronic insomnia, treating the cause is crucial. If you're depressed because of a bad marriage, you might sleep better after marital therapy, for example."

Stop Worrying

Dr. Hauri observes that many insomniacs worry about being unable to sleep. "We find it crucial to change distorted beliefs about sleep and insomnia. The more you worry about not being able to sleep, the more you will have insomnia."

Herbs to help you sleep better

In some situations, herbs can help bring on a desire for refreshing sleep and help you awake with more energy. Your herbalist has these products that can be enjoyed as a soothing tea or potion:

> *Celery Seed.* It contains phthalides, substances that have soothing effects in animals. While animal findings do not always apply to humans, if you're anxious or wakeful, try this herb and see how it works for you.
>
> *Motherwort.* Herbalists often recommend it to bring on natural relaxation and a desire to sleep. Its leaves, flowers, and stems have the ingredients that should help you feel more peaceful and sleepy.
>
> *Valerian.* Parts of the root contain substances called valepotriates that help create a more natural desire for sleep.

More important, this herb improves sleep quality so that you are able to awaken with vitality and energy. Valerian seems to have good results with older individuals who consider themselves poor sleepers.

CASE HISTORY—
Herbs Help Bring on Natural Sleep and Supercharged Energy

Recurring insomnia drained Brian V. to the extent that he would fall asleep while behind the wheel of his car as he made his rounds delivering hardware supplies throughout the district. He had tried sleeping pills, but they so upset his equilibrium, he felt the treatment was worse than the illness!

While on his route, he stopped off to deliver supplies to a medical facility. A casual chat with one of the physicians alerted him to the possibility of using herbs as "natural medicines" to help him sleep.

He tried celery seed, which helped him rest enough to enjoy some sleep, but he was still bothered with much tossing and turning. He changed to valerian, which he used in the form of tablets and also as a tea. (He gave up his habitual caffeine beverages.) The valerian helped him enjoy more thorough sleep until he gave up all drugs. Brian V. was able to overcome his insomnia and enjoy refreshing sleep with natural herbs and an improved life-style.

The biggest reward was his renewed energy. He was alert, active, and energetic and was soon given a "safe driver award" because he had sharp senses and instincts behind the wheel . . . and during his waking day.

WHAT TO DO BEFORE THE LIGHTS GO OUT

Insomnia experts with the Better Sleep Council advise, "The best time to get a headstart on a good night's rest is long before you get into bed. Here is a set of programs that are good for you—and your sleep."

Exercise. Daily physical activity works away tensions as well as inches. But don't exercise vigorously late in the evening, or you'll raise your heart and breathing rates, preparing your body for action, not rest.

Guard against Sunday night insomnia. An erratic schedule can disrupt your biological rhythms and cause problems such as insomnia. It strikes people who stay up late and sleep later on weekends and then try to switch back to their usual bedtime to prepare for Monday morning.

Stay away from stimulants. Coffee, tea, soft drinks, chocolate, and some medications contain caffeine which can interfere with your sleep. Nicotine may be an even more potent sleep disrupter. Smokers take longer to fall asleep and wake up more often in the night than do nonsmokers.

Eschew late meals. Heavy or spicy meals at bedtime force your digestive system to work overtime—keeping you awake, too. But an empty stomach can be as uncomfortable as a too-full one, so you can have a small late night snack. If you're dieting, make sure it's low in calories.

Eliminate heavy drinking. Perhaps a glass of wine will shorten the time it takes you to fall asleep, but overindulgence can shatter your normal sleep pattern. Heart pounding, dry mouth, aching muscles, you wake up before dawn, a hapless victim of the wrath of grapes.

Turn off worrying. Set aside a time for worrying, planning, or preparation several hours before bedtime. Use this time to focus on problems, think over events of the day, or make a list of things to do tomorrow. If daytime pressures follow you into bed, tell yourself you'll deal with them during the next day's worry time.

Change your presleep rituals. If you follow the same routine every evening, your activities will become well-rehearsed cues for rest. You might try writing in a diary, listening to soft music, or reading a not-too-exciting book. Prayer and meditation help many end the day in peaceful slumber.

Check room temperature. You'll feel more comfortable with a temperature in the mid-60s. The temperature of the room air matters more than whether it is fresh (which it should be, too).

Ensure quiet. We never do adjust to traffic and other night noises. Even if we don't wake up, we shift to a lighter, less restful sleep stage. To block out noise, try wearing ear plugs or playing tapes of soothing sounds, like ocean waves or wind in the trees. A white noise generator (available in some sound system stores) that sounds like an air conditioner on the "fan" setting may help if you live amidst noisy people.

Block out light. This may be the most sinister sleep saboteur, since your biological clock relies on light as its strongest clue. Light is a signal for action; darkness, for rest. If you're trying to sleep late in the morning or during the day, use heavy draperies or light-blocking shades in your bedroom.

Sleep—it's a wonderful energy booster

Your sleep ritual can be as simple or as elaborate as you choose. Whatever you select, do the same things every evening until they become cues for your body to settle down for the night. You'll be able to face the day ahead with a burst of energy that will make you feel glad all over!

Highlights

1. Sleep is essential to refresh your body and mind. Check the guidelines as to how much sleep you need and about those bad nights that lead to bad days!

2. Sleep better with tryptophan, an amino acid that helps bring on refreshing sleep so you awaken with youthful energy.

3. Four basic techniques (easy to follow) help bring on restful sleep without pills and boost your potential for energy the next day.

4. Barbara P. gave up pill addiction and used a magnesium-calcium program that overcame her insomnia-caused fatigue. Simple and effective.

5. Adjust your circadian rhythm for better sleep. Reset your biological clock.

6. Are you an "owl" or a "lark"? No matter. You can still have healthy sleep and better energy with the guidelines offered.

7. Try herbs to help you sleep better. They're "natural medicines."

8. Brian V. used herbs to bring on natural sleep and also benefited with supercharged energy.

9. A set of easy programs help you invite natural sleep. Prepared by sleep experts. And . . . be wary of sleep-inducing drugs!

Ten

How to energize climate fatigue

It happens on schedule as the short days and long nights of winter draw near. A feeling of fatigue as well as sadness. *Symptoms:* Irritability, boredom, lack of energy, a tendency to oversleep and overeat, frequent confinement to the home because of the weather—the constant tiredness is often accompanied by feelings of depression.

This condition has a name: seasonal affective disorder (SAD). Martin B. Keller, M.D., director of outpatient research in the Massachusetts General Hospital Psychiatry Service, says that to be diagnosed as having SAD, a person must have:

- Experienced episodes of depression within the same 60-day fall or winter period during three years, at least two of them consecutive.
- Endured at least three times as many instances of depression within that two-month time frame as during other times of the year.
- Recovered from the depressive states during another 60-day period occurring at the same time during each of the years in question.

(You are excluded if there is an obvious effect of seasonally related stress, such as being unemployed every winter.)

Dr. Keller explains, "We find that three or four particular symptoms stand out in this condition. SAD patients typically sleep and eat more than usual and gain weight. They also have a real sense of loss and energy."

Winter, Light, Gland, Fatigue

During winter, the decrease of daylight has an influence on your *pineal gland*. Pronounced pie-nee-ul, this pea-size organ located near the center of your brain has an influence on your energy-fatigue levels. You are either energized or fatigued by blood levels of *melatonin*, a hormone released and regulated by your pineal gland.

Light is the triggering factor in the release of melatonin. Photoreceptors in the retina of the eye are linked to the pineal gland. The greater the light, the lower your level of melatonin and the more energy you have. The lesser the light, the higher your level of melatonin and the more fatigue you have.

Simple Test: If you shut your eyes and lie down, the darkness brings forth more melatonin and you feel groggy, sleepy, tired. But . . . when you open your eyes, get out in the sunshine, you have less melatonin and you feel energetic.

Some SAD patients can energize themselves by adding bright, white lights to extend winter's daylight. Dr. Keller says that responses were noticed after two to four days of the light treatment. "The patients did best if they continued treatment for a couple of weeks. Those who discontinued the treatment after getting an initial response found their depression recurring within another two to four days."

Some reports have told of relief from SAD by changing latitude, traveling in winter from a northern state with short days to a southern clime with longer days. *Problem:* If you go south for a vacation, the question is: Was it the good time or the longer days that led to your sense of renewed wellness?

How to Energize Yourself in the Dark Days of Winter

Winter may bring on some social stress. There tend to be fewer activities available and reduced occasions to socialize and seek social support. When this happens, you may feel "under the weather." You can get out from under that dark cloud of fatigue with some simple self-energy tips:

1. Get outside and keep yourself physically active. Inactivity worsens the symptoms of SAD and lethargy and fatigue.

2. If you have a craving for carbohydrates, try some fresh fruit or chewy raw vegetable chunks. In particular, very ripe fruit has a good supply of sugar that will help ease some of the fatigue of "winter hormones."

3. Break your routine. Get out of your residence. Take a brief vacation to a sunny climate. Not possible? Recharge your batteries with a weekend getaway.

4. It's the middle of the dark days of winter. You've been feeling tired and blue. To self-energize, flip on the lights and recharge your spirits.

Bright Lights Help Boost Your Energy

You are likely to become more energetic when you are exposed to longer periods of light. One reason may be that sunlight controls production of the hormone melatonin, which, at its high winter levels, tends to make you feel sleepier and less energetic.

Light Controls Energy

Dr. Norman Rosenthal, a staff psychiatrist at the National Institute of Mental Health (NIMH), tells of a woman who was always bright and cheerful during sunlight-drenched summer but changed with the dark days of winter. "She grew very depressed. She overate and was so tired all the time she could hardly go to work. When springtime came, she perked up as if by magic. I helped her to feel better by using very bright artificial light to lengthen the day."

Some researchers believe that ultraviolet rays (found in sunlight but missing from most artificial light) could be the reason for seasonal fatigue. One remedy is to install brighter than normal lights as a means of helping brighten moods and improve energy levels. While not as effective as sunlight, it is somewhat helpful in boosting energy to an appreciable level.

CASE HISTORY—
Strong Light Helps Improve Energy

Dr. Norman Rosenthal tells of treating John Z., a 63-year-old manic-depressive whose gloomy periods almost always began in midsummer and peaked around year's end. During his winter depression, he withdrew, became stressed and self-critical. He was chronically tired, afraid to go to work. He tried medications, but they had to be discontinued because of side effects. How could the doctors help him become more energetic and cheer up?

They created springtime conditions. During the first week of December, shortly before his fatigue-depression was going to reach a peak, the doctors woke John Z. out of bed at 6:00 a.m. and exposed him to very bright artificial light—about ten times as bright as customary indoor light—for three hours. Then at 4:00 p.m., they exposed him to the same type of light for another three hours. They were lengthening his days. The treatment continued for ten days.

Within four days, the man started to get out of his depressive cocoon. He declared he felt better. Although the beneficial effect ended four days after the treatment ended, the doctors established that "strong artificial light can have as great an effect on emotional health as does natural sunlight."

How to Keep Energetic Even if It Is Dark and Gloomy

You can maintain high energy levels by following these suggestions as soon as the darkness approaches:

- Keep yourself active. Enjoy excitement whether it is a visit to a new area or simply splurging on a luxury. You can fantasize about travel plans as you sit back and dream a little.
- Acclimate yourself to cold weather by maintaining an outdoor exercise program in the early fall. Always start with warm-up

exercises and end with cool-down exercises. Dress lighter than usual since exertion raises your body heat.

- Even during the cold temperatures, allow some fresh air to circulate regularly throughout your residence. This helps prevent toxic bacteria from building up.
- Keep warm with layers of loose clothing for the best insulation. Remove a layer if you feel warm.
- Overweight? You are at a greater risk of tiredness.
- Too thin? You need more clothing to stay comfortable in the cold.
- Even if it is cold, drink several glasses of water daily to prevent dehydration and to keep your body temperature at a steady level.
- In cold, dark weather, eat moderate amounts of protein. This may come from seafood, poultry, legumes, and peas, and not necessarily from high-fat meats.
- Schedule at least one pleasurable social activity a week or even every day. This extends a "playful" feeling to make you feel energetic.
- Air pollution and heating deplete the supply of soothing negative ions in the air. Try to get into a fresh air region and enjoy this refreshing treat to boost energy.
- Whenever possible, get plenty of sunshine. Keep out of the rain. Dress comfortably. Don't get overheated or overchilled.
- Brighten your indoor living space with lots of full-spectrum light (bulbs and lamps are available at your lighting or hardware store) plus as much daylight as possible and lots of color.
- Enjoy all available sunlight—especially in the winter. It is needed to inhibit excessive production of the hormone melatonin, which, at its high winter levels, tends to make you feel sleepier and less energetic. A healthy dose of daily sunlight is energizing because it controls the drowsy melatonin. Wake up your body and mind with at least one or two hours of sunshine daily in the winter.

WHEN TO ENERGIZE WITH LIGHT THERAPY

You need full-spectrum lights which are as close to natural sunlight as possible. Give yourself light therapy in the early morning to advance the time that melatonin is produced. Light given in the middle of the day does not have that much effect. Morning light convinced your brain that it is not dark winter but another season, and you tend to have more energy, as well as a lighter mood.

You may spend about two hours every morning in front of several very bright full-spectrum lights. You may talk, read, or do something to occupy yourself, if you prefer. It is helpful if you will look at the lights for a few seconds every few minutes. For some reason, the retinas should be exposed to light for the energizing treatment to work.

You may also take the light therapy at the end of the day if you want to extend the length of your schedule and activities.

Which Type of Light?

Fatigue-causing melatonin can be inhibited with 2,500 lux-intensity light. (*Lux* is Latin for "light," or a unit of measure for brightness.) As an example of the intensities of the light sources used to overcome fatigue, think of a bright, sunny day. The light falling on your eyes is equal to 100,000 lux. A set of lights that produce 2,500 lux should help reset your body clocks to have more energy and less fatigue. Again, ask your light specialist as well as your health practitioner for guidance on which lights are available for use at home. You may also find such light therapy available at major medical universities.

CASE HISTORY—
Light Makes Life Worth Living Again

Al Lewy, M.D., professor of psychiatry at Oregon Health Sciences University in Portland, worked with others at the National Institute of Mental Health to help find out why so many become fatigued and depressed when dark days come along.

Dr. Lewy treated Herb K., a 63-year-old engineer who was troubled with mood changes. He told his doctors that as the days got shorter, he "just wanted to crawl into a hole and hibernate. I finally latched on the thought that sunlight was the key. When the days got longer in summer, the wheels of my brain would spin again." But Herb K. says his doctors would not believe him.

When he came to Dr. Lewy, the advice was to lengthen Herb K.'s winter days by sitting him in a room under bright full-spectrum lights for six hours—three before dawn and three after sunset. *Results:* Herb K. says he felt as if he were in springtime! He was no longer tired; he felt energetic and not depressed, either. He continues to take two hours of light treatment at 6:00 a.m. from fall through spring. "Since using the lights, I have been able to manage my depressions very nicely."

Should You Use Ordinary Light for Therapy?

No! Standard home lighting fixtures are nowhere near bright enough (150 to 250 lux). Some standard superbright lights can damage vision when you look at them. If you think you have SAD, discuss it with your health practitioner and ask about phototherapy.

You can use incandescent lighting (cool-white fluorescent is a "cold" light) and as much wattage as you can afford around the home and workplace. If you must get up in the dark, put a light or two on a timer set to turn on a little before the alarm goes off. You'll feel more energetic awakening to some light.

Make the most of daylight. If possible, move your desk to a window or location that provides a window view. Go for a noonday walk. If possible, leave your home early enough for a walk during sunrise. It's important to enjoy as much sunlight as possible.

Let There Be Light!

With the use of available and indoor light, you can overcome the doldrums of climate/winter darkness. You'll become energized and active as light eases SAD and makes you glad. The point is, don't let the condition overwhelm you. When it gets dark at 4:30 p.m., your lights shouldn't go out, too.

Highlights

1. Feel fatigued in dark winter? It could be SAD. Energy specialists have found the reason for this tiredness and how to correct it.

2. A simple four-step basic plan helps you energize yourself in the dark days of winter.

3. Bright lights stimulate glandular function so you are able to cheer up and feel a surge of energy.

4. John Z. was a manic-depressive with chronic tiredness that responded to a doctor's light therapy. He soon became energetic and more responsive to the world around him.

5. A set of suggestions helps you keep energetic even if it is dark and gloomy.

6. Several hours daily of full-spectrum light therapy helps boost your energy levels. Note which type of light is effective. (There are differences!)

7. Herb K. corrected his mood changes and feelings of depression and fatigue with a doctor-prescribed light program.

···Eleven

Carbohydrate power – the fuel that energizes your body and mind

· · · ·

Food is a source of superenergy—if you eat the right kind! The quality and amounts of food have a direct bearing on your levels of energy. The main source of energy comes from carbohydrates—they act as rechargers of your body and mind.

How Carbohydrates Boost Energy—in Minutes

"Carbohydrate is the key fuel source for your body," says David L. Costill, Ph.D., director of the Human Performance Laboratory of Ball State University in Muncie, Indiana. "Once food is consumed, most carbohydrate energy, in the form of glucose, is converted to storage forms—glycogen and fat. Together, carbohydrate consumption, muscle glycogen, blood glucose, and the duration and intensity of muscle work (load) play important roles in determining exercise performance and training capabilities."

Improve Energy with Carbohydrates

Dr. Costill explains that energy production depends largely on the availability of muscle glycogen and blood glucose. "Although it is possible to perform light exercise with low levels of these carbohydrates, depletion of these fuels makes it impossible for your muscles to meet energy requirements and sustain the contractile tension needed for work performance."

What About Fat and Protein?

"They contribute to the energy pool used during muscular activity, but these fuels alone cannot support the demands of acute activity: *carbohydrate is the primary fuel for exercise.* Even in the presence of

149

adequate muscle glycogen, only minor demands are placed on protein and fat reserves of the body." Dr. Costill cautions that during activity, less than 1 percent of the body's total fat and protein stores might be oxidized, whereas total glycogen depletion (from carbohydrate) may occur during the activity.

And it is this depletion that is a major factor responsible for fatigue and exhaustion. He recommends eating complex carbohydrate foods in adequate amounts to give you much-needed energy of body and mind.

Caution: Because your body stores only small amounts of this energy giver, you must replenish your supplies on a daily basis. If your carbohydrate stores become inadequate (such as from much physical activity), your body can adjust and permit the use of fats and proteins to fill your energy needs. *Problem:* The use of fats and proteins as a carbohydrate substitute is less efficient; they can become depleted and other body functions start to decline. You cannot run this risk of overall decline and premature aging.

Which Carbohydrates Boost Your Vitality?

Carbohydrate-containing foods are typically grouped in two categories: (1) *Simple carbohydrates* are found in sugars and sweets, including candy, soft drinks, cookies, cakes, and most processed desserts. They provide a quick surge of energy . . . and a quick letdown. (2) *Complex carbohydrates* also known as starches are found in whole fruits, vegetables, grains and cereals, as well as legumes (dried peas and beans). They provide a slow-but-steady infusion of energy that can last for hours and hours, sometimes for most of the day.

Complex Carbohydrates for Steady Energy

These foods allow for a steady stream of energy—releasing about two calories of energy per minute. This rate is ideally suited to the needs of your body and mind.

The Magic Power of Complex Carbohydrates

How can these foods work like a time clock—ticking away two calories of energy per minute to give you a feeling of exhilaration and vitality? Basically, carbohydrates increase the amount of muscle glycogen. This surge delays the time when such stores may be depleted. Therefore, you have a much longer level of energy and are less likely to feel prematurely tired. Consider the automotive analogy: carbohydrates increase the capacity of your fuel tank, therefore increasing your movement range.

Want to wake up and feel energetic? Start the day off with complex carbohydrates. Want to feel an energy boost during the day? Or when faced with a lot of work—physical and/or mental? Reach for complex carbohydrates. Where are they found? In lots of tasty and convenient sources:

- *Breads, grains, cereals, and pastas*—wild rice pilaf, salads made up of different types of pasta, whole wheat or buckwheat pancakes, sandwiches made with bagels or pita bread.
- *Fruits, vegetables*—sun-dried fruit mixes; baked potatoes stuffed with broccoli; kiwi fruit, mangoes, papayas, and other tropical fruits; raw vegetables with low-fat yogurt dip.
- *Legumes* (chickpeas, kidney beans, split peas, pinto beans, black beans, lentils, and other dried peas and beans)—bean enchiladas, black bean and split pea soups, vegetarian baked beans, baked potatoes topped with vegetarian chili.
- *Sweet foods and desserts*—if you must have them, try these energy-boosting, high-carbohydrate foods: frozen low-fat yogurt topped with fresh fruit; graham crackers or oatmeal-raisin cookies; puddings made with skim milk or low-fat milk; homemade breads made with figs, dates, applesauce, zucchini, or bananas; fresh fruit salad.

Your primary supply of complex carbohydrates should come from a variety of fresh, whole fruits and vegetables, as well as whole grains. Don't gorge yourself! More is not necessarily better. Instead, your basic energy-boosting plan is to have reduced amounts of meat and fatty dairy products and proportionally increased quantities of fruits, vegetables, legumes, and whole grains.

How to Wake Up and Feel Youthfully Energetic

"You can start off your day with a superburst of energy when you have a revitalizing breakfast," says Dr. Jack Soltanoff, chiropractor-nutritionist of West Hurley, New York. "Be sure to choose as your complex carbohydrate a whole grain cereal, whole wheat bread, buckwheat or millet pancakes, or waffles with fresh fruit juice; you'll also be taking lots of vitamins and minerals in your system. This combination provides a slow, steady supply of energy that gives you youthful vitality in the morning and lasts for many hours.

"The idea of oatmeal 'sticking to your ribs,' for example, may have some scientific basis. Oatmeal has a nice balance of nutrients with complex carbohydrates that slow the rate of digestion. As a result, your blood sugar levels rise slowly, peak later, and stay at a high level longer. You have more energy that can last until noon . . . or more.

"Start off your day with this basic breakfast and see your energy levels zoom upward so that you feel vigorous for much of the day."

Carbohydrate Balance Is Important

When you eat a complex carbohydrate food, add a small amount of protein to help produce the needed energy boost. *Example:* Add some low-fat milk to your breakfast cereal. Or add a bit of cheese to your whole grain bread. You'll then provide a balanced metabolism for prolonged energy.

Superenergizers

Consider a whole grain bran muffin with salt-free natural nut butter, cold broiled chicken with grapes, and California fresh figs with low-fat cottage cheese.

CASE HISTORY—
They Called Me an Old Woman . . . and I'm Only 51"

She was headed for several promotions in the hotel chain where she worked as office administrator. Something went wrong. Muriel J.D. had always juggled different tasks ranging from reservation clerk to convention hostess—even helping out in the restaurant when called upon. She was being groomed for a partnership until she started to feel tired—in the morning! She started yawning when talking to clients. Her eyelids drooped and she fought against an urge to sleep when it was hardly 11:00 a.m. There were times when the bellhop paged Muriel J.D. to attend a special meeting and found her in a spare room—fast asleep. Again, it was not even noon and she felt an overwhelming urge to collapse on a bed and sleep. Making it worse, she had to take four, five, and even seven different "breaks" throughout a short day . . . because she was always tired. What was happening?

Muriel J.D. was only 51—yet she felt a stab of hurt when someone in an adjoining room called her an old woman! All because she had this constant chronic fatigue problem. What was wrong? She knew her future was in jeopardy. She would be passed over for promotion unless she could overcome her fatigue. But how?

As luck would have it, there was a gathering of nutritionists and dietitians in the hotel. She spoke to the chairperson about her tiredness, and the diagnosis was simple: give up your "no breakfast" habit and improper eating. Instead, have a solid whole grain plus fruit breakfast in low-fat milk or fresh juice. Boost intake of complex carbohydrates as part of the daily food plan; keep amounts of protein and fat *small*. With this basic change, her energy levels would be boosted. (She admitted eating a lot of fatty foods that acted to depress her energy.) Muriel J.D. followed the simple change. Within four days, she enjoyed a power surge!

She bounced back with vigor. She was active and bubbling over with joy—no more yawning and no more forced naps during the day. Instead, the only "break" she took was for a complex carbohydrate snack for an energy boost. Her supervisors noted the change, and she was soon given the coveted promotion—and they passed over someone who was 15 years younger! So nobody would ever call her an "old woman" again!

How to Double, Even Triple, Energy with a "Glucose Tolerance" Boost

In brief, each food is digested and absorbed at a different rate, which yields a unique glucose tolerance curve. *Energy Secret:* The more gradual the glucose tolerance curve, the more steady the supply of energy you enjoy (in body and mind). Which foods can double or triple your energy with this secret method?

A team of nutritional researchers tested the glucose tolerance curves of commonly eaten carbohydrate food in humans. The results were as follows:

Energy Booster Foods: This category included legumes (beans), dairy products, fruit, whole grain cereals and biscuits, breakfast cereals, vegetables.

Superenergy Food: Lentils at breakfast were able to improve glucose tolerance and cause a longer-lasting energy boost by the time the next meal arrived. This means the people who had lentils at breakfast could enjoy superenergy for five, six, or seven hours until the noon meal. Power from dynamic food!

Good Glucose Tolerance Foods: The researchers found these foods also helped control glucose tolerance to provide steady energy: whole rye kernels, whole wheat kernels, bulgur, pumpernickel bread, whole meal wheat bread.

Want More Natural Energy? Try More Natural Foods!

The more refined, ground up, or processed a food is, the more sporadic the blood glucose curve will be. That means you will have a surge of energy with processed foods . . . and then a drop or slump. This is just another reason to eat foods in as close to their natural state as possible.

Pectin + Grains = Quick Energy Boost

Pectin is the substance best known for making fruits gel—as in making apple jelly. It is also found in the inner rind of citrus fruits—oranges, grapefruits, lemons, and limes.

Pectin is known to slow the emptying rate of the stomach, which is good insofar as energy is concerned. This provides a gradual infusion of carbohydrates into the bloodstream and a more gradual balance in blood glucose.

Grains also help balance what is known as a glycemic response so that your glucose tolerance curve helps provide a gradual and comfortable supply of energy throughout your bloodstream.

A *combination* of pectin with grains is a simple but powerful source of dynamic energy boosting that lasts and lasts and lasts.

To help experience this surge, try these combinations in the morning—or whenever you know you will be needing more energy:

- Whole grain cereal with a grapefruit (eat the inner rind).
- Millet cereal with an orange (again, eat the inner rind).
- Shredded wheat with grapefruit and orange wedges (eat inner rinds, of course).
- Ready-to-eat whole grain cereal with the same citrus fruit wedges . . . and inner rinds, of course.
- Whole grain breads of any type with several smaller oranges—and you guessed it, eat the inner rinds!

It is this *combination* that will send a welcome surge of power via a balanced glucose tolerance level.

You can start off the day with a "big bang" with this combination . . . or use it at any time of the day or evening when you feel you will need mind/body energy. It works in minutes and lasts for many hours!

Pasta for Super Energy Power

How do runners and athletes develop so much energy? One secret is *pasta*. Here is a whole grain food that can give you the energy of an athlete. While you may not want to run a marathon, you will still want to enjoy similar energy . . . or as much as possible . . . as the athletic runners. The trick is to include more pasta in your meal plan.

Why Pasta Is an Energy Booster

How could something that tastes so good be so energizing? Basically, pasta is low in fat and calories but high in carbohydrates. One-half cup of uncooked pasta provides 80 calories and 15 grams of complex carbohydrates. (Remember, you need a daily supply of these carbohydrates). Since pasta is low in fat and calories, but so rich in carbohydrates, it makes a perfect food for those who want energy— marathon runner or housewife!

With more than 600 different shapes, you could eat this easyto-prepare energy-boosting food as a main course on a regular basis and never become bored. Whether pasta, macaroni, spaghetti, or noodles, they are all superenergy boosters . . . and they do taste good!

Because of the power of pasta, athletes, runners, and sportspeople use them for a precompetition meal. That is, before getting into the race—they reach for pasta . . . for power!

CAUTION: AVOID EXCESSIVE FAT AND PROTEIN

Why will a fatty high-protein meal drain your energy? The answer is the rush of blood to your stomach, an "emergency call" to help with the large amounts of invading fat and protein. With the blood go oxygen and glucose, depriving your brain of needed support.

Basically, blood is marshaled and sent to your stomach in proportion to the number of calories ingested. Your body then digests the different nutrients and different times, stretching out your energy-using times.

Carbohydrates start being absorbed by your body 15 to 20 minutes after consumption.

Proteins start being digested 30 minutes to 1 hour later, and reach their peak about the time carbohydrate absorption is starting to slow down.

Fats take over where the proteins leave off, so absorption is still occurring 3 to 5 hours after the meal, depending on your personal metabolism.

Energy Danger

The more fat you eat, the longer you will feel fatigued. Your body is working hard to handle not only the fat but the excessive protein. Your energy levels are in danger!

Simple Energy-Boosting Plan Using Pasta

That's it—eat pasta! But—avoid covering the pasta with very fatty meats, sauces, dressings. Go easy on any protein with the pasta. These have given pasta a bad name insofar as fatigue is concerned. (High fat and high protein are not cleared from the stomach too easily and bring on that tired feeling. Eliminate them from pasta, and you have a terrific energy booster.)

Suggestions

Try pasta primavera, which is simply pasta combined with cooked vegetables. Add zucchini, red pepper strips, green pepper strips, minced garlic cloves, and a very small amount of Parmesan cheese. For a fat-free tomato sauce, use tomato tidbits or make your own sauce: steam tomato wedges in a small amount of water until smooth enough for the dressing. Add some herbs and you have a pasta dish that will give you the energy of an athlete!

A Little Goes a Long Way

No need to gorge yourself on pasta. If you take in too many carbohydrates via a "loading," you could end up getting puffy and feeling stiff because carbohydrates stored as muscle glycogen tend to bind a lot of water along with it. A cup and a half of pasta with vegetables and tomato sauce will help fuel your muscles . . . and your mind, too.

ARE CARBOHYDRATES FATTENING?

Unfortunately, starch has a bad reputation that it does not really deserve. As illustrated below, gram per gram (or ounce per ounce), carbohydrates have fewer than half as many calories as fat.

> Carbohydrates—4 calories per gram
> Fat—9 calories per gram
> Protein—4 calories per gram
> Alcohol—7 calories per gram

Carbohydrates have about the same amount of energy per gram as protein, but they are low in fat and usually free of cholesterol, while containing much-needed fiber.

A word of caution here. Although carbohydrates themselves are not high in calories, you may have been adding butter and sour cream on potatoes, butter on bread, and cream cheese on bagels. Prevent energy drain through fattening calories by avoiding these added fats!

CASE HISTORY—
Uses Pasta Power for More Energy than His Children

The college-aged children of Joseph DiG. were recipients of athletic scholarships. They had amazing energy. Granted, they were 30 years younger . . . but why was Joseph DiG. always falling asleep after a meal? Why did he complain that "I'm not as young as I used to be. Can't walk more than a block or two and I'm winded"? He otherwise appeared to be in good health.

His daughter, a marathon runner, was also studying sports nutrition and kept a log of what she and her brothers ate and what her "always tired" father ate.

She noted that while she and her brothers ate pasta with lots of vegetables and also adequate amounts of carbohydrates with minimal fats and modest protein, they all had energy to compete in marathons . . . and frequently win.

But her father heaped heavy, fatty sauces with lots of meat and oil on his pasta. That was the clue to his fatigue. He had overloaded his metabolism with fats and protein.

His daughter suggested a simple change—no fat and very little protein with his favorite pasta. Joseph DiG., not wanting to be called "old," readily complied. In six days, he had unbelievable energy. He could walk 1 or 2 or even 3 miles and still have vitality. He even joined a senior jogging group. While he was not a jogger or marathon runner, he was rewarded with increased energy. Carbohydrates via pasta and vegetables (but no fat and animal protein) had made him youthfully energetic!

Meet your super energy booster

Complex carbohydrates are made of twisty, labyrinthine bunches of glucose molecules. Starch is the preeminent member of that family (cellulose is a less notable one). Starch is found solely in plants; seeds are the richest source. Starch foods also contain fiber to give you a feeling of fullness. Also, starch foods are less calorically dense than fat; per unit weight, carbohydrates have less than half the calories of fat.

A 5-ounce potato has 22 grams of carbohydrates, 3 grams of protein, but no fat. A 2-ounce serving of spinach noodles has 41 grams of carbohydrates, 7 grams of protein, and 1 gram of fat. One full-sized shredded wheat biscuit has 19 grams of carbohydrates, 2 grams of protein, and 1 gram of fat. Four ounces of brown rice has 22 grams of carbohydrates, 2 grams of protein, but no fat. See how big a selection you have for carbohydrate energy boosters?

How to feed yourself super energy

Here are combinations that are high in carbohydrates, modest in protein, and low in fat—to give you super energy . . . almost within 30 minutes:

- Chili made with kidney beans and served with whole grain bread.
- Vegetable stir-fry with tofu served over brown rice.
- Soft-shell corn tortillas filled with legumes and topped with tomato sauce or low-fat cheese.
- Grilled fish kabobs (chunks of fresh fish alternating with cherry tomatoes, green pepper, and pineapple on a skewer) served on brown rice.
- Lentils (alone or mixed with brown rice) in spaghetti sauce on whole wheat pasta.
- Green peppers stuffed with brown rice. Add a mixed green salad and finish the meal with angel food cake topped with strawberries.
- A baked potato, steamed carrots and cauliflower, and whole wheat rolls.
- Vegetable salad (made with reduced-calorie mayonnaise, lemon zest, and tarragon) on rye bread with tomato slices and bean sprouts. Serve with vegetable soup, whole wheat crackers, and cantaloupe slices.
- Noodle soup, bread or crackers, a baked potato, and a vegetable juice.
- Whole grain pancakes topped with sliced strawberries and nonfat yogurt, and fruit juice.

CARBOHYDRATES GIVE YOU ENERGY OF AN ATHLETE

But you need not be an athlete or runner to benefit from the natural energy booster power of carbohydrates. You can meet your increased energy needs with the preceding simple carbohydrate choices. Food will give you great energy—with carbohydrates at the head of the list to recharge your body and mind.

HIGHLIGHTS

1. Looking for more energy the easy way? Try boosting carbohydrates with less fat and protein as your food program. Select the right type, though—the complex carbohydrates are your energy boosters.

2. Try the tasty breakfasts recommended by a leading chiropractor-nutritionist to enjoy "get up and go" power in the morning.

3. Muriel J.D. was labeled an "old woman" at 51—until she discovered the youthful energy-giving power of carbohydrates and became much younger insofar as vitality is concerned.

4. You can double—even triple—your energy with certain foods that boost your glucose tolerance curve. Tasty and energizing.

5. Pectin combined with grains gives you a surge of vitality.

6. Pasta, the carbohydrate food used by marathon winners for energy, can give you a boost of vitality. But guard against adding fat or excessive protein.

7. Carbohydrates (popularly called starch) are not as fattening as you may have been led to believe. The extras you heap on are the villains.

8. Joseph DiG. used pasta to develop more energy than his marathon-running children.

9. Enjoy the tasty food combinations that give you power-packed energy almost from the first luscious bite and swallow.

···*Twelve*

How to beat the monday morning blues

The weekend is over. It's Monday morning and a week of obligations is staring you in the face. How do you feel? Eager to tackle the work load? Or, more likely, blue at the prospect of another five days to get through? Do you feel as if you just want to stay in bed and pull the covers over your head? Fatigue appears to be most overwhelming on Mondays when few people want to shoulder responsibilities. If the tired feeling persists, you need to start your energy sizzling to brighten up your blue Monday.

The Cause: Week-Long Build-up

"The Monday morning blues have much to do with the way you spend your entire week," explains Ronald Pies, M.D., staff psychiatrist of counseling and psychological services at Penn State University. "The blues are influenced by your lifestyle and the way you cope with things from Monday to Friday. You probably have the attitude you want to 'save up' for good times during the weekend. The rest of the week is 'terrible' or 'rotten,' and something you have to put up with. It's this 'job dislike' that makes you crowd a week of fun into a few days. And it makes you feel blue to have to go back to work."

Adjust Your Lifestyle

Dr. Pies says you need to avoid burning yourself out during the other days of the week. "The Type A personality is always driving, pushing, competing to stay ahead of others. You're obsessed with time, using every minute to the fullest. This person develops heart and blood pressure troubles, ulcers, etc."

Make These Changes

"Change your week-long style," advises the psychiatrist. "Reassess your priorities. Ask yourself, 'What do I want out of life? Do I really want to be company president at the expense of my family, my leisure, my health, my life? Or wouldn't it be better to blend these desires into my lifestyle? How can I begin changing?'"

How to Brighten Moods and Enjoy More Energy

Restructure your lifestyle to help boost your energy with these effective remedies:

"First, do *not* set high standards for Monday morning. You may not meet them and feel all the more blue! Next, build little pieces of pleasure into every day," advises Dr. Pies. "Example—instead of working through the night without a break, take 30 or 60 minutes off to do something enjoyable. Listen to music. Jog. Talk to friends. Have a light snack. Meditate. These things help ease your workweek stress."

Enjoy Some Energizing Sunshine

Let bright sunlight wake you up to a cheerful day. Get out of bed, open your blinds, and absorb a good dose of sunlight. Morning depression may occur when your body's circadian rhythm goes awry and its inner clock runs too fast or slow. Very bright light at an important moment in the early morning hours could jolt your internal clock and relieve the fatigue of Monday morning.

Sunshine, Calcium, Energy

The sun's rays help stimulate your hormonal system to boost absorption of calcium and help you feel alert and energetic on Monday as well as other mornings. (While not as energizing as sunlight, in its absence strong artificial light can be helpful.)

Keep Active to Stimulate Energy Sources From Within

Exercise helps stimulate your inner energy sources. When you exercise regularly, you will be able to ease the problems of confusion, anxiety, tension, and fatigue. You will be rewarded with an increase in energy and overall feeling of well-being. The most effective energizing exercises are rhythmic, aerobic activities, performed five times a week for about 60 minutes per session.

You probably overeat on the weekend and feel tired on Monday. Starting your week with a 60-minute exercise session lessens the effects of binge eating; you'll start your week on an upbeat note.

Exercise Boosts Energy

Regular exercise promotes inner cleansing. Drink lots of liquids, especially water, before, during, and after exercising. Maintain a regular schedule. Don't cheat or you'll feel a slump on Monday morning . . . and other mornings, too!

Aerobic exercise (swimming, cycling, dancing, running) activates the production of important chemicals—endorphins and adrenalin—which create short- and long-term energizing mood changes. These body chemicals produce what is known as the "runner's high," a euphoric mood condition that most long-distance runners and aerobic exercisers experience.

These body chemicals change your mood into positive directions, boost energy, and decrease depression. In particular, energy produced by adrenaline helps you feel better, which in turn produces even more positive feelings about yourself.

Improve Your Nutritional Picture

If you are regularly fatigued, depressed, catch cold easily, or have allergies, it may be wise to add to your diet a good multivitamin-mineral supplement and additional beta-carotene, B-complex, and C vitamins, which boost your immune system and give you a steady "rush" of energy. Vitamin B6 may also help to chase the blues away.

Careful: To guard yourself against any energy fluctuations, avoid artificial mood-altering substances such as alcohol, caffeine, and tobacco. They make it tougher for you to cope.

Do's and Don'ts for Energy

Eliminate refined sugar. It could trigger hypoglycemia or low blood sugar in which you have an up-and-down swerve of emotional and physical energy. A switch to whole grain foods, fresh fruits and vegetables and their juices, and legumes will give your thoughts a brighter outlook and body more energy.

Become More Sociable

Make contact with people you care about. You say you do not feel like socializing? Too tired? Mix with others who will listen, lift your spirits, and show you warmth and affection. They will help distract you from your feelings of the blues on Mondays and other days, too.

Start smiling. Studies show that a smile can send positive signals to a fatigued nervous system in need of an energizing lift.

Relax. Try such relaxation techniques as meditation or yoga to reduce stress and create a sense of energetic well-being to counteract the blues.

ADJUST YOUR ATTITUDE, ENERGIZE YOUR BODY AND MIND

Here are tips to help send a supply of energy throughout your body and mind:

- You may be having difficulty shifting gears after a relaxing weekend. It's nothing unusual. Stop feeling puzzled or guilty.
- Plan ahead. Save an enjoyable piece of work reserved for Monday morning.
- Do less work, have more fun on the weekend. Relax your cleaning and cooking standards. Do enough around the home

so you feel in control of things, but not so much that your feel fatigued, haggard, and resentful on Monday morning. Take time to refresh yourself and "fill your cup" so that you don't head into Monday feeling tired and empty.

- Remember that when you're having a blue Monday, just getting out of bed is an energizing start. Once you start moving, you begin feeling brighter. Try it and see!

- Begin tasks you do not enjoy on Friday while you are still in a productive mood to ease the prospect of psyching yourself up come Monday.

- Treat yourself to something enjoyable so that your Monday gets off to a good start. Indulge in a favorite healthy food. Read or listen to something you enjoy on the way to work. Try a different route. Use a more pleasant means of transportation.

- Give yourself extra start-up time. Report to work 15 to 30 minutes earlier. Take time to socialize with coworkers. Organize your desk or worksite; straighten out your priorities before the day starts.

- Avoid grouchy feelings by noticing whatever is nice about others in your surroundings. Decide to say "Good morning," and keep smiling, even if you may not want to do so. Flatter someone. Give thanks for suggestions given to you. Praise another person's accomplishment. You'll feel better.

- Take a few moments for a brief chat with your boss. Discuss your chores and your ideas. Ask if there is anything special you can do. Plan for a diversion at the same time during the afternoon.

- Make specific plans for lunch. It will give you something to anticipate. Plan to meet a friend or colleague. If time permits, take in a lunchtime event occurring near your workplace. Even 15 minutes of a musical event is energizing. Check the morning paper to locate any available events in your vicinity.

- Tackle the least pleasant tasks first. Your sense of accomplishment will make the rest of your work seem much easier and less of a burden.

CASE HISTORY—Chases Away Fatigue with a Smile and Self-esteem

Helen N. was grumpy until she had her morning coffee. Even then, she was somewhat jerky, given to mood swings, complaining of always feeling tired. This led to a binge of more coffee and even soft drinks. The caffeine and refined sugar gave her a burst of energy. But like a balloon, it was punctured when the caffeine and sugar wore off. She plunged and felt deflated. It was a seesaw energy. The worst occurred on Mondays. She had a responsible job at a travel agency but had to struggle to control her moods . . . temper . . . fatigue.

A local psychotherapist who used her travel agency for frequent trips listened to Helen N. lament that she hated Mondays because of her tiredness . . . and she wailed she hated Tuesdays, too. Why was she so exhausted?

The psychotherapist "prescribed" that she smile, even if she didn't feel like it. Then he recommended regular exercise, doing less over the weekend to store up energy, and when Monday arrived, to rearrange her schedule so that she would have less pressure. The strongest "prescription" was for her to develop more self-esteem, to convince herself she could manage with a better attitude. It took three weeks, but Helen N. changed into a much happier person, and Monday morning was filled with sunshine, not the blues.

The final "prescription" was to give up her caffeine (coffee, tea, soft drinks, chocolate) and switch to herbal beverages or seltzer with a bit of fruit juice for flavor. When she went off the caffeine roller coaster, she became energetic—her smile was captivating. She had banished the blues!

HIGH-ENERGY BREAKFASTS TO BRIGHTEN MONDAYS . . . AND OTHER DAYS

Eat a power breakfast! One that includes complex carbohydrates, a bit of protein, and minimal fat will keep your blood sugar at a consistently high level through the morning (Monday and other days of the week), increasing your productivity, energy, and sense of well-being.

Caution: If you skip breakfast, you will not be able to charge your energy batteries. Downing a fatty doughnut, coffee, or a glass of juice on the run is not likely to give you the power you need in the morning. Make it a rule to have breakfast! It should have complex carbohydrates–some protein–little fat. Avoid salt or sugar, which can be destructive to your energy curve.

Selection of Energy-Boosting Breakfast Foods

To meet the requirements, try low-fat cottage cheese, low-fat milk, low-fat yogurt, whole grains, fresh fruits, scrambled egg whites on a bagel.

Three Energy-Boosting Foods

Wheat germ (rich in energizing B-complex vitamins), brewer's or nutritional yeast (powerhouse of B-complex and complex carbohydrates with a tiny amount of fat), and lecithin (high-protein, B-complex, and complex carbohydrates) are all available at most health food stores.

How to Use

Sprinkle a half-teaspoon of each over your breakfast cereal or scrambled egg whites or in your fruit salad . . . or add to a cup of plain yogurt. You'll be supercharging your energy reserves to send forth much-needed vitality in the morning. And long lasting, too.

Banana Yogurt Energizer

Combine the following in your blender: 1/2 cup nonfat plain yogurt, 1/2 cup skim milk, 1 banana, 1/2 teaspoon of wheat germ, 1/2 teaspoon of brewer's yeast, 1/2 teaspoon of lecithin. Process until smooth. Drink slowly.

Within moments the complex carbohydrates, the protein, the vitamins, minerals, and enzymes combine to send a stream of vitality shooting through your body. Within a half hour, the blues give way to a sunshine day filled with vitality!

Energy Booster Breakfast

The night before, place an assortment of sun-dried fruit slices (apricots, figs, raisins, dates, pitted prunes) in a glass container. Cover with water. Close the container. Let it stand overnight.

Next morning, put the rehydrated fruits in a bowl. Sprinkle one-quarter teaspoon each of wheat germ, brewer's yeast, and lecithin into the bowl. Add nonfat milk or else the water that is left over in the container. Then eat and enjoy.

Energy Surges Through Body and Mind

The concentrated vitamins and minerals of the fruits and grains combine to help alert your endocrine glands. Energy streams through your body and mind because of this unusual combination of nutrients. Monday (or any other day) morning becomes a "glad to be alive" day brimming with energy, thanks to this *Energy Booster Breakfast*.

Case History—
"Tired" Couple Send Monday Morning Blues into Oblivion

It was sad enough for Leonard Q. to feel grouchy, sluggish, and half asleep on Monday morning, but his working wife, Anna Q. had the same feeling of lethargy and a sad case of the blahs.

Both were in their early fifties and should have had more energy . . . but instead they were troubled with constant fatigue. When Leonard Q. almost lost his direction while commuting in the morning, he let Anna Q. do the driving since both left home at the same time for their respective jobs. Then his wife dozed off at the wheel. They narrowly avoided hitting another car on the road. It was the constant feeling of tiredness, especially in the morning, that made both of them feel drowsy . . . often, until noontime!

A nutritionist was consulted only when someone said they could have some nutritional deficiencies. They were a two-career couple and could not afford to risk their jobs because of this Monday morning fatigue . . . that was extending into the rest of the week.

The nutritionist immediately insisted they have breakfast at home (they always skipped it and had coffee and doughnuts from a vending machine at their work sites). They would have the *Energy Booster Breakfast* since both said they could not eat in the morning. (Skipped breakfast was a cause of their tired blues.) They tried this breakfast . . . and both of them bounced back with so much energy, they soon became more youthful and alert moments after the special breakfast. Later, they began to eat other foods that were high in complex carbohydrates, moderate in protein, and minimal in fat. They adjusted their emotional attitudes and were soon able to send the Monday morning blues into oblivion . . . to be replaced with bright feelings of energy.

No TIME FOR BREAKFAST?

That's what many victims of Monday morning blues say, but you can energize yourself with these power breakfasts:

- Fresh fruit and vegetable juices.
- Fresh and sun-dried fruits.
- Leftover poultry, fish, and meat; canned fish such as sardines or salmon or tuna.
- Leftover main dish casseroles such as macaroni and cheese.
- Ready-to-eat breads, muffins, rolls, and the like.
- Quick-cooking instant hot cereals.
- Ready-to-eat cold cereals.
- Quick breakfast drinks or shakes in a blender made from skim milk and fruits or spices such as cinnamon.

- Top cereals with favorite fruits. Try minted pineapple chunks, blueberries, cantaloupe, peach slices, figs, or a combination such as bananas and strawberries.
- Add fruits such as peach, apple, banana, or pear slices or berries to hot cereals.
- Stir chopped nuts, pecans, or walnuts into cooked cereal.
- Try a mug of hot tomato juice or tomato soup flavored with herbs, such as oregano or basil.
- Top broiled tomatoes with heated condensed mushroom soup.
- Top a cantaloupe half with low-fat cottage cheese or plain yogurt.
- Broil a grapefruit half topped with cranberry or orange juice.
- Drain canned peaches or pineapple and heat under a broiler. Serve with waffles or pancakes.
- For pancakes, try adding nuts or fruits such as bananas, strawberries, chopped apples, blueberries, or crushed pineapple to the batter.
- Add cinnamon to French toast batter.
- Make a breakfast sandwich using French toast or waffles with tomato slices, sliced bananas or cheese between them.
- Sprinkle grated cheese over cooked waffles and broil.
- Serve leftover cooked fish fillet, flaked and seasoned with Italian dressing on whole grain crackers.

Not hungry yet?

You can eat a little in the morning if you can't do it as soon as you get up. Late breakfasts are as energizing for you as early ones.

If you still don't eat breakfast because eating in the morning bothers you, start lightly with juice or a piece of fruit. Add bread or crackers. Then add a food such as nonfat milk, cheese, nut butter. Before you know it, the energy you experience will give you the incentive to greet the day with a power breakfast . . . in a glass or on a plate!

Yo**U CAN BRIGHTEN YOUR MONDAY MORNINGS**

The alarm clock jangles into the Monday morning silence. You groan, reach over to snap off the alarm, and roll over for just a few minutes of sleep. You wish you could stay home. If only the weekend could include Monday, it would be perfect. You feel you are a victim of the Monday morning blues. You are *not* "allergic" to Mondays. You can bounce out of bed and face the day with energy.

Wake up your sluggish metabolism with energy-boosting attitudes and foods. You'll soon wake up and live!

Highlights

1. Activities of the week and the weekend often drain your energies so that you are exhausted on Monday morning. Make some suggested changes, as described by a psychiatrist, and you'll tap your hidden sources of morning (and day-long) energy.

2. Keep yourself active to help stimulate inner energy sources. Simple exercise can work wonders in boosting vitality.

3. Improve your nutritional picture with the do's and don'ts for better morning energy.

4. Adjust your attitude and you energize your body and mind.

5. Helen N. was able to chase away fatigue with a smile and improved self-esteem.

6. Want morning energy? Try high-power breakfasts—don't leave home without them! Check the three unique energy-boosting foods.

7. Leonard and Anna Q. tried a special energy booster breakfast and no longer felt like a "tired" couple.

8. Enjoy a variety of easy-to-prepare energy-boosting breakfasts and send sizzling vitality coursing through your body and mind.

...Thirteen

How to avoid mid-afternoon slump

It's 2:00 p.m., but it feels like 7:00 p.m. Your eyelids are drooping. Your mind is in a slump. You feel like falling asleep. You are a victim of the midday slump. To keep awake, you reach for a "quick fix"—coffee, cola, ice cream, candy bar, cookie, or even a cocktail. These are the worst possible solutions. They give you a quick jolt of caffeine, sugar, or alcohol, but just as quickly there's a dropoff—brought about by the state of low blood sugar as your body deals with the overload. Most likely, low blood sugar made you feel drowsy in the first place.

Danger of Slump

If you're behind the wheel on the open road, you'll nod and doze off and risk an accident in broad daylight. If you're at home, your foggy thoughts will forget a lit stove, a running faucet, a crawling baby. More dangerous accidents can occur. If you're walking across traffic-filled intersections, your muddled mental state obscures your sense of direction; you could be the victim of a pedestrian crash. A midday slump, whether at work or at home or in the outdoors can be dangerous . . . to yourself and to others!

ARE YOU A VICTIM OF THE MIDDAY BLAHS?

No matter what your age or activity, if you're not eating properly, late afternoon can bring about a major energy fadeout. Suddenly vitality evaporates, body and mind slump, you face the blahs; you are in desperate need of energy boosters. This lethargy can strike any time between noon and four—usually after lunch. Few people can escape its consequences. You may feel irritable, restless, depressed, or dull-witted. Emotionally and physically, you feel drained. Does it sound familiar?

Why Does It Happen to You?

Nutritional scientists call it the *postprandial* (after-eating) *dip*. It is characterized by a drop in body temperature, blood sugar, work efficiency, and mood. It happens because you need a stockpile of energy to be fueled from the time of breakfast every morning. *Caution:* Skip a breakfast or gulp down coffee or soda with some pastry and you play havoc with your energy stores and bring on dangerous midday slump.

SIMPLE MEAL PLAN GIVES YOU SPEEDY ENERGY BOOSTERS

Energy comes from burning calories, the "fuel" you get from food. Refined sugar calories will give you a jolt of energy but followed by a plunging letdown. Your plan is to strive for a balance. Here is a simple meal arrangement that gives you steady energy and protects against the midday slump:

Breakfast

For a balance of protein and complex carbohydrates, select from lean meats, poultry, egg whites, low-fat cottage cheese, a whole grain natural cereal, and low-fat milk or yogurt with some fresh fruit. Say "No" to pastries, refined pancakes, or sugary syrup or (worse) going without breakfast!

Lunch

A light but adequate lunch is best for a heavy afternoon work schedule. Some studies show that people who eat a heavy lunch suffer impaired judgment and are less able to detect signals. They cannot distinguish between different sizes and light intensities. "An excellent antidote for the afternoon slump is to eat a hundred percent raw lunch," says Ray C. Wunderlich, Jr., M.D., of St. Petersburg, Florida. "Overeating at lunch time is one of the biggest causes of fatigue in the afternoon. A heavy meal will drop you down, making you feel tired and heavy afterward. Even if your lunch isn't totally raw, many people should get rid of refined foods and sugars. Eat a salad for lunch, one containing such things as watercress, sprouts, chickpeas, tofu, tuna, sardines, seeds, and nuts. Or have a chickpea special (hummus) and sprout sandwich on whole grain bread."

Dinner

Plan for a balance of calories and include some protein, complex carbohydrates, and minimal fats. Examples could be a whole grain bread product, lean meats, poultry, seafood, low-fat cheeses, peas, and nuts, with a salad containing a bit of oil-vinegar dressing; finish with fresh fruit.

How to Enjoy Day-Long Energy

Balance is the key—plan for the three calorie (fuel-energy) sources: complex carbohydrates, proteins, and fats. *Tip:* For superenergy, complex carbohydrates are great boosters—whole grain pasta, brown rice, whole grains and cereals, fresh fruits, and vegetables. These carbohydrates speedily convert to glucose (sugar for energy) without those awful leaps or drops in your blood sugar level.

For day-long energy, balance carbohydrates with protein (from lean meat, low-fat dairy products, tofu, egg whites, peas, beans, nuts). Protein enables carbohydrates to burn more slowly throughout the day. Fats are necessary but in small amounts; fats convert slowly to energy, and those not burned are stored as unwanted pounds . . . so a small bit of fat goes a long way!

Simple Energy Booster Formula

To protect against midday slump and avoid the dangerous blahs, plan for this energy-boosting formula meal plan: 15 percent protein, 60 percent complex carbohydrates, and about 25 percent fat . . . or less. You'll discover you will function more energetically if you also schedule four or five smaller balanced light meals throughout the day instead of one or two heavy ones. Your metabolism remains at top energy level, and you will have energy throughout midday and even in late evening.

CASE HISTORY—
Overcomes Dangerous Sleepiness with Simple Meal Change

As a payroll administrator, Jerome D. needed to be alert to negotiate with pension planning services and deal with long columns of figures requiring his verification. Working for a large plastics firm, he also had to do some local traveling. But the problem was that even though Jerome D. may have begun his day with a "bang," he faced a "slump" before noon. This was dangerous. He almost fell asleep behind the wheel of his car and narrowly missed a crash.

A chemist at the plastics firm heard of Jerome D.'s low energy curve and asked for a rundown of his eating methods. He saw that Jerome D. would gulp down coffee and some pastries in the morning, then take some more coffee with sugary confections a few hours afterwards. No wonder he had the midday slump. He was overdosing on refined sweets and caffeine and would have a burst of energy, followed by a plunging decline of vitality so that he was in a midday slump.

Jerome D. was told to follow the simple meal plan as outlined earlier. Tasty, satisfying, and, most important, energy boosting! Even more important than that—the energy on this meal plan would last from morning until sunset!

Jerome D. made the change. Within two days, he started the day with vitality that endured throughout his work schedule . . . into the evening. Now he could negotiate with a clear head, could drive while youthfully alert, and have day-long energy! A simple meal change . . . but a powerful energy booster!

How to Self-energize with Complex Carbohydrates

You can revitalize your body and mind and enjoy youthful vitality with the joy of complex carbohydrate foods. This was first discovered by athletes who underwent "carbohydrate loading" in which generous amounts of spaghetti, whole grain breads, sweet corn, potatoes, brown rice, and all-grain cereals would be consumed to perk up energies and avoid a letdown.

Energy Benefit

The purpose is to nourish the cells, tissues, and muscles with glycogen, an energy-producing compound: the more carbohydrates, the more glycogen, and thus more energy for the athletic event ahead.

Brown rice and potatoes cause a slow, gradual rise in blood sugar levels because both are great sources of energy-boosting complex carbohydrates; in some tests, these foods have been found to send levels shooting up faster than a candy bar . . . and keep energy high for a longer time span.

Be Careful with Fat

If you spread 1 ounce of cream cheese over two crackers, you eat 1 gram of carbohydrate, 2 grams of protein—but 10 grams of fat. But if you cook up 1 ounce of dry pasta, you have about 20 grams of energy-boosting carbohydrates, 4 grams of protein, and no fat. *Remember:* It is fat that makes you groggy, so you want to keep it to a minimum. (Animal foods do contain many nutrients and protein but carry a high-fat price tag.)

How to Enjoy Carbohydrates with Less Fat

When using carbohydrate foods, minimize the addition of any fats. Instead of sour cream, use low-fat yogurt; instead of meat sauce, use plain (salt-free) tomato sauce, or make a simple pasta primavera, with vegetables sautéed with a little olive oil in a nonstick pan.

Complex carbohydrate salads are energizing but can be fatty if you are not careful. Regular potato salad with its fatty mayonnaise can be an energy-destroyer. A simple adjustment calls for salads with potatoes, brown rice, pasta, and beans with some oil, but in amounts that only lightly *coat* the ingredients, not drench them.

Quick Energy Booster in Midday

To give yourself a longer-lasting energy booster, try some of these quick "throw together" salads or luncheons: baked potato sliced in thick rounds with a little fruity olive oil drizzled on with herbal seasonings; some orzo (rice-shaped pasta), leftover peas, and slivers of red pepper combined with chunks of water-packed tuna or salmon; or lentil salad made with a vinaigrette, diced onion, and favorite herbs.

Secrets of Energy-Boosting Nutrients

Carbohydrates start being absorbed by your body 15 to 20 minutes after consumption. Proteins start being digested 30 to 60 minutes later and reach their peak about the time carbohydrate absorption begins to slow down. Fats take over where the proteins leave off, so there is absorption still taking place three to five hours after the meal, depending on your metabolism. *Tip:* The more emphasis on carbohydrates, the more energy. Keep protein at a good balance and minimize fat.

Avoid big meals, especially if high in protein and fat. A heavy meal sends a rush of blood to the stomach to help with the large amounts of invading ingredients. Along with the blood go oxygen and glucose, depriving your brain of needed support. Your brain loses its fight for blood and you start to feel groggy. At midday, a big meal is an invitation to the penalty of a slump!

Sources of Energy-Boosting Complex Carbohydrates

Brown rice, whole grain pasta, potatoes, whole grain bread, sundried raisins, California fresh figs, papaya slices, pears, beans, corn, whole grain pancakes, dairy products, legumes, nuts, fresh raw vegetables, fresh fruits, whole grain crackers, seeds, and whole grain cereals—all are sources of energy-boosting complex carbohydrates.

Protects Protein

Carbohydrates also have a protein-sparing action in your body. Without an adequate supply of carbohydrate, your body uses protein as an energy source. Protein is necessary for the growth and maintenance of cells. *Careful:* The use of protein for energy over an extended period of time can cause unfavorable reactions. But if carbohydrate intake is adequate, protein is *not* diverted and can be used for cellular growth and maintenance.

Carbohydrates, Fat Metabolism

Another important function of carbohydrates is for fat metabolism. If you are deficient in carbohydrates, then fats are metabolized too rapidly. This leads to an accumulation of by-products of fat metabolism or ketones. If your body cannot get rid of these ketones fast enough, an excess can cause dehydration and even coma. So you can see that a deficiency of carbohydrates can be life threatening!

THE FOOD THAT HELPS GIVE A STEADY SUPPLY OF ENERGY

Yogurt is a carbohydrate-protein food that is able to boost your energy levels. Plain yogurt is refreshing, but you will boost its carbohydrate power if you add such energy toppings as wheat germ, bran, sliced figs, papaya, bananas, granola, sun-dried raisins, various diced nuts, seasonal berries, or citrus fruit sections.

Within moments after eating a cup of this energy booster food, you'll feel fatigue lifting from your senses and enjoy youthful exhilaration of a steady supply of energy.

CASE HISTORY—
Eats on the Run but Still Has Day-Long Energy

No matter how she tried, Esther Q. could not take time for very careful meal planning. Even if it is simple, as has been just described, she had to juggle responsibilities as director of retail merchandising for a large chain with family responsibilities. Also, she was taking night courses on sales management, which added to her activity-filled life-style. How could she take time to plan special types of meals? She wanted an easy program that would help her feel energetic with these various obligations.

Her primary health care practitioner listened to her complaints about feeling tired in midafternoon when her day was hardly over, since she often worked late into the evening. How to boost her energy?

Esther Q. was told to follow the simple meal plan of more complex carbohydrates with modest protein and minimal fat. No sugar, caffeine, or refined foods. Furthermore, she was told to eat frequent "yogurt snacks" for energy. A cup of plain yogurt (low-fat) together with any of the desired energy toppings listed would help send a surge of vitality streaming through her body and mind and help keep her alert when she had to be vital and clear-headed.

Esther Q. made the simple change, and when she cut down on her sugar, caffeine, refined foods, and also reduced fats, she began to perk up. With a meal plan, she was soon able to fulfill her obligations as a retail merchandiser, not to mention night courses and also manage her family obligations.

She enjoyed a steady supply of energy, thanks to the carbohydrate program.

KEEP YOURSELF ACTIVE FOR MORE ENERGY

A short spurt of activity, whether a brisk walk or more vigorous exercise, will help energize your body and mind, especially after lunch. Ever notice college kids? Many of them are seen playing

Frisbee on the lawns after lunch! You need not be so energetic, unless you want to. Instead, try any light exercise after you have your lunch.

Try a brisk 10-minute walk. Gradually extend to 30 minutes. And breathe deeply. Get some fresh air and sunshine. Try standing up and doing a set of 10 to 20 to 30 jumping jacks. One or 2 minutes of jumping jacks will:

- Double your body's intake of revitalizing oxygen.
- Convert blood fats into energy.
- Boost your calorie-burning rate speed as much as 75 percent.

If jumping jacks are not for you, try a brisk walk, stair climbing, even housework. Keep moving—and keep energetic!

FIVE STEPS FOR DAY-LONG SUPER ENERGY

1. Keep a daily log of what you eat. Do not fool yourself. Eliminate foods that are heavy and burdensome such as refined sugary sweets, caffeine, and fats. Be honest!

2. Balance caloric intake with emphasis on complex carbohydrates, proteins, and minimal fats in each meal, beginning with breakfast. Feature fresh fruits, vegetables, whole grains, and legumes.

3. Plan ahead. Bring along energy-boosting snacks for a midday pickup instead of sweets. *Tips:* A container of fresh fruit or vegetable chunks sprinkled with your favorite herbal seasonings is always energizing. Low-fat yogurt or cottage cheese with wheat germ or bran and fruit or vegetable pieces will fill you up and give you a lasting energy supply.

4. Say "No" to caffeine, sugar, and alcohol to guard against roller-coaster mood swings. Diet sodas may increase sugar cravings so try water flavored with a spritz of lemon or lime juice . . . five to six glasses throughout the day.

5. Keep moving. Your body and mind need lots of oxygen—it's the "flame" used to burn calories. Exercise accelerates oxygen consumption. If you feel groggy, take a 15-minute walk (or longer). It washes away fatigue (and tension) and sends a fresh flow of energy-boosting blood streaming throughout your brain and body.

Avoid alcohol

Drinking alcohol, a nervous system depressant, is a completely no-win situation. In concert with a large meal, it will make you more likely to nod off later. Alcohol also gets to its destination very fast; it starts being absorbed into your body as soon as it enters your mouth. *Careful:* Alcohol stimulates your appetite so you eat more! Avoid alcohol and avoid fatigue!

The midday slump can be a crippler! Your immune system weakens and renders you vulnerable to infectious invaders. Revitalize your body and mind with improved nutrition and emphasis upon complex carbohydrates. You can feel alive in midafternoon (and afterward) with corrective nutrition and more activities to oxygenate your cells and tissues.

Highlights

1. Beware of midafternoon slump; it can be dangerous if you are behind the wheel or in the midst of responsibilities.
2. A simple (tasty) meal plan gives you speedy energy boosters in the middle of the day . . . or any other time.
3. To enjoy day-long energy, try the simple formula with balanced carbohydrates, protein, and fats. The secret: proper amounts as described.
4. Jerome D. overcame his low energy curve during midday with a change in the foods he ate.
5. You can self-energize in minutes with certain delicious complex carbohydrate foods.

6. Yogurt is a smooth delight that helps give you a steady energy supply, especially when enjoyed with listed carbohydrate foods.

7. Esther Q. was a typical "eat-on-the-run" career housewife who was troubled by fatigue. She discovered the secret of healthy day-long (evening, too) energy using yogurt snacks.

8. Follow guidelines for exercise to revitalize your body and mind.

9. A five-step plan helps give you day-long superenergy. And you must avoid alcohol to avoid slumps . . . midday or any other time!

···Fourteen

**Energy secrets from
the million dollar
health spas of the world**

● ● ● ● ● ● ●

When you think "spa," what comes to mind? Fashionable turn-of-the-century Britons sipping sulfurous spring water at an exclusive European facility? Arthritic patients bathing in warm mineral waters in Europe or in America?

Today, health spas are found in all parts of the world. While many have bubbly water baths or swimming pools, they are more dedicated to rejuvenation and energization of their pampered guests. Leading celebrities pay top dollar to receive so-called secret remedies to enable them to feel energetic and vibrant.

These programs are "secret" in the sense that they are used almost exclusively at these health spas . . . and only some visitors are able to discover what they consist of.

You can create a home spa and supercharge your body and mind with the same remedies used at these exclusive million-dollar facilities and emerge all the more vibrant and alert. And for only pennies . . . or less!

YOUR GOAL: TO REMAKE YOUR BODY AND MIND

Plan for a total body-mind makeover. In some situations, a simple remedy, a potion, a special food, a tonic, a herbal scent can work miracles in giving you a youthful energy surge. But for overall benefits, plan to use the comprehensive programs outlined throughout the book. Remake your body and mind with these energizing programs, and you will have the health, vitality, and good looks of the leading celebrities—without leaving your home.

Energy Secrets from Switzerland

Nestled in the snow-capped peaks of Switzerland, a million-dollar health spa has been able to rejuvenate and revitalize the most "tired" of patrons with a basic regeneration program. Here are some of the basic energy secrets you can follow at home:

Energy Breakfast

Also known as Swiss muesli, the rule is that you must have this breakfast before starting your day.

How to Make: For each serving, soak three tablespoons of oatmeal in cold water and cover overnight. Next morning, add one tablespoon of fresh lemon juice, one tablespoon of yogurt, and one or two grated (unpeeled) apples. Sprinkle with a tablespoon of grated nuts (almonds, hazelnuts, pecans, or walnuts are recommended). Add a bit of honey, according to personal taste, and top with sliced seasonal fruits and berries.

Have this breakfast in the morning. It reportedly is a powerhouse of nutrients that stimulate your energy reserves to give you "get up and go" to face the day with youthful vitality.

Popularly known as the "Swiss Breakfast," it has traditionally been enjoyed by hard-working peasants who are said to be the healthiest of Europe. *One reason:* They start off the day with this superpowered *Energy Breakfast.* And it is this meal that is served to the top-paying celebrities and members of royal families of the world who come here for regeneration. You can make it in your own home for only pennies . . . and receive a million dollars' worth of energy!

Basic Energy Program

This exclusive Swiss health spa boosts energy of their high-paying guests with these guidelines:

- Minimal amount of cooked food throughout the day and more raw food. The rule is to cook only that which has to be cooked. Animal foods are almost minimal . . . or nonexistent.

- Elimination of all saturated fats . . . and modest (very modest) amounts of any fats.
- *No* refined sugar. Natural fruit sugar is a source of complex carbohydrates.
- Reduced amounts of animal foods. The Swiss energy doctors feel that high protein injures the vital organs and drains energy. Some protein, of course, comes from meatless sources (peas, beans, nuts).
- Each day, at least 60 minutes of exercise, which can be as mild as brisk walking, to doctor-approved aerobics.
- Herb-scented baths daily—sometimes twice a day. Comfortably warm baths must steam open pores to detoxify the system and rid the body of poisons that drain energy. This form of inner cleansing is a key remedy in helping to regenerate your source of energy.

Schedule time for recreation, indulging in your favorite hobby, socializing with friends, and healthy bed rest. With this basic energy program (for which socialite guests paid in the many thousands of dollars per week), energy is boosted almost from the start. You can follow it at home for speedy results . . . at almost no cost!

ENERGY SECRETS FROM ITALY

At 1,600 feet above sea level, in a chalet-style residential villa, within sight of glistening snow-clad Alpine peaks, a meadow-fringed million-dollar health spa offers a unique energy-boosting program. This exclusive spa in the Italian Alps has a special program—raw food!

Why Cooked Foods Drain Your Energy

Energy specialists at this Italian spa maintain that overprocessed and cooked food is devitalized . . . and drains your energy. Toxins from cooked foods disturb the balance of your body and make you look and feel prematurely old and tired. The belief is that an accumulation of uric acid and other toxins tend to cause constant friction and erode your basic health. Switch to a raw food program to revive and regenerate.

What Are Raw Foods?

At this exclusive Italian spa, only fresh, unspoiled plant food from healthy soil is used. The spa experts say that only fresh, vital raw foods will restore the energy-boosting conditions essential to vitality. Raw foods, they tell us, will revive and regenerate the regulative systems and that of the endocrine glands.

Raw foods increase microelectric vitality and cell respiration, stimulating cell metabolism. There is an increase in the power of the immune system, and metabolism proceeds more youthfully. Raw foods improve the bloodstream so that the body is able to build immunity against fatigue-causing toxins.

The Italian health spa has a rule that at least one-half of the day's meal should consist solely of raw foods. This program has helped regenerate and energize some of the world's leading celebrities. (And aren't they always bubbling over with energy? Now you know the secret!)

ENERGY SECRETS FROM THE MEDITERRANEAN

Dotting the blue Mediterranean, sparkling in the warm sunshine, basking in the balmy atmosphere are several little-known health spas that have been able to double, even triple, their guest's energy with an amazing program: green leaves! That's it—green vegetables. Guests check in for a few days (and pay astronomical prices) to regenerate with the green leaf energy booster program.

"No Day Without Green Leaves!"

For an entire day, guests are given green leaves—in the form of freshly prepared juices and salads or combined with a few seeds or nuts or sprouts as part of a main meal. Guests are also allowed herbal tea, some grains, lots of fresh water, and minimal fruit juices. The idea is for the nutrients in the green leaves to metabolize *without interference* of other foods.

How Green Leaves Promote Superenergy

The secret from these Mediterranean health spas has been revealed. Raw enzymes, vitamins, minerals, and trace elements in *uncooked* green leaves promote the formation of red blood cells. They stimulate respiration and nitrogen metabolism of the cell tissues. These green leaves nutrients improve utilization of protein, normalize blood pressure, balance blood sugar, and boost circulation.

Small wonder that the world's leading celebrities undergo only one or two days on green leaves and emerge all the more energetic . . . with little effort! And you can do the same by devoting several days per week to green leaves as your nutritional energy booster plan.

ENERGY SECRETS FROM FRANCE

In the warm sunshine-splashed south of France, within view of rolling hills and pastoral farmland, a unique hideaway spa caters to members of the nobility and those who frequent the plush Riviera. This spa does not advertise. It is not listed by travel agents. It shuns all publicity. The therapists accept guests *only* by recommendation!

This exclusive spa has jealously guarded its energy booster secrets for many years, but through certain means, they have been revealed. You can follow the program at home and be part of the inner circle, with nary a cost. (If you were able to check into this exclusive and restricted spa, it might cost upwards of $1,000 per day. That is, if they accepted you, which is unlikely, unless you are a member of the European nobility.) Here are the rules:

Recommended are raw or steamed vegetables and fruits (taboo are spinach, rhubarb, and tomatoes, under this program); brown rice, barley, or farina cooked with water; and herbal tea with a bit of milk. (When boiling vegetables, you may add salt-free bouillon cubes to the water.)

You may have milk that is slightly warm but never cooked to the boiling point, very lean grilled beef or grilled fish, and a quarter teaspoon of oil on your raw salad.

Absolutely forbidden is whatever is fat—butter, oil, egg yolks (whites are approved), cheese, salt, cooked milk, pastry— as well as sugar, coffee, and commercial tea. Also taboo are fruits with pits, on the grounds that they create negative reactions in the body to induce tiredness because of impaired metabolism.

This may seem restrictive but notice that you do have a variety of foods that will help you regenerate and feel more energetic as your metabolism is adjusted. This program reportedly has worked for an exclusive circle of the rich, famous, and beautiful from all parts of the world. And the proof is in the results—they keep coming back— paying top prices!

Energy Secrets from California

Snug and protected in a deep valley, surrounded by multiflowered hills, bathed with scents and a fresh ocean breeze, this very private spa boasts of having the secret of superenergy.

"One or two days and you will have the energy of a youngster!" is the claim. And it is true! But to find out the secret and to experience the regeneration, you need to be recommended by another privileged guest . . . as well as pay a very hefty fee. And the secret is one that you can follow in your own home—without spending a single penny!

It calls for spending one or two days per week (more or less, depending upon your energy needs and toxic build-up) on a water fast. That's it!

Your Energy-Boosting Water Fast

All that is required is one day at home. Prepare in advance to have a gallon of bottled spring water. You may also have a few lemons or limes and some honey. The lemons put taste in the water and seem to help wash out the toxins from your system. This waste tends to cause sluggishness and tiredness, hence the power of the water fast in boosting your energy.

To one 8-ounce glass of bottled spring water, add two table-spoons of lemon juice and one-half teaspoon of honey. Stir vigorously. Then drink slowly.

Hints, Tips, Suggestions

When you flush out accumulated poisons in the morning, you may have to make frequent bathroom trips. Once you adjust, by noontime, you will help stabilize your metabolism. Do not gulp down the water. Take up to 15 minutes to finish a glass. Repeat throughout the day. Take in no other foods! Obtain adequate rest. Relax. Think about a more energetic benefit. Best not to do any heavy work . . . or work of any sort. (Neither do guests at the exclusive California health spa do work while on this detoxification fast.) Take frequent naps, if desired. By nightfall, you will feel pressures being lifted and a lightness together with energy. The water fast has boosted your energy.

Easing Out of the Fast

Breaking the fast properly is important. Next day, start with a large salad of shredded carrots and cabbage. For dressing, the juice of one whole orange. Drink hot herbal tea, if desired. If hungry, have a few slices of very thin whole wheat toast. The basic rule is that the day after your water fast is a strict diet of fresh fruits and vegetables. After the change, you may add other foods—but be careful with animal fats, sugars, caffeine, or you will only overburden your metabolism and become fatigued again.

Do this one- or two-day water fast, once a week and be rewarded with month-long energy!

ENERGY SECRETS FROM MAINE

Celebrities, politicians, million-dollar-earning film stars, and the ultrawealthy women of our new society all experience an energy revitalization at this very special spa in Maine. It is difficult to find—made invisible by forests that protect it with thick foliage, surrounded by impassable woods. Yet there is a winding path known only to those who are privileged to be accepted as guests.

The secrets of this spa's program are simple—a set of ten basic revitalization steps:

1. Avoid white sugar from the bowl or in foods of any sort.

2. Avoid white flour from any source.

3. Avoid any greasy foods—potato chips and French fries, for example.

4. Avoid greasy meats—and most meats that contain cell-destroying nitrates.

5. Avoid sugar—in cereals and in any other foods.

6. Avoid all cola drinks or bottled beverages made with or without chemical sweeteners. Drink plain seltzer.

7. Avoid any artificial or chemical sweeteners.

8. Avoid any hardened (hydrogenated) fats.

9. Avoid any frozen dinners.

10. Avoid any flat-tasting or overcooked foods; instead, opt for slightly steamed foods. Keep cooking to a minimum.

With these rules, you can supercharge your metabolism, cleanse away toxic wastes, and emerge looking and feeling youthfully alert and energetic—just as do the rich and famous.

Energy Secrets from Texas

A former cattle ranch was transformed into a plush, exclusive resort with almost no publicity. The rich and famous (or anyone else who can afford the high prices) are able to enjoy comfortable rooms with private entry foyers, colorful decor, and a view of an exotic jungle landscape, scalloped into a series of interior gardens and patios bathed with warm western sunlight.

The Texas health spa has a food program that is designed to stimulate your metabolism and help you cleanse away fatigue-causing toxins. The program is as follows:

Breakfast consists of whole grain toast, no butter, with scrambled egg whites, herbal tea with honey and an assortment of fresh fruit.

The *noonday meal* is a small portion (about 4 ounces) of lean steak, a small tomato, diced vegetables with parsley sprigs, and citrus fruit slices; herbal tea with honey; and if you must have it, one half of a bagel.

For *evening*, enjoy gazpacho, lentil roast (or any meat substitute), vegetable broth, and brussels sprouts with pimiento sponge cake, and again, if you must have it, one half of a bagel.

Vary the Foods for Taste Satisfaction

Each day, you can make changes but follow the basic structure of this Texas health spa meal plan. Namely, for breakfast, you can have whole grain cereals of all sorts; for noonday, try a small portion of chicken or seafood with different vegetables; for evening, try a different meat substitute whether chick peas, string beans, or legumes of all sorts, and in all combinations.

You can supercharge your system with this basic meal plan that helps you eat your way to energy.

CASE HISTORY—
Feels Like a Million with Health Spa Secrets . . .
That Cost a Million!

Bit by bit, Bridget McK. felt her energy slipping away. She worked as a private maid, helping a woman who was recovering from a slight stroke and a bout with diagnosed chronic fatigue syndrome. Bridget McK. felt worried—she was supposed to be energetic, helping this always tired and stiff-limbed woman. How could she succumb to the same fatigue and limitations?

As luck would have it, the woman's family suggested she improve her recovery with a one-week visit to a Texas health spa. Of course, Bridget McK. would go along as her personal caretaker.

So it was that she discovered the basic nutritional program that revitalized the ailing woman—and when she, herself, followed the program, she could experience a complete body makeover: when she returned home, she was spry and flexible and alert. And her ailing patient had also recovered and now insisted Bridget McK. remain as her personal secretary, even though she no longer needed care as an invalid. With this set of basic guidelines, Bridget McK. felt like a million—and life became energetic again!

Keep Yourself Fit and Energetic

All health spas require at least 60 to 90 minutes daily of fitness programs. If you want the benefits to endure, plan to do exercise every single day. Otherwise, your efforts will dissipate and you will become fatigued again.

Although exercising regularly is not the easiest habit to form, once you've got it, once you feel the surge of power surging through your body and mind, you will continue with it.

At health spas, exercise may be as simple as walking or more advanced, as aerobics or gymnasium workouts. Proceed at your own pace. Consider joining a group at a local health center. Self-discipline is essential.

Exercise is a terrific energy booster. All that deep breathing and muscular activity fills your bloodstream with healthy oxygen and stirs up your circulation. Once you set up an exercise schedule and feel the vitality, you'll find that the 60 or 90 minutes goes by so quickly, you'll wonder where the time went! Go to it!

ENERGIZE WITH AROMATHERAPY

Health spas make full use of water therapy—different types of baths ranging from comfortable soaks to whirlpools. Nearly all employ the ancient art of aromatherapy, or scents.

How Scents Boost Energy

Your olfactory (smelling) system helps give you a surge of vitality when in the presence of aromas. Scents stimulate the olfactory bulb in your nose to send electrical signals to the area of your brain concerned with energy. These signals directly affect your emotions. Olfactory signals, called *pheromes*, send a whiff into your system so that you experience a revitalization that helps you think and function with more vitality.

The million-dollar health spas know of this secret and utilize scented baths as part of their energy-boosting program. Nasal nerve cells located high in your nose reach into that part of your brain involved in energy. You can stimulate your energy levels with these particular essential oils available from almost any herbal pharmacy:

Energy-Boosting Scents

Basil, cinnamon, geranium, hyssop, marjoram, nutmeg, pine, chamomile, clove, jasmine, rose, thyme, cypress, frankincense, lavender, orange, sage, sandalwood, vanilla: when you inhale any of these scents, the limbic area of your brain reacts to arouse your body and mind, to stimulate your metabolism.

You can boost energy by inhaling these scents as part of a perfume that you wear, or else in the form of essential oils in a tub of water and luxuriate for 30 minutes. The aroma penetrates your nasal passages, stimulates your brain, participates in detoxification, and gives you a feeling of youthful vitality. In short—you feel glad all over!

CASE HISTORY—
Peps Up "Instantly" with a Whiff of Perfume

In charge of customer service for a large mail order company, Ruth G.A. was subjected to frequent spells of fatigue. There were times when she could not answer telephone queries properly and her low energy made her so lethargic she was unable to fill orders correctly. Ruth G.A. was a supersaleswoman, highly regarded, even in charge of others in the department, yet her recurring fatigue made her groggy, even "dopey" as someone said, thinking she was out of earshot.

The cure came by a strange coincidence. Her company advertised a special set of fragrances on a nationwide television program; the promotion said these scents were used at several leading health spas to revive and regenerate their tired guests. Whether inhaled from a flagon or added to bathwater, they would stimulate the senses and actually "breathe away fatigue."

Ruth G.A. started taking orders for this special package of energizing fragrances . . . and then decided to sample them herself. "It is a miracle," she would say to coworkers and even to customers who queried. "I was tired, too, and just a few whiffs every hour helped boost my energy! I'm going to use them in my bath every night . . . and wear the perfumes daily." She was no longer called "dopey" as her energy doubled with the use of these scents! A single whiff can give you instant energy!

FEEL LIKE A MILLION WITH YOUR HOME HEALTH SPA

You are an individual, as personal as your fingerprints. You can become supercharged with energy with one, two, or more of the health spa secrets just outlined. Set your own program. When you feel energy, you will know your personal health home spa is helping you feel supercharged with energy. You'll feel like a million—from the million-dollar health spas right at home!

HIGHLIGHTS

1. Remake your body and mind and enjoy supercharged energy when using health secrets from the world's exclusive spas.

2. You can easily prepare an *Energy Breakfast* and follow the energy secrets from a Swiss health spa.

3. A raw food program, as prepared in an Italian Alps spa, can help you enjoy renewed energy and better health, too.

4. A green leaves vegetable program from a Mediterranean health spa may well give you energy in a short time.

5. A simple set of do's and don'ts at a French health spa can give you youthful energy as it does for the rich and famous.

6. Try an energy-boosting water fast, the secret therapy at a special California health spa.

7. A ten-step revitalization program from a Maine spa will give you energy you thought never existed. Tasty, too.

8. A Texas health spa's secrets will give you more energy. Bridget McK. felt like a million when she followed the programs at home.

9. Include fitness and aromatherapy as part of your energizing plan. Ruth G.A. was able to pep up "instantly" with a whiff of perfume.

Fifteen

Brighten depression with cheerful energy boosters

CASE HISTORY—
Nutritional Therapy Overcomes Chronic Tiredness

In early springtime, Arthur T.K. found himself feeling blue. Very blue. He dragged himself around, feeling depressed and anxious. He had to force himself through his daily duties as an inventory control systems manager for a large midwestern conglomerate. This feeling of constant tiredness coupled with depression began to worsen. There were days when he could scarcely get out of bed. "What is happening to me?" he wondered, feeling all the more blue. Constant tiredness interfered with his obligations. His wife and family worried at the way he nibbled at his food, became lethargic, almost like a robot. He was sinking into the depths of depression. Everyone was worried, and it took a company nurse to rescue him from what might have been hospitalization.

The nurse brought him to an orthomolecular physician, who used nutrition as therapy, especially for emotional problems. Arthur T.K. was diagnosed as having certain nutritional deficiencies that were responsible for his emotional unrest and his constant fatigue . . . even upon awakening after a sleepless night. Certain nutrients and foods were prescribed. Arthur T.K. responded speedily and, within one month, was as bright as springtime. He was alert and energetic, played golf regularly, joined the company bowling team, and entered the social whirl with his wife and children. He had brightened his depression and overcame tiredness with nutritional therapy.

DEPRESSION CAN MAKE YOU TIRED

It's not *all* in your mind! But most of it (tiredness) can stem from mood feelings, glooms, blues, and depression. It can sap away your energy reserves. Depression can upset your routine, causing sleep problems, fatigue of body and mind, weakness in your ability to concentrate, changes your appetite, and many more symptoms.

Are You Tired Because of Depression?

Everyone feels "blue" at certain times. In fact, transitory feelings of sadness or discouragement are perfectly normal, especially during particularly difficult times. But if you cannot "snap out of it" or get over these feelings within two weeks, you may have a sad case of depression. In addition to the symptoms of fatigue, you may have feelings of sadness, helplessness, hopelessness, and irritability.

ARE YOU DEPRESSED?

The following checklist, offered by the American Psychiatric Association, can help you assess whether you have serious depression:

- Noticeable change of appetite, with either significant weight loss or weight gain, though not dieting
- Noticeable change in sleeping patterns, such as fitful sleep, inability to sleep, or sleeping too much
- Loss of interest and pleasure in activities formerly enjoyed
- Loss of energy, stubborn fatigue
- Feelings of worthlessness
- Persistent feelings of hopelessness
- Feeling of inappropriate guilt
- Inability to concentrate or think, indecisiveness
- Recurring thoughts of death or suicide, wishing to die, or attempting suicide

- Disturbed thinking, a symptom developed by some severely depressed persons

You Are Not Alone

Each year at least 10 million people are troubled by clinical depression often during their most productive years. With the newer knowledge of nutritional healing, you need not feel depressed and fatigued. There is hope and help for this problem.

YOUR EMOTIONS AND NUTRITION: CAUSE AND CURE FOR DEPRESSION

Runaway emotions upset brain chemistry to disturb chemical signals between nerves in the brain. These neurotransmitters are influenced by your brain waves. The process of transmission is assisted by electrolytes, neurohormones, biogenic amines, norepinephrine, serotonin, dopamine, and acetylcholine along with many other transmitters.

Some depressed persons show an excess of one or more of these neurotransmitters, while others show a deficiency. Too much or too little can cause mood swings of fatigue-depression. For example, electrolytes—minerals in the body such as sodium, magnesium, calcium, and potassium—are directly involved in neurotransmission; thus imbalances or nutritional problems with electrolytes have been correlated with certain types of depression.

When you are subjected to stressful situations or thinking negatively, troubled by the "blues," or feeling bored, alone, or tired, your brain waves cause disturbances in neurotransmission, and you are vulnerable to mood swings.

BRIGHTEN MOODS WITH NUTRITION

In some situations, nutritional deficiencies can lead to disturbances in brain chemistry and subsequent fatigue-causing depression. Can you be "depressed today" and "cheerful tomorrow" with the use of nutrition? Very possible, since you will be feeding your brain with the nutrients needed to help you correct imbalances responsible for negative thinking.

Dr. Brian L. G. Morgan of the Institute of Human Nutrition of Columbia University, New York City, tells us, "There are two popularly held explanations for the feeling of sadness, withdrawal, or lethargy, characteristic of depression. Both explanations have to do with the levels of neurotransmitters or chemical messengers in the brain.

"One theory attributes depression to a low level of one such messenger, called serotonin, and the other to a low level of another called norepinephrine.

"Deficiencies of vitamins B1, B6, C, and A, as well as folic acid, niacin, copper, magnesium, and iron, can all cause depression by affecting serotonin and norepinephrine metabolism.

"Brain levels of norepinephrine can be raised by taking supplements of tyrosine and phenylalanine, since they are converted into norepinephrine in the brain. The same is true of tryptophan, which makes serotonin, and you can raise its brain levels when you get enough of it into your body.

"Both tyrosine and tryptophan have shown startling results in treating the *unipolar depression* that causes you to swing from a normal, well-adjusted mood to a period of withdrawal, sadness, and lethargy. However, these substances are of no value in treating *bipolar depression*, in which mood swings range from irrational elation to total depression."

Six NUTRITIONAL STEPS FOR TREATING FATIGUE-CAUSING DEPRESSION

Dr. Morgan offers these suggestions:

1. Your diet should provide adequate amounts of calcium and protein.

2. Be alert to deficiencies of vitamins B1, B6, C, and A; folic acid; niacin; copper; magnesium; and iron.

3. If you crave carbohydrates, go on a high-carbohydrate diet, supplemented with 500 to 1,000 milligrams of L-tryptophan, taken three times a day with juice.

4. If you are lethargic and depressed, and do not crave carbohydrates, take 1 gram (1,000 milligrams) of tyrosine three times a day with meals.

5. If you are taking monoamine oxidase inhibitors (MAO inhibitors), be sure to consume a tyramine-restricted diet. Avoid, for example, aged cheese, nuts, bananas, beer, wine, chocolate, and cultured dairy products.

6. If you are on antidepressants, watch your weight carefully.

Dr. Morgan offers a thumbnail nutritional program: "To be on the safe side, anybody with depression should be taking a one-a-day vitamin supplement containing the recommended dietary allowance of vitamins and minerals. The B vitamins are often the problem, and a one-a-day supplement will correct any B-complex deficiency."

THE VITAMIN THAT EASES DEPRESSION AND PROMOTES ENERGY

In many situations, one vitamin helps heal depression and act as a speedy emotional booster. In particular, vitamin B6, or pyridoxine, is recognized as having such powers, according to Alan Gaby, M.D., who practices family medicine with a nutritional emphasis in Baltimore, Maryland, and is author of *B6, The Natural Healer*. He tells us, "The brain's metabolism is extremely complex. Dozens of different molecules found in the brain are known to affect mood and behavior, and their interactions are complicated and poorly understood. Brain metabolism can go awry in countless ways, any number of which might trigger depression. Some of these abnormalities, and the depression they produce, can be corrected by vitamin B6."

Dr. Gaby observes that a deficiency of neurotransmitter molecules can cause depression. These neurotransmitters (serotonin and norepinephrine, for example) affect moods, behavior, and thoughts. "A deficiency might occur in several ways: The brain may not manufacture adequate quantities of these molecules; the enzymes that break down the neurotransmitter might be overactive, or the neuron on the receiving end may have lost its ability to respond to the chemical message." This could bring on the problems of fatigue-causing depression.

Vitamin Helps Lift Moods

Dr. Gaby believes that vitamin B6 will help improve the balance of neurotransmitters and thereby "lift moods" and help boost energy.

Dr. Gaby explains it is more rational to treat depressed patients via the neurotransmitters themselves. In some cases "trytophan and tyrosine do indeed have antidepressant activity. In some cases tryptophan has worked as well as the tricyclic antidepressant imipramine. In a few cases, tyrosine was found to be effective even after standard drugs had failed."

The happy news is that "Vitamin B6 is the cofactor for enzymes that convert tryptophan to serotonin and tyrosine to norepinephrine. A B6 deficiency could presumably lead to depression by impairing the production of brain amines from their precursors. By the same token, vitamin B6 supplements might favorably affect some cases of depression by raising the level of these neurotransmitters.

"It has been well documented that large doses of B6 not only raise blood serotonin levels in hyperactive children, but also eliminate their symptoms in some cases."

Do you need more iron?

Severe cases of iron-deficiency anemia can bring on chronic tiredness, depression, and feelings of being listless and lethargic. Even mild anemia could make you tired. This is a problem in women of childbearing age, but the condition is seen in older women too. Ask your health practitioner for a hemoglobin test and then see about increasing iron intake.

Boost ENERGY, BANISH DEPRESSION WITH CARBOHYDRATES

Judith Wurtman, Ph.D., a nutritional researcher at the Massachusetts Institute of Technology and author of *Managing Your Mind and Mood Through Food*, believes that a diet high in complex carbohydrates boosts serotonin levels, which helps to boost energy and banish depression.

Watch the Proper Combination

If you always eat your complex carbohydrates—rice, b
cereal—together with protein, you may not boost energy.
man speculates, "That's because the amino acids in protei
tryptophan from getting into the brain. And tryptophan i
for producing serotonin, the brain chemical that keeps yc
stable."

Dr. Wurtman believes that when eaten alone, comple
drates boost serotonin production in the brain, help yo
energy boost, and wash away depression and fatigue.

Doctor's Energy Booster Plan

Dr. Wurtman recommends getting at least one meal a day
high in complex carbohydrates, with little or no protein.
potatoes, and plain pasta are good choices.

What About Fruit?

For depression, fruit may not be effective since they contain simple sugars which do not stimulate serotonin release.

How EVERYDAY FOODS CAN BANISH DEPRESSION . . . AND BOOST ENERGY

James F. Balch, M.D., of Greenfield, Indiana, and author of *Prescription for Nutritional Healing*, agrees that "depression begins with a disturbance in the part of the brain that governs moods . . . . It has

been discovered that foods greatly influence the brain's behavior."
He offers these remedies that use everyday foods (and avoids some
of them, too) to help banish depression and boost energy:

1. Avoid foods high in saturated fats; consumption of pork or fried
   foods, such as hamburgers and French fries, leads to sluggishness, slow thinking, and fatigue. *Danger:* "Fats inhibit the syn-
   thesis of neurotransmitters by the brain in that they cause the
   blood cells to become sticky and to clump together, resulting in
   poor circulation, especially to the brain."

2. A raw vegetable diet, with soybeans and their by-products, is
   important. Diets too low in complex carbohydrates can cause
   serotonin depletion and depression.

3. Tyrosine is also needed for brain function. This amino acid may
   be good for those who have prolonged and intense stress.
   Uncontrollable stress may thereby be prevented or reversed if
   this essential amino acid is obtained in the diet.

4. Chromium (trace mineral), helps in mobilizing fats for energy.
   About 300 micrograms daily is recommended.

5. Vitamin B6 (pyridoxine) is needed for normal brain function.
   About 50 milligrams, three times daily, is recommended.

6. Vitamin B5 (pantothenic acid) is an "antistress" vitamin that
   may help depression. About 500 milligrams daily is recommended.

7. Vitamin C, plus rutin, a by-product of buckwheat, boosts the
   immune function, helps increase energy, and helps to ease and
   erase depression. About 2,000 to 5,000 milligrams daily, in
   divided doses, is recommended.

With these basic nutritional guidelines, you should be able to
feed yourself more energy while banishing depression.

CASE HISTORY—
Beats Depression, Boosts Energy, Improves Diet

The moody blues threatened to put Noreen E. into a rest home. She was troubled with irritability, decreased energy, fatigue, poor concentration, and poor memory retention. She complained, "I get tired for no reason. I feel so hopeless about the future. There are times when I can hardly get out of bed. What's the purpose?"

Noreen E. was sinking into serious depression that was diagnosed as debilitating as the fatigue that threatened to make her helpless. Must she face the bleak future of being confined to an institution? She had tried medications but complained that the side effects were so uncomfortable she would rather remain depressed and fatigued. Not a good choice. But did she have another?

Yes, said a psychiatrist who was called in by her anxious family. She had upset her mental equilibrium with careless eating. The brain disturbance could be corrected with certain nutritional adjustments.

The psychiatrist told Noreen E. to go on a low-fat diet: raw vegetables, high complex carbohydrates, prescribed amounts of supplements such as tyrosine, chromium, the B-complex group with emphasis on B6, B5, as well as vitamin C. When her meal pattern was adjusted to eliminate refined sugars, minimal protein, very little fat but with more complex carbohydrates and wholesome foods, she began to respond.

Within three weeks, Noreen E. felt the dark mood lifting. She was even-tempered and had better powers of concentration and improved memory. Her energy levels had so increased, she was eager to return to the work force and manage a busy household too. Thanks to nutritional therapies as recommended by her psychiatrist, she had been able to banish depression and boost her energy . . . and avoid the threat of institutional confinement!

TRY A DOSE OF COLOR THERAPY

The effects of color on your moods, health, and way of thinking have been studied by scientists for many years. Your personal preference for one color over another most likely had something to do with the way that color makes you feel. But it has been noted that photoreceptors in the retina of the eye, called cones, translate light waves into color vision that stimulate different pigments and create certain responses.

It is believed that colors can stimulate the pituitary and pineal glands to influence hormones and other physiological systems in the body. Colors may well help ease depression and boost energy.

Color Boosts Energy

Color supercharges the nervous system. Its action upon the millions of nerve terminals in the skin causes electrical currents to arise in them which stimulate you to greater energy and activity.

Under the influence of color, your skin releases a certain hormone that is carried by your blood and increases the functional capacity of your muscles and sense organs.

Color Is Part of Your Personality

You may not be aware of the power of color, but note these common statements: "You see *red* when you are angry." "You become *green* with envy." "You feel *blue*." "You are in the *pink*." "You have a *rosy* future."

COLOR IN YOUR LIFESTYLE

In some situations, it has been found that:

> *Red:* can be exciting, even disturbing. Blood pressure, eye blinks, palm conductivity, and breathing rate are accelerated. It could turn your bedroom into a nest of passion.

Blue: can be calming, eases stress, and calms the breathing rate. It may act as a tranquilizer and bring on sleep.

Soft warm colors: these include peach, tan, orange, that are conducive to the intellectual pursuits; said to be good choices in schools, libraries, and wherever studying is done.

Soft cool colors: these include green, blue-green, and light from cool fluorescence; favorable for movement and ideal in a gymnasium. The deeper, brighter blues have a tendency to focus your thoughts more inward.

The Power of Red

The knowledge that red eases depression and boosts energy has been put to use by some school coaches: they have the home team's locker room painted red. The visitors' team has a low-energy blue! Get the picture!!

CHROMOTHERAPY: HOW TO USE COLOR TO BOOST YOUR ENERGY

Color therapists believe that when your body is in balance, it filters out of white light those healing colors that are needed. When something is wrong, colors may be applied in a variety of ways—for example, wearing a light blue sweater on a day when you feel depressed will be comforting. Green, for instance, is thought to build muscle and tissue, and likewise, they attest, eating green foods will also help. Considering that green vegetables are a rich source of nutrients needed to improve your mood and boost energy, the color therapists seem to have a point.

Practitioners point out that certain colors produce energy boosting in a depleted system. Chromotherapy stimulates subsequent emotional change that improves the physical side. Chromotherapy as treatment often uses these colors to initiate physiological responses:

Orange—increases energy levels, soothes depression.
Green—soothes the nerves, boosts self-esteem.

Red—stimulates nervous system and blood flow.

Pastel blue—improves memory and thinking powers.

Yellowish orange—invigorates the digestive system.

Navy blue—improves potential of energy boosting and emotional happiness.

Flame red—stimulates the libido.

The Color That Boosts Energy

Of all the colors, orange is said to be the most energizing. It helps stimulate energy, reduce fatigue, and soothe emotional upsets. Orange may well be the superenergy-boosting color. Make it part of your life!

Whether on your walls, part of your furnishings, your clothes, or jewelry, color can have an influence on your emotional well-being and energy boosting. Try a variety of different colors. One that boosts your energy may not be effective for another person. This only emphasizes that you are an individual. You need to find what works for you—and stay with it.

THE HERB THAT EASES DEPRESSION AND BOOSTS ENERGY

European herbalists have long recommended St. John's wort as an energy booster, simultaneously helping to clear the mind of feelings of depression. The leaves and flowers of St. John's wort contain special glands that release a red oil that has the energy-boosting power. To prepare, use one to two teaspoons of the dried herb per cup of boiling water. Steep 15 minutes. Drink up to three cups per day.

The technical name for St. John's wort, available at most herbal pharmacists or large health stores, is *hypericin*, a natural substance in the red oil that helps protect against biological reactions involved in depression. It soothes this feeling of gloom. And it also helps stimulate the physiological system to boost energy. The effect is not always felt immediately. It may take two months of daily use, but the benefits are slow and sure. St. John's wort should also be used in amounts approved by your health practitioner.

Feel gloomy? depressed? always tired? It's not all in your mind. You can wipe away the debilitating depression and supercharge your system with energy boosters. Start now!

HIGHLIGHTS

1. Arthur T.K. overcame near-debilitating depression with the use of nutritional programs as outlined in this chapter. They can help you, too.
2. See the checklist of symptoms of depression. Don't wait until they increase. Start energy boosting right away.
3. A doctor offers a set of six nutritional methods for treating fatigue-causing depression right at home. All natural. Quick acting.
4. Vitamin B6 may, by itself, correct your metabolic defect and ease depression while boosting energy.
5. A nutritional researcher at the Massachusetts Institute of Technology suggests a simple energy booster plan.
6. Eat your way to freedom from depression and more energy with a doctor's seven step program.
7. Noreen E. won the battle against depression and boosted energy with a simple nutritional program.
8. Try a dose of color therapy. It may well brighten your lifestyle.
9. A traditional herb has been found to ease depression and give more energy.

···*Sixteen*

For women only

··········

Why do women complain of being tired? Because certain factors, including irrational diets and hormonal changes tend to sap away much needed energy. With corrective energy boosters, you can build your immune response so that you can heal these disorders and feel alert and active. And some of these energy boosters are amazingly simple!

CASE HISTORY—
Restores Energy with Simple Diet Trick

Pauline LaK. went to her doctor complaining of debilitating fatigue. She had to stay home from work for several days and spent the time in bed, too exhausted to do simple tasks. She would not even get dressed until noontime. "Even if I do very little. I'm still exhausted. What's wrong?" she lamented.

Pauline LaK. was quizzed by her physician about her diet and exercise programs, whether she was taking medication, and if she was satisfied with her lifestyle, job included.

Before long, the physician isolated the basic cause of Pauline LaK.'s tiredness. She had been on a reducing diet: high-protein, low-carbohydrate for a few weeks. The diagnosis: "You're carbohydrate-deprived and most likely dehydrated. On that diet, you lose a lot of water and energy. My prescription: go home and have a big dish of pasta primavera for dinner. Tomorrow morning, have a whole grain breakfast with fresh fruit slices. And drink about eight glasses of water throughout the day. You will feel more energetic within a day or two."

Pauline LaK. followed the program. She became energetic almost from the beginning. She would now be able to maintain her weight and her energy on a high-complex carbohydrate diet, with modest protein and minimal fat. She had discovered why she was so tired: carbohydrate deprivation.

Why women complain of tiredness

The two-career couple or the single parent today struggles to manage work with family and home care. This could lead to improper food programs, lack of exercise, and addiction to fast foods and caffeine. Alcohol is another problem. Excessive work and home responsibilities cut into sleep. Little personal time is another energy drain. These deficits in lifestyle are largely to blame for the increasing numbers of women who complain of tiredness and fatigue.

Twelve energy booster steps for women

To enjoy energy boosters, you need to feed your body the fuel it functions on best, says Holly Atkinson, M.D., former staff physician with the Rockefeller Foundation of New York and author of *Women and Fatigue*. She offers these basic energy boosters:

1. *Aim for nutritional balance.* Beware of diets that are low on carbohydrates or fruits and vegetables or too low in protein, since you need these nutrients and foods for energy boosting.

2. *Focus on complex carbohydrates.* The main part of your meals should consist of complex carbohydrates: pasta, whole grain breads and cereals, potatoes, brown rice, peas, and beans. Choose those that are natural or minimally processed. You need carbohydrates for energy. Without them, your body must burn fats and protein (including muscles and organs) for energy. This leads to the formation of toxic substances that bring on fatigue and exhaustion.

3. *Avoid simple carbohydrates.* Any form of sugar, from the shaker or in a food, should be avoided. Sugar will give you a speedy pickup to be followed by a quick let down. If you have a craving for a sweet, indulge in naturally sweet fruit, whether fresh or sun dried.

4. *Shun fats.* A fatty meal brings on immediate fatigue; you know the situation of someone who finishes such a meal and falls asleep almost at once. Eating fat temporarily raises blood fat levels that cause blood sludging. Fewer oxygen-transporting red blood cells are able to reach muscles and other tissues; waste products accumulate and fatigue comes on. A typical woman eats eight tablespoons of fat daily—only one tablespoon of vegetable oil is needed daily!

5. *Monitor protein intake.* You need it but not in excessive amounts. The average woman can thrive on about 40 grams of protein daily. Too much stresses the kidneys.

    Sample Protein Plan: Three ounces of flounder, two cups of pasta, one cup of nonfat or low-fat milk gives you close to 40 grams of protein. A good amount for good energy boosting.

6. *Boost your intake of fruits and vegetables.* Take advantage of this great source of energy-boosting complex carbohydrates. Very low in calories, but also rich in vitamins and minerals. Have them daily!

7. *Ingest iron for energy.* Enrich your bloodstream with iron-rich foods such as very lean meats, green leafy vegetables, sun-dried fruits, dried beans and peas, potatoes, and whole grain breads and cereals. *Tip:* For better absorption, eat a food rich in vitamin C (citrus fruits, juices, tomatoes, peppers) *together* with an iron-containing food. You'll feel an energy surge right from the start. Remember to take folacin (especially for women taking oral contraceptives) and also vitamin B12. These nutrients are found in organ meats, dark green leafy vegetables, wheat germ, dried beans and peas. Include some fish and milk as well as brewer's

yeast, also known as nutritional yeast, for good vitamin B12 intake if you want to avoid meats.

8. *Plan your meals with care.* Schedule food intake to meet your energy needs. Carbohydrate plus some protein is helpful to wake you up in the morning and give you energy at noon. In the evening, a complex carbohydrate meal with very modest protein is satisfying. *Tip:* You'll enjoy more energy on a plan that calls for several small meals throughout the day instead of two huge ones. You'll avoid sleepiness and sluggishness with this basic plan.

9. *Never skip meals.* You'll play havoc with your blood sugar. Hunger causes these levels to plunge; you become tired, nervous, irritable. *Careful:* No binge-purge eating schemes either or you deplete your energy and threaten your life, too!

10. *Avoid alcohol.* It's a depressant. It makes you groggy. Female metabolism is such that you may become sleepy before men who drink as much or more than you do! At a social function? Try plain seltzer on the rocks with a slice of lemon or lime.

11. *Avoid caffeine.* It's an addictive drug that gives picks you up and then dashes you to the ground when the effects wear off. You'll feel fatigue between drinks. Feel midafternoon fatigue? Take a catnap.

12. *Exercise regularly.* Regular exercise—about 60 minutes daily— helps keep you energetic. It also helps metabolize foods. Tone up your muscles. They'll be able to accomplish tasks much easier and with less fatigue. Exercise helps wash away toxic wastes that induce tiredness. A great way to cleanse your system. As someone remarked, "Exercise doesn't take time, it makes time!" A great way to lose weight, if need be.

With these basic 12 energy boosters, you will be able to enjoy more vitality—and you'll look younger, too! Isn't that all part of being a woman?

ENERGY ROBBER—PREMENSTRUAL SYNDROME

Premenstrual syndrome, also known as PMS, occurs once a month, about two weeks before the menstrual period. The two hormones—estrogen and progesterone—that regulate your menstrual cycle tend to cause upheaval. For several days, there are mood swings, food cravings, irritability, and emotional and/or physical exhaustion. Some women go through PMS with few reactions; others have more throbbing reactions with fatigue and energy drain.

Energy Boosters

Some research suggests taking doctor-approved supplements; in particular, vitamins A and D help control premenstrual skin problems (acne and oil). Vitamin B6 is believed to ease symptoms such as mood swings, fluid retention, breast tenderness, bloating, sugar craving, and fatigue. Vitamin C reduces stress, while vitamin E balances the hormonal system and appears to promote natural energy. Two minerals—calcium and magnesium—ease problems of cramps and pain, ease unnatural (and unhealthy) food cravings, and stabilize moods. Be sure to go easy on fats because they contribute to very high estrogen levels, and you don't need this during PMS. Control dairy foods. Small portions are all you need. The lactose in dairy may block your body's absorption of magnesium, which is needed to balance estrogen and help its excretion. And eliminate salt, which also causes you to retain water. Avoid caffeine, alcohol, stress. More fiber is needed to help your body clear out excess estrogen. Good fiber foods are vegetables, whole grains, and beans. *Tip:* Try barley, buckwheat, and millet, which are high not only in fiber but also in magnesium, which helps your body absorb calcium to prevent PMS cramps and pain.

ENERGY ROBBER—YEAST INFECTIONS

Candida albicans—yeast—is a fungus that grows naturally in women's vaginas can become a problem in the case of an alteration of the normal pH balance of the vagina. When this pH balance changes from its normal, slightly acidic nature to the more alkaline pH, the environment becomes more susceptible to harmful fungi and bacteria. *Symptoms:* Intense itching, accompanied by an odorless, white, cheeselike discharge. A yeast infection is often provoked by pregnancy; the taking of birth control pills, hormones for menopause, or antibiotics; chemical douches; spermicides; nicks in the vaginal wall from tampons; poor lubrication; or intercourse with someone who has a yeast infection. It is annoying and causes a drain of energy because of the infection.

Energy Boosters

William G. Crook, M.D., of Jackson, Tennessee, who specializes in female fatigue disorders and is the author of *The Yeast Connection*, offers these energy booster suggestions for yeast infections.

Avoid refined carbohydrates. Avoid sugar-containing foods and beverages. Avoid yeast and foods containing yeast. Avoid alcohol. Monitor your intake of cheeses. "The more aged, the more yeast it contains. Some doctors allow cream cheese, cottage cheese, ricotta." Avoid products of yeast fermentation: all vinegars and products containing vinegar (pickles, mayonnaise, catsup, many salad dressings, barbecue sauce), soy sauce, sour cream, and buttermilk. *Tip:* You may have sugar-free, fruit-free yogurt because it is fermented with the friendly bacteria lactobacillus, not yeast. Avoid processed foods: bacon, ham, lox, beef jerky, and smoked meats and fish. And avoid food additives or foods made with synthetic flavors, colors, preservatives. You may have all vegetables, whole grains (brown rice, wheat, oats, barley, millet), poultry, fish, seafood, lean meats, unprocessed vegetable oils.

ENERGY ROBBER—VAGINITIS

Vaginitis is an inflammation of the vagina; redness, swelling, and irritation of the vaginal tissues. It causes discharge, burning, itching, and odor. The cause may be germlike bacteria or fungus which can occur with or without sexual contact. Your menstrual period, birth control pills, douching too frequently, use of tight pantyhose without a cotton crotch, and other assorted conditions such as diabetes and pregnancy are some other causes. A change in the acidity of the vagina can allow potentially harmful organisms living in this area to grow rapidly and lead to symptoms which include fatigue and tiredness.

Energy Boosters

To bring vaginitis under control, Martin Gubernidk, M.D., assistant professor of obstetrics and gynecology at Cornell Medical School in New York, recommends the following:

- Avoid scratching; it will only irritate the area and cause the infection to spread.
- Dry the vaginal area after showering, bathing, or swimming. Change out of wet bathing suits or sweaty exercise outfits as soon as possible because the organisms that cause vaginitis thrive in moist conditions.
- Wipe from front to rear (away from the vagina) following urination and after a bowel movement.
- Wear cotton underwear. Nylon and other synthetic fabrics retain heat and moisture, providing harmful bacteria with a damp environment in which to grow. Choose pantyhose with a cotton crotch.
- Avoid sexual activity, which can irritate inflamed tissues, and force harmful bacteria into the uterus and fallopian tubes.
- When menstruating and using vaginal antifungal medication, avoid using tampons because they may absorb the medication and/or increase inflammation of the vagina.
- If symptoms do not alleviate within three days, or the infection is not cured in seven days, see your doctor.

ENERGY ROBBER—ENDOMETRIOSIS

Endometriosis is a condition in which the lining of the uterus (the endometrium) grows outside the uterus, mostly in the pelvic cavity.

The endometrium can attach itself to the fallopian tubes, through which the egg travels to the uterus; ovaries, intestines, and other organs may also be affected. Symptoms can range from mild to severe, including energy loss, cramps, pain in the lower back, and a feeling of tiredness. Endometriosis may also affect fertility.

Energy Boosters

Keep a calendar. Chart your cycle. Prepare for when symptoms and fatigue are at their worst. You'll be able to rearrange your schedule to minimize fatigue during these times. For some, eating more fish is helpful; fish contains omega-3 fatty acids, which suppress prostaglandins—those substances that cause pain and also fatigue. To ease pain, try bed rest, moist heat, or warm drinks. Be sure to exercise as a means of bringing down estrogen levels, which may slow the growth of endometriosis. *Tip:* Exercise stimulates your body's production of endorphins, those natural pain-blocking substances. *Careful:* Jarring exercise can pull on adhesions and scar tissue—try simple walking. Avoid caffeine (coffee, tea, soft drinks, some chocolates, over-the-counter medications, prescribed medications) because this drug may worsen pain and cause more fatigue.

ENERGY ROBBER—MENOPAUSE

Also called the "change of life," it is the point at which you stop ovulating. Estrogen secretion slows, then stops. Monthly menstruation becomes irregular, then ceases. Normally, women reach menopause by age 50 and the symptoms may last for four or five years. The energy-draining symptoms include hot flashes, dizziness, headache, difficulty breathing, and heart palpitations. Depression accompanies fatigue to cause distress.

Energy Boosters

Nutritional suggestions include certain nutrients that help your body cope during these trying times. Evening primrose oil, a herb available at health stores, helps soothe symptoms and gives you a feeling of alertness and exhilaration. Vitamin B6 (pyridoxine) minimizes water retention and eases symptoms while restoring energy. Vitamin E helps you cope with the hot flashes, minimizing their fatigue-causing distress. It's also important to have enough calcium and magnesium to balance hormonal upset and promote a feeling of well-being.

To improve energy, minimize intake of animal products, switch to complex carbohydrates, moderate protein intake, and increase the amount of legumes in your diet. Sometimes ginseng is said to help ease fatigue-caused depression and upheavals in estrogen production. A cup or two of ginseng tea daily may help keep you feeling energetic and less discomforted. For itching in the vaginal area, use vitamin E cream (without fragrance) or else open a natural vitamin E capsule and apply. This natural emollient helps stop the itching almost from the start.

You may also find comfort in taking vitamin E, about 400 international units taken twice a day. It may help cut the frequency of hot flashes. While the vitamin is generally considered safe, it can have a blood-thinning effect, so use with the guidance of your health practitioner. Use mild (fragrance-free) deodorant-free soap or cleansing bars. Avoid personal hygiene sprays that can irritate dry, sensitive vaginal tissues. After bath or shower, dry thoroughly. (Bacteria could multiply in a damp area and invade vulnerable vaginal tissues.) Wear cotton-crotch underwear (it "breathes" better than nylon), which permits moisture to evaporate.

To boost energy, keep yourself active. Daily walks, bicycle rides, and aerobic exercise will boost blood flow to your brain and make you feel vigorous. At least 60 minutes daily will keep you in an energetic mood. And because menopause brings on hormonal changes that could thin your bones, be sure to take at least 1,200 milligrams of calcium daily—either a doctor-approved supplement or low-fat dairy products, broccoli, kale, sardines (with bones), mackerel, and tofu. And drink lots of water or juice, especially if you see you are sweating profusely or losing body water. The "change of life" can be a welcome new future. Be ready and sail forth into the happy and energetic years ahead.

CASE HISTORY—
Menopause Almost Makes Her an Invalid

When the hot flashes started shortly after her fifty-second birthday, Theresa W. had severe stomach pains, mood swings, chronic tiredness, and insomnia. Her distress kept her tossing and turning. Just when she was ready to start a new job, since her children were grown and out of the house, and do more traveling with her husband, she was almost bedridden because of symptoms. Her main complaint was "always wanting to sleep." She had always feared the change of life (her emotions made it worse) and felt like "crawling in a hole and hiding from the world."

Her husband almost dragged her to an endocrinologist who outlined an energy booster plan: more complex carbohydrates, little fat, moderate protein, prescribed vitamins, and more exercise. Theresa W. feared being an invalid, not to mention losing her new job. She followed the doctor's advice. In five days, she felt more alive and youthful. The ginseng tea also helped give her pep and minimize discomfort. She was soon feeling better, with more natural energy, and was able to work vigorously on her new job. She had used natural energy boosters to help ease the menopause, a threat to her vitality. And she planned many car trips with the boast, "I'll do the driving . . . across the country . . . because I'm overflowing with energy!"

Because women are becoming increasingly active—joining the work force and accepting more responsibilities—the risk for fatigue could be serious. But with the use of energy boosters, you can be fatigue free and have vitality forever!

HIGHLIGHTS

1. A woman doctor offers a 12-step plan for women who are troubled with fatigue and seek energy boosters.

2. Women can help ease and erase fatigue-causing problems of PMS, yeast infections, vaginitis, endometriosis, menopause. A set of energy boosters will help almost from the start.

3. Pauline LaK. was able to restore energy with the use of a simple diet trick. It rescued her from debilitating fatigue.

4. Theresa W. was saved from being an invalid during menopause. She followed a nutritional energy booster plan that made her a powerhouse of energy—in the midst of the menopause. It was a change for the better!

···Seventeen

For men only

● ● ● ● ● ● ● ●

Is male energy related to the levels of testosterone in the body? Endocrinologists, who study the delicate science of hormones, caution that if testosterone levels slump as men grow older, there follows a broad range of fatigue symptoms. These include a decline in muscle mass and strength, accumulation of fatigue-causing body fat, a loss of bone density, reduced energy, lowered fertility, and fading virility.

Body Rhythms and Hormone Levels

In younger men, hormone levels are at their energetic peak early in the morning and level off slightly as the day goes on. But in middle-aged men, there is a slowing up of circadian rhythms that lower testosterone supplies, bringing on tiredness and weakness. It would appear that the key to maintaining good circadian rhythms is to have an ample supply of testosterone, the "energy" hormone for men.

How the Male Hormone Influences Energy

The production of testosterone is governed by the brain's pituitary gland, which secretes hormones that prompt the male sex organs (testes) to generate this energy substance. *Problem:* In some men, especially if there is nutritional deficiency, testicular tissue becomes gradually less responsive to the pituitary hormones; this leads to a dropoff of testosterone production, which, in turn, reduces sperm output and weakens the mobility of sperm. Further loss of testosterone leads to more body fat, less muscle mass, and thinner bones than those who have adequate amounts of testosterone. This hormonal decline affects a man's mood, bringing on bouts of fatigue, loss of initiative, and weaker concentration powers. It appears that this vital male hormone has quite an influence on energy.

THE MINERAL THAT NOURISHES THE MALE HORMONE

Zinc is a little-known but powerful mineral that nourishes the male glands to release an adequate amount of testosterone. The male prostate gland accumulates high levels of zinc—more zinc than any other organ in the body. In some situations, a deficiency of zinc leads to disorders of the prostate and a decline in testosterone. Zinc is also concerned with youthful growth processes (hair included) and tissue respiration, and participates in utilization of insulin secreted by the pancreas; therefore, zinc becomes involved in the body's use of carbohydrates to produce energy. The greatest concentration of zinc in the body is found in the sex organs, where it is used to manufacture much of the testosterone the male needs for energy and vitality.

Sources of Zinc

Herring, milk, meat, and egg yolks (but also high in fat and cholesterol) are sources, and the zinc in whole grains, while not totally absorbed, does provide a substantial contribution. Brewer's yeast is another good source. A daily supplement of zinc gluconate is considered a reliable source, giving you the zinc in an absorbable form and as much of it as you require.

PROSTATE GLAND: KEY TO MALE YOUTHFUL ENERGY

Do you have problems with getting up at night to go to the bathroom? Throughout the day, do you notice you have to make many more trips to the bathroom? It could be your prostate, the gland that influences your youthful vitality.

What Is the Prostate? What Does It Do?

The prostate is a walnut-sized gland of the male reproductive system. It is located in front of the rectum and just below the bladder, the organ that stores urine. The prostate is quite small—it weighs only about one ounce. It produces fluid that helps to nourish and transport sperm. The prostate wraps around a tube called the urethra, which carries urine from the bladder out through the tip of the penis. It is involved in a man's youthfulness—and it has often been said that a man is as energetic and youthful as his prostate.

When the Prostate Weakens

During the middle years, the prostate may become enlarged and block the flow of urine through the urethra, leading to more frequent urination and a loss of energy. Symptoms of failure include hesitancy, or difficulty, in starting urination, weak urinary stream, interruption of the stream, and feeling of incomplete bladder emptying. *Danger:* Blockage of urine from an enlarged prostate can also cause infections of the urinary system and damage to the bladder and kidneys.

Risk of Prostatitis

Also known as inflammation of the prostate, it is caused by bacterial infection and may lead to serious disorders such as cancer of this vital male gland.

The symptoms of prostatitis often mimic those of other urinary tract or prostate disorders. You may experience no symptoms or symptoms so sudden and severe that you seek emergency medical care. Symptoms, when present, can include any of the following: fever, chills, urinary frequency, frequent urination at night, difficulty urinating, burning or painful urination, perineal (referring to the perineum, the area between the scrotum and the anus) and low-back pain, joint or muscle pain, tender or swollen prostate, blood in the urine, or painful ejaculation. It is essential to obtain prompt medical treatment for such a condition.

The prostate is unusual in that it enlarges with age, unlike many other organs. The loss of energy is obvious: premature "old age" is brought on with a malfunctioning and malnourished prostate—the key to your youthful energy.

How to Nourish Your Prostate for More Vitality

Zinc, say Dr. Jonathan V. Wright of Tacoma, Washington, is needed for the prostate gland and sperm cell production. These sites have more zinc than any other organs or tissues. This is reflected in the many men who have prostate problems with low zinc stores.

Dr. Wright prescribes this basic treatment to his fatigue-troubled prostate-weakened patients:

1. Chelated zinc, 50 milligrams, one tablet three times a day

2. Essential fatty acids, 400 milligrams, one capsule three times a day

3. Bee pollen tablets, three a day

With these nutrients, Dr. Wright believes that you can nourish your prostate gland and sperm cells to keep yourself feeling energetic and vigorous. (These supplements are available at health stores.)

Is Stress Hurting Your Prostate?

Relaxing the muscles is essential as part of the treatment of nonbacterial prostatitis. Ira Sharplip, M.D., urologist in private practice and assistant professor of urology at the University of California, San Francisco, says that in many cases, the symptoms of prostatitis are related to muscle stress.

"The cause is an increase in the tone of the urethral sphincter muscles due to stress," says Dr. Sharplip. "Often, just understanding the problem is enough to keep the man from being so uptight." He believes it is possible to maintain prostate health and overall energy by eliminating stress.

Another physician who sees a link between prostatitis and stress is Donald M. Rudnick, M.D., of Pomona, California, who tells us:

"In my practice, where 'prostatitis' comprises 15 percent of patient visits, the one common thread binding all patients together is chronic, unrelenting stress. The stress may result from problems in any of life's spheres—work, education, or family. The various constitutional symptoms from the disease respond best when patients are removed from their source of stress—at vacation time, when the big job is finally done, or when the family dispute is settled."

Beware These Prostate Energy Thieves

Dr. Rudnick cautions: "Prostatitis patients are invariably heavy smokers, heavy caffeine partakers and spicy food eaters. The substances are known urothelial irritants—elimination of them from your diet always prompts symptomatic improvement."

Treat the Whole Person

Dr. Rudnick comments, "I have always felt that prostatitis is a disease of the person, and not simply an inflammation of the prostate. I have, therefore, always given advice regarding both dietary and physical and mental hygiene along with antibiotic therapy to more effectively eliminate the chances of relapse or recurrence."

SLANT BOARD REJUVENATES PROSTATE GLAND

Want to rejuvenate your prostate and regenerate yourself? Try an unusual treatment recommended by Jay Cohen, M.D., a San Diego, California, physician, which he used for his own condition!

Dr. Cohen was diagnosed as having chronic nonbacterial prostatitis. For five years, he had been plagued by symptoms ranging from lower-back pain, muscular soreness, and aching in the area below the genitals to occasional painful urination.

"Most distressing," says Dr. Cohen, "was a constant pain on both sides of my groin, which progressed to a swollen and tender epididymis (sperm storage sites in the scrotum) and a pain so intense, that it severely limited my activity."

Pain, Fatigue, Medications, Treatment

He sought the help of many specialists, including three different urologists. He tried antibiotics, heat, ice, prostatic massage, physical therapy, and anti-inflammatory drugs. Nothing worked. He does say that the antibiotics (tetracycline and trimethoprimsulfa-methoxazole) provided "significant relief" for more than a year, but then he developed reactions to the drugs. He was almost going to start another antibiotic (carbenicillin) when "something surprising" intervened and he was offered an alternative to established treatment methods.

"Having noticed that my epididymis swelled and ached the more I was on my feet, I thought I would try using my wife's slant board, which raises the feet above the head at an angle of 30 degrees," says Dr. Cohen. "Understand that I had always laughed at my wife for her unconventional ideas, and I felt quite strange the first time I found myself looking up at my toes.

"But my embarrassment faded as my symptoms gradually but steadily disappeared. Now, over a year later, I am virtually asymptomatic. I am far better than when I was taking the antibiotics. A long day will still evoke some tenderness and swelling, but it disappears quickly once I am back on the slant board."

Why Slant Board Regenerates Prostate

Dr. Cohen explains that he uses the slant board for 20 minutes, three times a day, and that he is now free of all medication and "fully active"—swimming, windsurfing, and sitting without discomfort. Why does it help? "Perhaps the tilted position may enhance the drainage of secretions and swelling, similar to the effect of elevating swollen feet." *Caution:* If you have problems of heart disease, high blood pressure, intracranial conditions, vascular fragility, glaucoma, or breathing disorders, get approval from your health practitioner before you try the slant board.

KEEP ACTIVE AND CUT DOWN ON MIDNIGHT BATHROOM TRIPS

Participate in some light activity one to two hours before going to bed. *Problem:* Inactivity causes bodily fluids (from blood and lymph) to pool in your legs, ankles, and feet, leading to swelling. When you lie down to go to sleep, the fluids drain, prompting the need to void. *Solution:* If you get up and get yourself moving for only 10 to 20 minutes between dinner and bedtime, the muscular action will pump and circulate fluids to your kidneys.

Also, while reading this book, keep legs elevated to prevent swelling. (Do it now.) Also keep legs on a hassock while watching television in the evening. You'll be more likely to void earlier and less likely to have to interrupt sweet dreaming.

Case History—
Revives Sluggish Prostate, Feels More Energetic
Avoids Surgery

Troubled with a slightly enlarged prostate gland, Warren MacD. had to keep going to the bathroom throughout the day. He was interrupted throughout the night for even more trips to the bathroom. He had a mild case of nonbacterial prostatitis and feared it could become worse if not treated. When he developed pain, he sought help from a urologist who told him that he might have to face surgery. He was given medications and told to return in two months.

The drugs offered temporary help. But when the effects wore off, he felt a return of discomfort, low-back pain, and annoying bathroom visits. He sought help from another urologist who was recommended as having found natural methods of care. Through it all, Warren MacD. was constantly tired. He would doze off in the middle of the day, often immediately after a meal. Was he getting old? (He was only 49.)

The recommended urologist put him on a basic revitalization program: daily, 150 milligrams of zinc, 400 milligrams of essential fatty acids, and 100 milligrams of bee pollen tablets. He was put on a stress-management program to ease tension. Then he was told to quit smoking and give up caffeine. Easy on spicy foods, too. He was put on a more healthful food program: very little animal fat, more complex carbohydrates, modest protein. Then he was told to try a slant board—from 20 to 30 minutes each day. Within two weeks, Warren MacD. felt ease of his groin pain. He no longer had to go to the bathroom excessively. "What a relief. Now I can sleep the night through." This also eased stress. When he detoxified his body of smoking, caffeine, and sharp spices, he experience a revitalization that gave him more energy than he had in his younger days. And the best news of all: his urologist said his nonbacterial prostatitis had cleared up and his prostate gland was a normal size. No surgery! He was as vital and energetic as a youngster!

A DOCTOR'S PLAN FOR PROSTATE HEALING

James F. Balch, M.D., of Greenfield, Indiana, offers nutritional energizers and herbal healers for prostate disorders:

- Herbal teas will often ease acute inflammation or prostate gland enlargement, but if no improvement takes place or symptoms recur, see a urologist.
- Mix together equal amounts of sea holly and hydrangea root and take three to four tablespoons three times daily. It is believed to ease inflammation and reduce the discomfort of urination. *Tip:* Add marshmallow leaves to this mixture if burning and heat persist; this last-named herb has demulcent benefits in cooling the heat.
- For frequent night urination (or if small amounts of blood are passed) use horsetail as an astringent. *Tip:* For an enlarged gland, combine with hydrangea. You will also ease frequent urination with such herbs as goldenseal root, parsley, juniper berries, uva ursi, and slippery elm bark. Ginseng is an excellent tonic!
- For prostatitis, increase fluid intake. Drink two to three quarts of spring water daily to stimulate urine flow. This prevents retention, cystitis (bladder infection), and kidney infection.
- Dr. Balch believes that to prevent the risk of prostate cancer, maintain a whole food diet. "Regular intake of zinc (15 milligrams daily) and polyunsaturated fatty acids (three to six capsules daily) in later life may help prevent development of problems. Consume more nuts and seeds, raw vegetables,

fruits, fresh juices, dried beans, peas, and brown rice. Avoid refined carbohydrates, coffee, strong tea, and alcohol. These have been linked to cancer of the prostate. Too much fat in the diet may result in prostate cancer as well. Chemical reactions occur when fat is cooked, leading to the production of free radicals. It is believed that these reactions play a major role in this cancer."

- Boost circulation in your prostate region and feel more energetic all over. Here is one helpful method: sit in a tub that contains comfortably hot water for 15 to 30 minutes once or twice a day. Another method calls for spraying the lower abdomen and pelvic region with warm and cold water; alternate three minutes hot, one minute cold. Or else—sit in comfortably hot water while immersing your feet in cold water for three minutes. Then sit in cold water for one minute while immersing feet in comfortably hot water.

- Eat one ounce of pumpkin seeds or take pumpkin seed oil capsules as directed daily. *Tip:* "Pumpkin seeds eaten daily are helpful for almost all prostate troubles because they are rich in zinc," says Dr. Balch.

CASE HISTORY—
Revives Prostate, Feels Energetic, Boosts Hormone Flow

In his early sixties, Chris P.J. was about to start on a world cruise with his wife when he started having difficulties with his prostate gland. Frequent urination, painful spasms, and a loss of energy put a hold on his long-awaited trip. How could Chris P.J. enjoy the trip when he was so weak?

Over a period of a few weeks, his discomfort increased: he had low-back pain, difficulties with urination, and energy loss. There were days when he was so lethargic, all he did was lie in bed and fall asleep while looking at television!

He resisted undergoing surgery when a urologist told him of his enlarged prostate. His brother-in-law and a younger brother both had the operations and had experienced so much pain that Chris P.J.

held off. But something had to be done. His symptoms worsened. It was through the suggestion of a naturopathic physician he consulted that he began to make changes in his lifestyle.

Chris P.J. used a variety of herbs. He then reduced his protein and fat intake and boosted his consumption of fresh fruits and raw vegetables. A meal would consist of cooked brown rice, whole grain pasta, and an assortment of beans or peas. No coffee, strong tea, or alcohol. He also devoted about an hour daily to a brisk walk. No cheating!

He also boosted his vitamin-mineral intake with adequate amounts of zinc to boost the health of his prostate gland. *Results:* A thorough examination after two months on this program showed his prostate was normal again. He had no problems with excess urination. He was filled with energy. His naturopathic physician pronounced him as fit as a youngster, thanks to this prostate rejuvenation program.

Chris P.J. and his wife went for a two-month well-deserved worldwide cruise, and he was so energetic, he won the dance contest on board, won the bowling prize, and beat out men half his age on the tennis court! The program aimed at rejuvenating his prostate, boosting his testosterone flow, and boosting his energy, too!

THE HERB THAT IS A DYNAMIC ENERGY BOOSTER

Used for thousands of years in the Orient, ginseng is regarded as the "ultimate energy booster" for all who want to feel more vibrant. (And who doesn't?)

Ginseng has a fleshy, multibranched root. With a stretch of the imagination, some roots resemble the human form, with limblike branches suggesting arms and legs. The ancients called the plant "man root," *jen shen*, which became "ginseng." It has been widely used to boost energy, helping to strengthen the body and mind.

Ginseng has several chemicals, called *ginsenosides*, that tend to stimulate the central nervous system, invigorate the glandular network, and boost a healthy and youthful release of hormones.

Ginseng appears to stimulate the immune system. It revs up the white blood cells (macrophages and natural killer cells) that devour fatigue-causing microorganisms. Ginseng also spurs production of interferon, the body's own virus-fighting chemical, and antibodies that fight off fatigue-causing bacterial and viral infections.

Some studies report that ginseng helps stimulate the male libido or sexual desires, but while this response has been observed in animals, the human is more involved insofar as emotions are concerned. That is, more complex social and psychological factors are involved in the libido. Still, ginseng may be able to rejuvenate and energize the glandular system, a major factor in energy.

How to Take Energy-Boosting Ginseng

Try root powder, teas, capsules, or tablets, which are available at herbal outlets and health stores. You may have about one teaspoon per day. You can also make a decoction from dried, pulverized root material. Use half a teaspoon per cup of water. Bring to a boil. Let simmer ten minutes. Drink several cups per day.

Ginseng has been hailed as an energy booster for thousands of years. Since it has been around so long, it must have value. Try it—and give your hormones a boost!

Is there a "male menopause" or "change of life"? Opinions are divided, but the man who starts to lose energy in his forties knows that such a change can occur. With the use of a variety of energy boosters, you can revive-regenerate-rejuvenate your body and mind and enjoy a youthful prostate—the key to vitality!

HIGHLIGHTS

1. As a man, your body rhythms and hormone levels start to change in your middle years. Your vital male hormone, testosterone, is your key to energy.

2. Zinc is an important mineral that helps balance your circadian rhythms and nourish your prostate for healthy testosterone.

3. A healthy prostate gland is a key to youthful energy. A doctor offers a three-step nutritional program to boost energy of fatigue-troubled, prostate-weakened men.

4. Be alert to stress as a fatigue-draining threat to your prostate.

5. A physician who had trouble with his own prostate recommends using a slant board that gave him recovery and an energy boost, too.

6. Warren MacD. avoided surgery and regenerated his prostate with a nutritional program.

7. A doctor offers a set of nutritional energizers and herbal healers for prostate disorders.

8. Chris P.J. followed a naturopathic physician's guidelines and boosted energy while healing his prostate. He was able to avoid surgery!

9. Ginseng is an ancient herb that has been used for thousands of years to boost energy and improve the immune system to overcome prostate disorders.

···*Eighteen*

How to enjoy high energy on a low-fat plan

The message is clear. You can enjoy youthful energy if you control the fat in your eating plan. While fats can be a source of energy, they are a double-edged sword. Too much will cause fatigue among other problems.

Why Fats Are Energy Thieves

Fats actually choke tissues by depriving them of oxygen. Whether saturated or unsaturated, fats form a suffocating film around the red blood cells and blood platelets, causing cells and platelets to stick together. This is a form of sludging that deprives red blood cells of oxygen and plugs tiny blood vessels (capillaries). Once the capillaries are blocked, the liquid portion of the blood is pushed through the capillary walls bringing on edema—further lowering the supply of oxygen available to the cells. This is a major cause of fatigue.

Fats, Energy, Ketosis

Suppose you go on a high-fat, high-protein, but low-carbohydrate reducing plan. On this high-fat diet, blood sugar is burned off rapidly, forcing your body to turn to fat reserves for energy. The fatty acids from the fat stores burn inefficiently, producing acid metabolites known as *ketones*. An increase in ketones brings on *ketosis*.

In ketosis, there is a decline of glucose—and glucose is your brain's only source of food. Fatty acids cannot be converted into glucose. Your brain becomes nutritionally starved, and you feel fatigue and tiredness. A problem is that ketones are acidic and could change your blood pH. This is a risk because if this balance is disturbed, if the blood becomes too acidic, your brain cannot function adequately. You develop fatigue and other difficulties, including irregular heartbeat and possible liver disorders.

A high-fat diet may raise cholesterol levels that clog the lining of your arteries. This chokes off oxygen to the heart, and you run the risk of cardiac problems. Fat can threaten your life!

You Do Need Some Fat

Yes, fat is important. A certain amount of fat will help you maintain a well-balanced energy level. During moderate activity, energy is drawn in equal amounts from your body's supply of carbohydrates and fats. If you are very active, your energy is drawn more from fats than from carbohydrates. So you need to store an adequate amount of both these nutrients. The successful burning of fat helps spare carbohydrate—and you enjoy more energy.

COUNT FAT, NOT CALORIES, FOR ENERGY

Ounce for ounce, dietary fat actually contains more calories (and is more speedily converted to body fat) than either carbohydrates or protein. So counting fat automatically counts calories. And you know that a high-fat diet increases fatigue, your risk of heart disease, diabetes, and cancer.

Control Fat Intake

That's the trick: limit the amount of fat you consume. Nutritional authorities recommend that you lower your fat intake so that fat accounts for less than 30 percent of total calories. Other energy authorities suggest even lower intakes, that is, no more than 25 percent of calories come from fat. How can you estimate your daily fat intake?

One method uses a calculator. Estimate the percentage of calories from fat for individual foods or your whole diet. For foods, check the labels for total grams of fat per serving and then multiply that number by 9, divide by the total calories per serving, and multiply by 100. (That's because each gram of fat has 9 calories.) For example, if you eat 1,800 calories a day, you should limit your intake to 60 grams of total fat.

But there is a simpler way, as is noted by the accompanying chart. Keep in mind that these fat limits are approximate and are designed for sedentary people. If you are very active or exercise vigorously, you are entitled to several more grams of fat (3 grams for every extra 100 calories you burn). The chart does not account for age at a time when metabolism slows down. That is why it is especially important for older individuals to become more active, participate in daily exercise, and cut back on fat calories.

You CAN Enjoy Some Fat

Your plan is to *limit* total fat intake but not to eliminate it entirely. You are entitled to an occasional pat of butter, a few slices of lean meat, a bit of oil, a splash of a salad dressing. But know your limits! When you stay within your boundaries, you'll have some fat along with energy.

Fat Goals
For limiting dietary fat to 25 percent of calories

Weight (Pounds)	Calorie Intake	Fat Limit (Grams)
WOMEN		
110	1,300	37
120	1,400	40
130	1,600	43
140	1,700	47
150	1,800	50
160	1,900	53
170	2,000	57
180	2,200	60
MEN		
130	1,800	51
140	2,000	54
150	2,100	58
160	2,200	62
170	2,400	66
180	2,500	70
190	2,700	74
200	2,800	78

Sandwich Guide

Use this guide to compare and to choose sandwich ingredients that are lower in calories, fat, cholesterol and sodium.

Food	Approximate amount per serving			
	Calories	Fat (grams)	Cholesterol (milligrams)	Sodium (milligrams)
Breads:				
2 slices whole-wheat	140	2	0	360
1 pita bread, 6½ inches in diameter	165	1	0	339
1 croissant, 4½ by 4 by 1¾ inches thick	235	12	13	452
Fillings:				
2 ounces home-cooked lean roast beef	110	4	46	37
2 ounces deli roast beef	145	9	47	234
2 ounces lean, boiled ham	75	3	27	815
1 slice (1 ounce) bologna	90	8	16	289
1 slice (1 ounce) process American cheese	105	9	27	406
2 tablespoons peanut butter	190	16	0	150
¼ cup tuna salad[1]	95	5	7	206
Sandwich Add-ons:				
1 teaspoon butter	35	4	10	39
1 teaspoon margarine	35	4	0	51
1 teaspoon prepared mustard	5	trace	0	63
1 teaspoon mayonnaise	35	4	3	26
1 teaspoon sweet pickle relish	5	trace	0	36

1. Tuna salad made with light tuna packed in oil, and mayonnaise-type salad dressing.

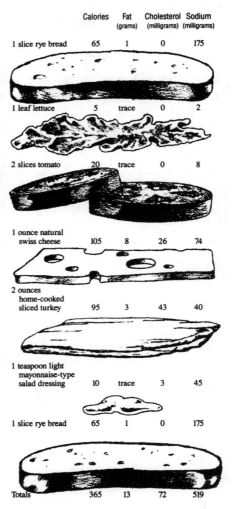

	Calories	Fat (grams)	Cholesterol (milligrams)	Sodium (milligrams)
1 slice rye bread	65	1	0	175
1 leaf lettuce	5	trace	0	2
2 slices tomato	20	trace	0	8
1 ounce natural swiss cheese	105	8	26	74
2 ounces home-cooked sliced turkey	95	3	43	40
1 teaspoon light mayonnaise-type salad dressing	10	trace	3	45
1 slice rye bread	65	1	0	175
Totals	365	13	72	519

Muncher's Guide

Eating Snacks and Desserts...
The Dietary Guidelines Way

Learn how to enjoy snacks and desserts the Dietary Guidelines way. Use this chart to find out more about the calories, fat, cholesterol, and sodium in your favorite snacks and to develop some new snack ideas.

FOOD	Approximate amount per serving			
	Calories	Fat (grams)	Cholesterol (milligrams)	Sodium (milligrams)
Breads, cereals, and other grain products				
½ cup corn chips	70	4	0	108
1 cup popcorn, unsalted, plain	30	trace	0	trace
1 cup popcorn, salted and buttered	50	2	5	213
4 whole-wheat crackers, 2 inches square	70	4	0	118
16 cheese crackers, 1 inch square	80	5	10	179
4 saltine crackers, 1⅞ inches square	50	1	4	165
Bagel, 3½ inches in diameter	200	2	0	245
Bran muffin, 2½ inches in diameter	125	6	24	189
10 thin salted pretzel sticks	10	trace	0	48
⅛ 15-inch cheese pizza	290	9	56	699
Milk, cheese, yogurt				
1 ounce swiss cheese	105	8	26	74
1 ounce Cheddar cheese	115	9	30	176
1 ounce process American cheese	105	9	27	406
1 cup skim milk	90	1	5	130
1 cup lowfat milk, 2% fat	125	5	18	128
1 cup whole milk	150	8	33	120
8-ounce carton plain lowfat yogurt	145	4	14	159
8-ounce carton lowfat yogurt with fruit	230	2	10	133

FOOD	Approximate amount per serving			
	Calories	Fat (grams)	Cholesterol (milligrams)	Sodium (milligrams)
Vegetables				
2 carrot and 2 celery sticks	5	trace	0	10
3 broccoli florets	10	trace	0	9
6 fluid ounces tomato juice	30	trace	0	658
6 fluid ounces tomato juice, "no-salt-added"	30	trace	0	18
1 medium dill pickle	5	trace	0	928
10 potato chips	105	7	0	94
10 salted french fries	160	8	0	108
Fruits				
Small apple	60	trace	0	0
Banana	105	1	0	1
6 fluid ounces orange juice	85	trace	0	2
1 small box raisins, ½ ounce (about 1½ tablespoons)	40	trace	0	2
Nuts and seeds				
¼ cup unsalted, roasted peanuts	210	18	0	2
¼ cup salted, dry-roasted peanuts	210	18	0	293
2 tablespoons peanut butter	190	16	0	153
¼ cup salted, roasted sunflower seeds	210	20	0	205
Desserts				
½ cup frozen yogurt	105	2	8	50
½ cup sherbet	135	2	7	44
½ cup ice milk	90	3	9	52
½ cup regular ice cream	135	7	30	58
Frosted brownie, 1½ inches by 1¾ inches by ⅞ inch thick	100	4	14	59
2 fig bars	105	2	14	90
2 oatmeal-raisin cookies, 2⅝ inches in diameter	120	5	1	74
Raised doughnut	235	13	21	222

Vegetables or Nachos?

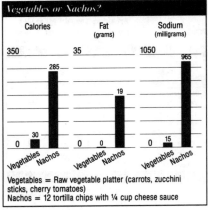

Calories	Fat (grams)	Sodium (milligrams)

Calories: 350, Vegetables 30, Nachos 285
Fat (grams): 35, Vegetables 0, Nachos 19
Sodium (milligrams): 1050, Vegetables 15, Nachos 965

Vegetables = Raw vegetable platter (carrots, zucchini sticks, cherry tomatoes)
Nachos = 12 tortilla chips with ¼ cup cheese sauce

SNACKING AT THE SHOPPING MALL

Snacks can be an enjoyable part of a shopping trip, and shopping malls offer a variety of foods and places to eat. How do these snacks fit into your total diet? Take a look at the calorie, fat, and sodium content of some popular items below:

	Calories	Fat (grams)	Sodium (milligrams)
Frozen yogurt, 1 cup	210	4	100
Ice cream cone, single dip	190	9	55
Popcorn, with salt and butter, 1 cup	105	8	145
Soft pretzel with cheese	275	8	1,175
Chocolate chip cookie, 1 large	190	8	160
Hotdog, with mustard, relish, and onion	240	14	835
Bran muffin, 1 large	140	7	210
Danish pastry	220	12	220
Mixed nuts, ¼ cup	225	21	240

Taking a Close Look At Desserts

Here are calorie, fat, and sodium values for a serving of some popular desserts. You will notice that serving sizes for different desserts are quite variable. For example, a serving of cheesecake is usually about half the size of a serving of apple pie.

Key:
F = fresh fruit cup
A = ⅙ apple pie
M = ¾ cup chocolate mousse
C = 1/12 cheesecake

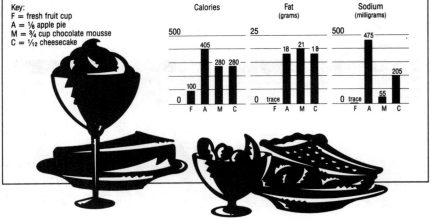

Calories: 500, F 100, A 405, M 280, C 280
Fat (grams): 25, F trace, A 18, M 21, C 18
Sodium (milligrams): 500, F trace, A 475, M 55, C 205

Benefit: Since you are going to limit fat intake, you aged to eat more of the delicious low-fat alternatives to fare, namely, the energy foods: fruits, vegetables, whole gra other complex carbohydrates. You'll keep fat intake (and we down—which is your key to more energy.

CASE HISTORY—
"Why Do I Feel So Tired All Day Long?"

Her dietitian heard Emma V.L. complain of her recurring fatigue. This 58-year-old housewife had many responsibilities she enjoyed. She had recently taken a part-time job as motel reception-ist, which brought her in touch with many people. She had pre-viously complained of being too isolated since her children were married and her husband went to work all day. Emma V.L. wanted to start her "new life" in the work force, but she kept feeling weary—even when awakening after what she believed was a good night's sleep.

The dietitian took a food profile, that is, a diary of what Emma V.L. ate throughout the day and evening. The profile showed an excessive amount of fats. Since Emma V.L. weighed in at 160, she was consuming some 2,500 calories and nearly 80 grams of fat every day. No wonder she was always fatigued.

She was put on a low-fat program—told to reduce to about 140. Her caloric intake was about 1,700 and her fat grams were limited to 47—even a bit less. Emma V.L. made the change even though she did like to eat more fatty foods than allowed. But her resolve was strong. She soon slimmed to 140 and with less fat intake, her energy started to increase. Before four weeks were over, she was vibrant, ambitious, cheerful. Everyone at the motel liked the lively receptionist, and customers praised her vitality. Emma V.L. controls her fat intake and is able to enjoy an energy boost that is the envy of younger people!

...are encour-
...higher-fat
...ns, and
...ght)

...| DOUBLE ENERGY IN MINUTES

...ler control, you can enjoy a meatless
...and cholesterol are largely found in
...louble your energy almost in minutes
...rogram.

...tired you feel after finishing a meat
...you are energetic after finishing a vegetar-
...you may want to follow a meatless plan three or four times
a week to help detoxify your body of fatigue-causing fat. Or you may
want to go on an "alternate diet" plan. Alternate days with animal
foods and vegetarian foods.

You may want to combine certain meatless foods to give you a
balance of the essential amino acids and other nutrients for production of energy. Try these energy booster combinations:

Legumes	Grains	Nuts or Seeds
lentils	brown rice	cashews
dried beans	whole wheat	pecans
split peas	corn	sunflower seeds
tofu	barley	sesame seeds
peanuts	oats	almonds

Suggestion: Combine any legume with any grain, nut, or seed
and you have a plant protein that is almost identical to the protein
found in animal foods. *Tip:* If you combine any of these with egg
whites or low-fat milk products, you have another top-quality protein.

Sample LOW-FAT, GOOD-PROTEIN, HIGH-COMPLEX-CARBOHYDRATE MEALS

Try any of these combinations, depending upon whether you want
strict vegetarian or some dairy and egg.

Black beans and brown rice

Tofu (soybean curd) with brown rice and mixed greens
Split pea soup with sesame crackers
Roasted soybeans and almonds
Chili garbanzos and mixed nuts
Oatmeal and low-fat milk
Macaroni and low-fat cheese
Bulgur wheat and low-fat yogurt
Garbanzo beans and sesame seeds in cheese sauce
Mixed beans and slivered almonds with yogurt dressing
Lentil soup made with low-fat milk
Sesame seeds mixed with low-fat cottage cheese
Chopped walnuts rolled in semihard cheese
Cooked black-eye peas with egg salad
Buckwheat (kasha) made with egg
Cheese omelet with sesame seeds

It's Easy to Energize on Low-Fat Plan

You need not abstain from meat or other animal foods, if you are tempted. But by relying less on fat-containing animal foods and increasing your consumption of vegetables, beans, and whole grains, you should feel satisfied and more energetic, too! You won't even feel the "sacrifice."

CASE HISTORY—
Loves Fat, Enjoys Superenergy on Simple Program

You could not tell Anna DeP. that eating fatty foods every day was to blame for her overweight and loss of energy. She loved fatty steaks, rich hamburgers, lots of butter in her mashed potatoes, a greasy breakfast, and heavy lunch, not to mention such a fatty dinner that she fell asleep in the chair, unable to clear away the dishes until she awakened a few hours later. She was a "fat lover" and stubbornly refused to give it up.

But when she started to stagger through the day, falling asleep in the middle of housework, she reluctantly went to see a dietitian at the local health center. An examination showed she was overweight and burdened by excessive fat intake. Still Anna DeP. complained, "I can't live without my favorite foods." The dietitian told her, "You're not going to live much longer if you keep eating those foods." She then outlined a program that called for meatless eating on alternate days of the week. Sunday, Tuesday, Thursday, and Friday were to be free of animal foods. The other days, Monday, Wednesday, and Saturday permitted animal foods, but fats were kept to a minimum. "A little bit goes a long way," the health center dietitian told her.

Anna DeP. reluctantly followed the plan. She had moderate meat portions on those days and then had the combinations (legume with any grain and nut or seed) on the other days. It was astonishing. She not only lost much weight, but her energy rebounded. In a short time, she had such a boost, she voluntarily cut back on animal foods, discovering that only very small portions were satisfying, instead of the large portions as before. She still satisfies her love for fat (in very small amounts) and has energy on the alternate program.

How to Spot Fatty Foods

As a rule, a food is likely to be high in fatty calories if it is:

- Greasy-crispy or oily—like fried tidbits and other fried foods, butter, margarine
- Smooth and thick—like rich sauces, cream cheese, peanut butter, cream
- Sweet and gooey—like candy, soft drinks, rich baked goods, and other desserts
- Anything alcoholic

HOW TO SPOT LOW-FAT FOODS

Look for these:

- Thin and watery—like tomato juice
- Crisp but not greasy-crisp—like celery, radishes, cucumbers, melons, and many other fresh fruits and vegetables
- Bulky—like salad greens

Be A DINNER DETECTIVE: TACKLE THE MENU MAZE

A restaurant's menu can provide you with the clues you need. The next time you eat out, put on your detective cap, get out your magnifying glass, and look for these terms, which clue you in on the fat content.

- *Higher-fat terms* are "buttered or buttery"; "fried," "French fried," "deep fried," "batter fried," "pan fried"; "breaded"; "creamed," "creamy," or "in cream sauce"; "in its own gravy," "with gravy," or "pan gravy"; "hollandaise"; "au gratin" or "in cheese sauce"; "scalloped" or "escalloped"; "rich"; "pastry."

Remember these words of advice when unraveling menu mysteries:

- Terms that usually mean *lower* fat include "stir fried," "roasted," "poached," and "steamed." Foods that are "grilled" or "broiled" can signal lower fat, too, if little or no fat is used during preparation and fat is drained during cooking.
- Words like "homemade" and "fresh" do not necessarily mean low fat.

How TO CONTROL YOUR FAT TOOTH

You'll enjoy more energy with these tricks to "fool" your fat tooth:

- Never eat when on your feet—dine only when sitting. This helps curb on-the-run eating, which tends to be high in fatty calories.

- Banish synthetic sweeteners—they tend to increase food cravings. Instead, use cinnamon in herbal tea, blackstrap molasses in cooking.
- Curb caffeine—it makes you jittery and more likely to munch fatty foods.
- Substitute flavored vinegar for fatty salad dressings.
- Watch out for hidden sources of fat such as frostings and sauces.
- Try substituting two egg whites for one whole egg in baked goods recipes.
- You love cheese? Keep skim milk cheese like mozzarella, ricotta, or cottage as part of your plan.
- Bean up your diet with these five ways:
  1. Puree cooked legumes in a blender or food processor. Stir in minced garlic, basil, and thyme to taste. Use as a low-fat spread for crusty bread or crisp vegetables.
  2. Chop cooked beans as a low-fat, high-fiber substitute for the meat in lasagna.
  3. Add cooked legumes to soups, stews, stir-fries, casseroles, meat loaves, and omelet fillings.
  4. Substitute cooked beans cup for cup for the bread cubes in poultry stuffing.
  5. Marinate cooked legumes in herbed vinegar with a bit of olive or canola oil. Toss into vegetable or green salads.
- Instead of using high-fat butter on toast, muffins, waffles, and pancakes, use all-fruit preserves. They're silky, smooth, and fat free. (Try spiced apple butter on a bran muffin or peach butter on oat-bran toast.) Always read labels of packaged preserves to see if sugar or fat has been added.
- With nonstick pans, you can avoid oil or butter in the pan as you prepare pancakes, crepes, or whatever. If you don't have nonstick pans, try no-stick vegetable spray. It adds a tiny trace of fat to the food.
- Look for fat content on packaged foods. Food labels with nutrition information make it easy to figure how fattening a food really is. Multiply the grams of fat by 9 to get the number of

calories from fat. Then divide by the total number of calories. If the percentage is under 30, the food should be good for your low-fat plan.

- Downsize and reverse portions. Are you a meat-and-potatoes lover? To eat lean, become instead a potatoes-and-meat lover. In other words, reverse it! Make potatoes (or other vegetables such as pasta, brown rice, grains, and legumes) the focus of meals. Use meats as smaller side dishes.

- You can control your fat tooth when eating at fast-food places with these tricks. While an occasional burger and fries won't be ruinous, you can have slimmer fare—even at these instant restaurants.

  1. Select restaurants offering salad bars, soups, baked potatoes, juices, and low-fat milk. Opt for a lightly dressed (or undressed) salad with fresh, crisp vegetables. Limit croutons or creamy salads. *Tip:* A baked potato minus rich toppings, skim milk, and citrus juice are good energy-boosting foods.

  2. Avoid those fatty sauces—and hands off fried fish and chicken. If you wish, try a lean roast beef sandwich with no sauce. *Careful:* Deep-frying makes fish and chicken as fat loaded as bacon cheeseburgers.

  3. Be fussy about breakfast. Taboo are fatty croissants, egg sandwiches, sausage, and biscuits. Opt for orange juice, pancakes, and plain toast.

- Use marinades of lemon juice, flavored vinegars, or fruit juices mixed with herbs when grilling or broiling and to tenderize leaner cuts of meat.

- Substitute plain low-fat yogurt in dips or sauces calling for sour cream or mayonnaise. Use low-fat yogurt to top baked potatoes and chili.

- Palm or coconut oils, sometimes called tropical oils, contain saturated fat. Limit or avoid products that list them as ingredients.

- When eating out, look for foods that are steamed, poached, broiled, or fresh rather than fried, creamed, crispy, breaded, or basted with oil or butter.

- Think "compact" when it comes to meat, chicken, or fish. If your portion is larger than a compact or a deck of cards (about three or four ounces), it's too much. Restaurant servings often exceed eight ounces. To save fat and conquer temptation, split the meat dish, or place half in a take-home container *before* the first taste. You would never dare take extra bites from the container.
- Avoid anything fried; obvious examples are French fries, chicken nuggets, donuts, and snack chips that absorb hidden fat.

Y OU CAN TAKE THE FAT OUT OF FATIGUE

Yes, fat is an energy robber and gives you FATigue. Keep fat under control and your body will be rewarded with more youthful energy. You'll have that "alive and well" feeling . . . when you take the fat out of your life and out of your FATigue.

HIGHLIGHTS

1. Fat is an energy robber. Counteract the fatigue with more complex carbohydrates, moderate protein, and low-low-low fat.

2. Some fat is necessary for health. Know your limits. Check the chart. Mark down your daily fat limit and stick to it.

3. Have snacks, desserts, sandwiches—but keep within your fat limits. Consult the accompanying at-a-glance charts.

4. Emma V.L. complained of constant tiredness that interfered with her "new life" once her children were married. The dietitian suggested a basic low-fat program that gave her new energy very quickly.

5. Try meatless meals to double energy in minutes. Look at the listing of delicious low-fat, good-protein, high-complex-carbohydrate (meatless) meals that satisfy and energize at the same time.

6. Fat-loving Anna DeP. followed a prescribed meal program that satisfied her every craving and reduced fat, but boosted energy.

7. Control your fat tooth with the tasty suggestions outlined; with these programs, you can take the FAT our of your FATigue.

•••*Nineteen*

Your minidirectory of power foods for instant pep

• • • • • • • •

Are you in need of a speedy burst of energy? Do you want to have more vitality to keep you going for most of the morning? What can you eat to give yourself more vim and vigor to accomplish your daily activities? The answers? *Foods!* More specifically—*power foods*. A snack or plate of different foods can give you an energy boost of your body and your mind.

How TO USE THESE POWER FOODS FOR MAXIMUM ENERGY

The key is variety. Your best approach is to build meals around a variety of these foods. That way, you'll tap into a wealth of nature's sources of energy boosters.

Remember: Choose Carbohydrates with Care

Beware of simple carbohydrates. These are energy robbers. They are much smaller chemical units and thus break down and enter the bloodstream rapidly. You are given an energy lift, but when sugar enters the blood faster than it can be absorbed by the muscles, rapid chemical changes occur in the body, resulting in a seesaw reaction. After rising rapidly, your blood sugar plunges to below the initial level, leaving less energy available to your muscles.

Select the complex carbohydrates that are low in fat. They consist of long strings of starches that slowly unravel when converted into your digestive tract. This chemical unraveling means that energy is released into your body and mind over a long period of time, an important consideration for longer-lasting energy.

Here is a minidirectory of such power foods that help keep you alert and vigorous for a longer period of time. Most are found at your local food market as well as health store. You now have a cornucopia of foods that help supercharge you with vitality.

Citrus Fruits. Rich in vitamin C, oranges, grapefruits, lemons, and limes tend to reduce the sluggishness of fat. Citrus fruits help liquefy and dilute the fat, flush it out of your body, giving you more energy. Additional fruits—apples and berries—contain a natural ingredient known as *pectin.* Pectin is a natural fat-fighter in that it limits the amount of fat that your cells can absorb. When pectin substances are released in your system, they tend to absorb water and bombard your cells, thereby releasing clusters of fatigue-causing fat.

Soybeans. They contain a substance—*lecithin*—that acts as a protective shield. Once metabolized, lecithin releases a by-product known as lecithin cholesterol acyltransferase (LCAT). This by-product serves as a barrier and defense mechanism for your cells. As fatty deposits are broken down, they become more easily flushed from your system. Remember, fats cause fatigue—so use soybeans to get the fat out of your body.

Asparagus. This vegetable contains an alkaloid, known as *asparagine,* that stimulates your kidneys and breaks down fatigue-causing fat.

Beets. Beets contain a form of low-level iron that cleanses blood cells and serves as a strong washing agent for flushing away fatty deposits. Beets also contain natural minerals which help wash away fats that accumulate in the cells of your liver, kidney, and gall bladder.

Cabbage. The high content of sulfur and iron in cabbage serves as a cleansing agent for stomach and intestinal tract to detoxify your system of fatigue-causing wastes.

Carrots. A good source of beta-carotene, a precursor of vitamin A that is able to "trap" certain fats before they clog your body and cause tiredness, carrots activate the metabolism by energizing your cells and promoting a fat-flushing reaction.

Celery. Fresh raw celery has a high concentration of calcium. This mineral energizes the endocrine system, producing hormones that break down fatty build-up in the cells. Celery also contains magnesium and iron, minerals that nourish blood cells.

Tomatoes. Rich in vitamin C and natural citric acids, tomatoes invigorate your metabolic processes. Tomatoes and the juice of tomatoes act as a diuretic by stimulating your kidneys. This combination, with enzyme-activated minerals, signals your kidneys to filter fatty deposits from your bloodstream.

Broccoli. This member of the cabbage family is rich in a little-known substance called *indole carbinol,* which breaks down compounds that might otherwise clog your cells and cause fatigue. This same compound helps to detoxify clogged arteries to give you more sparkle and vigor.

Bananas. Bananas are an excellent source of potassium, vitamin B6, and biotin, another B-complex vitamin, a trio of nutrients that helps to sweep away fatty deposits and promote a feeling of longer-lasting energy.

Beans. A great source of complex carbohydrates, beans help to give you a feeling of energy that can last for hours and hours. Be careful about adding any fat to a bean dish—a small amount will be sufficient but keep it to a minimum.

Peppers. Which has more energizing vitamin C: an orange or a pepper? Bet on the pepper. One of these green beauties contains twice the vitamin C of an orange. Include green or red peppers (rich in beta-carotene) in a salad daily and enjoy more sustained energy.

Seeds. High in zinc and protein, seeds (such as sesame, sunflower, pumpkin) also contain something called a *protease inhibitor.* This substance inhibits the accumulation of fat and boosts the metabolism of carbohydrates that will promote more enduring energy.

Wheat Germ. Rich in the B-complex vitamins, this food is also a prime source of B6, which is needed to help promote a feeling of emotional and physical vigor. This versatile food need not be confined to breakfast cereal. Use it in everything from baked foods to soups, stews, salads, and breads.

Barley. Competing with high-profile complex carbohydrates such as oats and brown rice, this humble grain does not get enough attention. Barley is rich in soluble fiber, which tends to soak up wastes that could make you feel sluggish. Try barley as a side dish, in casseroles and salads, or in soups. As little as one half a cup of cooked barley a day may be sufficient to help detoxify your system of fatigue-causing toxemia.

Chili Peppers. Ever notice how hot, spicy food makes your eyes water? That's because of a dynamic ingredient—*capsaicin*—that triggers natural reflexes that flood your respiratory system with watery secretions. This extra fluid thins toxic wastes that otherwise clog your breathing passages, allowing you to oxygenate your system for more energy. A small chili pepper a day helps boost your metabolic rate and give you a much-needed power surge . . . in minutes.

Garlic. This superfood has active sulfur-derivative compounds that cleanse your system of toxic wastes that reduce energy. Garlic also acts as a blood thinner. It contains *allicin*, an active ingredient that can revitalize your metabolism, whip up your energy, boost your immune system, and give you a feeling of youthful health. One or two cloves daily should act as a power booster.

Kale. A dark, leafy green that offers you beta-carotene to detoxify wastes that could otherwise cause sluggishness. In particular, kale has a substance called *indole-3-carbinol*, which is needed to rev up your metabolism and provide youthful energy. What makes kale so energetic is its high amounts of absorbable calcium to help stabilize your energy hormones in a proper balance.

Spices. Cinnamon, cloves, and turmeric in particular are able to regulate blood sugar, the key to energy. These spices improve the effectiveness of insulin production, a hormone that helps keep blood sugar in a balance that gives you sustained energy. *Tip:* Sprinkle a little bit on your salads and add a little spice to your life!

Strawberries. A sensuous taste, it is true, but there is another bonus. Strawberries contain *ellagic acid*, a compound that helps alert your metabolism, boost your immune system, and revitalize your body and mind. A bowl of strawberries with some low-fat yogurt—or just as a snack or dessert—will work wonders in giving you a power boost.

Onions. The sulfur compounds of onions enter your body's cells, stimulate your metabolism, rejuvenate your immune response, help protect against blood sludge. A few sliced onions in a salad can give you a "lift" that acts as a well-needed power burst—and it is long lasting, too.

Alfalfa Leaf. Once said to be fit only for cattle, it is now recognized as one of the best systematic alkalizers available. It is a prime source of vitamin K, needed for a healthier bloodstream; it has rich sources of calcium, potassium, phosphorus, nitrogen, and magnesium which improve your metabolism and give you improved energy.

Leeks. Leeks stimulate your glands and thereby clean your system of sludge that could cause fatigue. In particular, leeks stimulate the muscles when they are overloaded with fatigue-causing uric acid. They are also a rich source of calcium, potassium, and B and C vitamins.

Mustard Greens. A valuable detoxifying food, this green contains energizing sulfur and phosphorus, among other elements. The greens are most effective when the leaves are young and when eaten raw.

Peas. The trick here is to eat raw peas with their pods—either chopped or juiced. The rich potassium and magnesium content will help act as a tonic for your glands to give you a feeling of exhilaration and energy.

Radishes. Rich in sulfur along with many other minerals, radishes help detoxify wastes (particularly mucus and phlegm) so that you are not "choked" with wastes that could cause fatigue. A few sliced radishes in your salad will help promote inner cleansing and more vitality.

Watercress. A powerful cleanser of the system, especially your bloodstream, it dissolves fatigue-causing fibrin coagulated in the blood vessels. Watercress is rich in many minerals that cleanse and invigorate your system.

Apples. Raw apple or apple juice is a valuable energizer. Apples tend to cleanse your inner organs, washing away impactations that are to blame for tiredness. Rich in a variety of minerals, apples are often recommended at health spas for a fasting of short duration. *Tip:* Eaten on an empty stomach, apples have a slightly diuretic and laxative effect to promote regularity. This natural cleansing will help boost your energy.

Apricots. Tree-ripened apricots are excellent sources of nutrients that rejuvenate your red corpuscles and strengthen your bones, teeth, nails, and hair. *Careful:* Cooking may weaken the effect of these nutrients. Plan to use raw apricots as part of a fruit or vegetable salad. You may also whip apricots to creamy consistency and flavor with lemon juice for a terrific energy booster. *Tip:* Apricots are more energizing if ripe, at which time the flesh yields to slight pressure of your fingers.

Dates. Dates are an excellent energizer because of their natural carbohydrates and high alkaline content, which helps give you a feeling of sparkling vitality. Date sugar (in moderation) is a good substitute for other sugars.

Figs. Rich in many vitamins and minerals, several California fresh figs as a snack or part of a dessert, will help give you an amazing power surge. They are a rich source of complex carbohydrates that enter the bloodstream promptly and promote a feeling of energy that can last for hours and hours.

Grapes. A valuable digestive stimulant, grapes will alert your metabolism to eliminate fatigue-causing uric acid from your system. Grapes further help reestablish the needed acid-alkaline balance of the body to give you sustained and prolonged energy.

Grapefruit. Raw grapefruit helps dissolve wastes and deposits in your cartilage and joints, while improving your digestive system. For stiffness of joints and muscle fatigue, grapefruit may well be the antidote to promote vitality and energy.

Papayas. Papayas are a valuable source of *papain,* an enzyme that dissolves stubborn wastes and helps wash them out of the body.

In so doing, your vital organs become cleansed and refreshed and you feel more alert. If you must eat meat, even if you trim away the fat, some remains to cause clogging, sluggishness, and a sleepy feeling. The antidote would be to have a half cup or more of freshly sliced papaya slices as a dessert after your meat meal. The enzymatic activity helps break down the fats to wash them out of your system to protect against fatigue from a meat meal.

Pineapple. A highly valuable cleanser, the pineapple has a rich supply of enzymes, especially bromelain, which helps detoxify the system of fat-causing wastes. The pineapple also offers you sulfur, citric, malic, and tartaric acids, which are needed to sweep away sluggish wastes. Pineapple is almost always more energizing if eaten raw . . . and fresh.

Blueberries. This product of nature's own vast garden of power foods is a good source of *myrtillin,* an amazing substance that helps balance your blood sugar, much as does insulin. This process helps improve a steady supply of energy. Blueberries are prime sources of manganese, which acts to cleanse the bloodstream and stabilize your blood sugar.

Buckwheat. An excellent complex carbohydrate grain that offers you a balance of vitamins and minerals that improve your energy flow. In particular, buckwheat contains rutin, a substance that occurs in vitamin C in foods. Rutin helps strengthen your capillaries so that you are less prone to fatigue.

Cucumber. Why do you feel "cool as a cucumber?" Because this vegetable has amazing power of cleansing your system of fatigue-causing uric acid. The high potassium content along with sulfur will give you a feeling of well-being by regulating your sugar metabolism. Try cucumber slices in a raw salad and feel yourself more balanced and alert in body and mind.

Horseradish. Oxygen is a key to overall energy. It is part of the aerobic principle to exercise and drench your cells and tissues with the energy-producing oxygen. Now you can eat a power food that could do the same revitalization as an hour of exercise. Horseradish, when used as a condiment for fish or a salad, dispatches a volatile oil that helps cleanse your respiratory tract so that you breathe much better and more thoroughly. Some have found that horseradish helps open up swollen nasal passages troubled by allergies such as sinus or asthma. You can breathe your way to more energy with the use of horseradish. A little bit—perhaps a half teaspoon a day—goes a long way in providing you with oxygen-producing energy.

Rice. Select brown rice, please. It has all the B-complex vitamins needed for energy that are washed out in processed white rice. Used as part of a salad or side dish or even as a main meal with added vegetables, it sends a rich supply of vitamins and minerals throughout your body to give you a feeling of vitality and energy.

CASE HISTORY—
Almost Loses New Job Because of Failed Energy

A failed economy created a minicrisis for Charles O'C. who still had school-age children to see through college as well as a household mortgage to pay off. He not only lost his job, but he was troubled with failed energy. "My energy dropped along with the economy," he would try to joke . . . but it was much more serious.

He was fortunate in joining a retraining program and was soon able to learn purchasing and inventory so that he was hired with a very large company. His salary was soon to be more than he earned previously as a machinist with an electronic company. So far, so good.

Except that Charles O'C. was always feeling tired. He had to take frequent rest breaks. His eyelids were heavy. He fumbled with his words. His supervisors told him he needed to show more enthusiasm if he wanted to remain with this company. A registered nurse who had recently been hired by the firm was aware of the importance of nutrition for energy. She asked Charles O'C. to provide her with an eating diary for one week. She would then see what could be done to help him become more energetic.

As she suspected, the eating diary showed excessive consumption of fatty meats and gravies, strong coffee, as well as caffeinated soft drinks. Charles O'C. was told to make a tasty change—plan meals around the power foods listed in this chapter. He was anxious to keep his job and followed the new eating program, namely, more complex carbohydrates, an assortment of the many fruits and vegetables just listed, but very little fatty food. *Result:* In six days, he was filled with vitality and pep. He impressed his superiors who admired his new energy and promised him advancement in due time. Charles O'C. had a simple energy plan as outlined by the company nurse: complex carbohydrate raw vegetable salad before a meal, low-fat and high-carbohydrate main meal, and raw fruit salad for dessert. Yes, he could enjoy an occasional hamburger but only as a side dish while the baked potato was the main fare. A simple plan, but it revitalized his metabolism and gave him the energy of a youngster.

And in the midst of economic difficulties, he was headed for a new career at pay increases. Power foods as part of a daily meal program had given him the vital energy!

> *Salad Greens.* Try a variety—the dark-green variety provides the essential nutrients needed to revitalize your sluggish metabolism. Available are endive, dandelion, escarole, leaf lettuce, lamb's lettuce, radicchio or red-leaf chicory, romaine, and watercress, to name a few. If at all possible, try to eat raw greens. If the leaves are too tough, cook briefly in stainless steel or noncorrosible metal pan. (Avoid aluminum pots; they will affect the color and flavor, particularly of varieties that are dark green and high in iron.) Cook quickly in as little liquid as possible or steam the greens in the water that clings to the leaves after washing.
>
> *Grains.* There are many complex-carbohydrate grains—brown rice, couscous (made of finely ground wheat meal, usually semolina), and polenta (a version of corn meal), to name a few. Mix and match. Since they are all complex carbohydrates with almost no fat, they will function as power foods when eaten regularly.

CASE HISTORY—
Refuses to Let Fatigue Make Her a Housebound Invalid

In her early fifties, Ida K.T. began feeling more and more tired. Now that her children were grown and out of the house, with only herself to take care of as a widow, she was careless about her food intake. She would eat canned meats and processed vegetables. "Why bother?" she would say. "I have only myself to satisfy. Who will complain?"

Her metabolism did complain! She became more and more fatigued, unable to do routine housework, and moped around with a hangdog expression. When someone suggested she hire a maid, she lost her temper. "Are you saying I'm too old to take care of my own house?" In truth, she was in her prime of life, but it was her careless meal planning that was turning her into a "fatigue-troubled invalid" before her time.

She attended a lecture at a senior citizen center that dealt with energy. The visiting nutritionist explained how fatty foods can drain energy; he suggested a basic program of more power foods (such as those listed in this chapter) and a moderate intake of fatigue-causing fats whether from meats or dairy products . . . or even from oils, themselves. "Less fat—more fresh fruits, vegetables, whole grains . . . and modest meats or animal foods. Try it . . . you'll become energetic very quickly. I promise!"

Ida T.K. realized her fatigue was due to her careless meal planning. She started eating (and enjoying) succulent fresh raw fruits, vegetables, steamed whole grains, small amounts of fat-trimmed meats, poultry, and seafood—but the emphasis was on the power foods listed. In three weeks, the promise made by the nutritionist came true. Ida T.K. was so energetic, she could do her spring cleaning—forget about any maid for her housework. "I can do twice as much work now, thanks to the power foods!

POWER FOODS . . . ENERGY SNACKS . . . QUICK PICKUP

Use the power foods as part of meal planning. But you can enjoy them as an energy snack. Want a quick pickup? Try some California fresh figs, some pitted dates, a bowl of grapes, an apple, an orange, a few apricots, or a fruit salad. Take these power foods along with you whether you are going to work or for any other outdoor purpose, and instead of a candy bar with its "yo yo" effect, try any of these natural snacks. You'll enjoy a quick pickup that lasts and lasts! Pep up with power foods!

HIGHLIGHTS

1. Look over the list of fruits, vegetables, and grains that are rich sources of energy—enjoy them instead of sugary sweets that offer a burst and a letdown soon after.
2. Charles O'C. was able to safeguard his new career by overcoming fatigue with power foods.
3. Ida K.T. refused to believe she was "old before her time" because of fatigue. She changed her eating plan to boost power foods and soon had more energy than someone half her age—which she admitted to be in the fifties.
4. Energize your life with power foods—as meals or snacks!

•••*Twenty*

High-energy raw juices that pep you up speedily

Wake up and live—with a glass of raw fruit or vegetable juice. Revitalize your body and mind as the ingredients in raw juices alert your senses and give you a feeling of "get up and go" in a matter of moments.

Why should you drink instead of eat raw fruits and vegetables? The answer is that you should do both—but the nutrient power of raw juices can energize your system like a lightening flash. Raw juices make little demand upon your digestive system, going to work in a matter of moments to give you vitality and a feeling of energy. In addition to vitamins and minerals, raw juices have enzymes— power-packed nutrients that act as energy boosters and givers of life, itself.

Enzymes in Raw Juices Are Energy Boosters

Enzymes are complex proteins that help you digest food and absorb it via your bloodstream, dispatching nutrients to every part of your body. Enzymes are more than substances. They possess a vital energy that is essential to the function of every part of your body. Without enzymes there would be no life!

Cooked Foods Versus Raw Foods

When you cook foods, you weaken or destroy various vitamins and minerals—but you're also destroying precious enzymes. Heating above 118°F. causes them to become weak and unable to perform their life-giving functions. Heating above 130°F. as in cooking, even for a short time, will kill the enzymes—and while the food you eat has some nourishment, it is depleted of these life-giving elements.

Fruits and vegetables and grains and seeds are prime sources of enzymes—but *only* when they are raw and uncooked. Dormant enzymes in seeds under proper conditions can remain in suspended animation for hundreds of centuries—but they become weakened when subjected to cooking.

Enzymes, Digestion, Body Energy

When you chew foods, then swallow, your digestive system uses enzymes to remove vitamins, minerals, amino acids, and other nutrients to be sent via your bloodstream throughout your body for building health and boosting body energy.

Without enzymes, the food would remain in your stomach as a solid mass! It would not be broken down or assimilated. If you have a depleted enzyme supply, you experience only partial metabolic reaction, and, obviously, partial energy production. Enzymes are catalysts. They create the biochemical change of metabolism but do not become part of that change. After finishing their work, they retreat into your cells and await the next call to transform the food you've eaten into energy-building elements.

A certain number of enzymes are used up or destroyed in the process, so you need a steady daily supply to meet the energy requirements of around-the-clock metabolism.

Whole Foods or Juiced Foods?

Whole fruits and vegetables that you chew thoroughly are, of course, the mainstay of health. Yet many folks chew improperly or have dental disorders that make it difficult or impossible to fully chew and withdraw the enzymes from whole fruits and vegetables. Your body receives only a partial supply of enzymes from improperly chewed produce.

Fresh raw juices are a richly concentrated source of enzymes along with other energy-boosting nutrients. When you use an electric-powered or strong hand-powered extractor, the blades break down the tough fibrous connective tissues and "veins" found in many raw fruits and especially in green vegetables. The centrifugal action of the sharp blades will cut right through the woody exterior of the produce to release the energy-boosting enzymes and nutrients into the juice you drink.

Even if you have excellent chewing ability, it could be difficult to break through the fibrous interior of many plant foods; the enzymes remain locked within, to be passed out with the undigested matter during bowel elimination.

Juices Provide Energy

With fresh raw juices, you break through the toughest of barriers as the whirring blades of the extractor penetrate and release an outpouring of these energy-boosting nutrients. These fresh juices are, obviously, uncooked, and therein lies their energy power, since enzymes have not been depleted or destroyed as they would when subjected to cooking, processing, or preserving with chemicals. You *drink* the rich energy powerhouse of *all* the life-giving substances in the produce as put there by nature. You receive total nutritional energy from whole foods that have been made liquid in a matter of moments.

How RAW JUICES BOOST ENERGY AND REBUILD HEALTH

Enzymes in raw juice are speedily used to boost energy and promote healing and regeneration. They improve your digestive power; they participate in assimilation and elimination.

Raw juice helps to break down other nutrients into simple substances that can be rapidly absorbed into the bloodstream. The enzymes in the juices easily perform these complex biological processes without heat and without themselves becoming part of the change. For this reason, they are called catalysts.

A variety of raw juices is used by your body to provide a continuous source of these enzymes. Each enzyme is specific; that is, it works upon one substance only. After its work has been finished, it is destroyed. *Note:* You need drink only several glasses of freshly squeezed juices daily to have an adequate supply of enzymes and other nutrients available to boost energy and rebuild health.

Juice for Energy

For example, if you have been feeling sluggish, the remedy is to drink a glass of freshly squeezed orange juice. The powerhouse vitamin C will speedily supercharge you with energy and vitality in a matter of moments. The enzymes will use this vitamin C to repair broken or damaged cells and strengthen your inner structure so you enjoy more vigor and youthful energy. This is the power of a raw juice.

Remember to Include Fiber in Your Energy Plan

If you have difficulties with biting into hard foods, you surely will benefit from drinking your fruits and vegetables. But juices are not good fiber sources. Dietary fiber is in the indigestible part of plant foods. You need fiber to act as a bulk producer in the large intestine to help protect against constipation, relieve hemorrhoids, and prevent diverticular disorders. The spongelike fiber absorbs water and allows the intestinal contents to move through the system quickly. And high-fiber fruits and vegetables and grains require chewing and do give a feeling of fullness. You will need to eat a certain amount of fiber foods daily; remember, juices do not contain much, if any, fiber.

How to Get Enough Fiber Easily

In addition to daily juices, eat those foods that provide fiber: try fresh fruits and vegetables you can chew easily, preferably unpeeled. Add seeds or nuts to a raw vegetable salad. Add bran to muffins, pancake batter, casseroles; top breakfast cereals and salads with bran or wheat germ. Use bean dishes like soups and casseroles in place of meat dishes occasionally. Lentils, lima beans, and split peas are the easiest legumes to digest; use them liberally in casseroles and soups.

In other words, eat other foods in addition to juice to give yourself sufficient fiber.

Getting Acquainted with Juicers

Juicers, available at health stores and housewares outlets, work on a variety of principles. Choose one that is appropriate for your needs.

Centrifugal juicers chew produce and spin it at high speeds in a basket, separating the juice from the pulp. This pulp remains in the basket until it is removed.

Centrifugal extractors work on the same principle, but the juice is passed out through the sides while the pulp is whirled over the top of the basket into a pour spout and collected in a container, which may be removed at any time.

Masticating juicers grind produce fibers and press this fine paste through a screen. The pulp is extracted in the front. The juice drops down into a bowl.

What to Do with the Pulp?

In juicing, nothing need be wasted. You may add pulp to soups, casseroles, cakes, salads, quick breads.

Do not confuse juicers with blenders or food processors. A juicer extracts the juice from plant foods and expels the fiber. A blender breaks the produce and provides a mixture of juice and mashed pulp. A food processor purees or liquefies the produce.

Juice Can Be a Speedy Energy Booster

By drinking a freshly prepared juice, you make it easier for your digestive system. You extract the liquid from the fiber and speedily give your body the needed nutritional energy boosters. That is, the juicer separates the juice from the fiber so that what you drink is free of pulp. Your body is supercharged with top-notch nutrients in a matter of minutes.

For example, one glass of energy-boosting pineapple juice may be the equivalent of ten pineapples! Now you know why juices are called powerful energy boosters!

Should You Try Packaged Juices?

Are they fresh? Are they pure? Read the label. The packaged juice may contain high-fructose sweeteners, corn sweeteners, or artificial sweeteners.

Deciphering the Label

Keep these tips in mind:

- "100% Pure Juice," "100% Fruit Juice," and "100% Fruit Juice Blends" mean that the juice is actually all fruit juice or a blend of fruit juices.
- "100% Real Juice" or "100% Natural" are meaningless and do not guarantee that the product is made from 100% fruit juice.
- Any label that lists sweeteners as an ingredient means the product has sugar added.
- Avoid products labeled "Juice Cocktail," "Fruit Drink," or "Juice Beverage." And definitely avoid products that list water before juice!

Nutrients Are Weak in Packaged Juices

Canned, bottled, or packaged juices have no enzymes since the juices have probably been processed, and enzymes cannot stand heat. If you must have packaged juices, do so in balance—with fresh raw juices.

Juices for Energy Power

Juices are absorbed and assimilated, and thus feed your thirsty cells all their energy power, within 20 minutes after being swallowed. Now you realize the value of drinking a glass of fresh raw juice to "get you started." It works immediately, free of interference by fiber.

Juices are not to be considered a substitute for an energy diet, but their use will boost the benefits of your regular diet. This balance helps give you the revitalization you want and need.

How to Plan Your Juice Program For Speedy Energy

When do you need more energy? In the morning? in the early afternoon? late afternoon? early evening? late evening? Or do you need more energy throughout the day? Chart your needs and then plan to have one glass of juice when you feel you will be needing more energy.

Plan Ahead

No time to prepare juice? Make it earlier and put in a thermos or else in a glass jar with a tight cover that you refrigerate. Juices are more effective if consumed as soon as prepared, but if this cannot be done, then prepare them ahead of time. The point is to enjoy different juices to help regenerate your body and produce more energy, among other benefits.

Here are several easy-to-prepare juices that will speed up your metabolism and give you a feeling of energy almost from the first sip.

Morning Energy Boost. Combine the juice of orange, grapefruit, and papaya with rose hips powder.

Vitality Tonic. Combine carrots, beets, figs, radishes, and tomatoes with one-half teaspoon lecithin granules.

Brain Booster. Combine seasonal grapes, berries, pitted prunes, papaya slices, berries.

Wake Up. Apples (cored), bananas, oranges, grapes.

Spice of Life. Tomato, celery, pinch of oregano, carrots.

Vim and Vigor. Peaches, apples, lemon wedge, nonfat yogurt, honey (to taste).

Sizzler. Radishes, red and green pepper, bean sprouts, cucumber slices, romaine lettuce.

Pep Up. Tomatoes, green pepper, carrots, onions, cabbage.

Energy Breakfast on the Run. Combine banana with two tablespoons soya powder, one tablespoon honey, one-half teaspoon vanilla, one pint bottled spring water. Makes a tasty and energy-boosting breakfast in a glass!

Yogurt-Tomato Mix. Tomatoes, one cup nonfat yogurt, lemon wedge, honey (according to taste). Gives a feeling of alertness in moments.

Freshener. Combine pineapple chunks, orange wedges, papaya slice, lime wedge.

Fatigue Eraser. Carrot slices, beets, celery, parsley, cucumber.

Alert Yourself. Carrot slices, beets, cucumbers, bean sprouts, lemon wedge.

With an assortment of so many fruits, vegetables, and bean sprouts, you can revitalize your taste buds and body with endless juices.

CASE HISTORY—
Juices Are Miracle Workers of Energy.

There were frequent slumps for Eleanor N., until she felt (or feared) something was organically wrong. She rearranged her eating program to include more complex carbohydrates and fewer fatigue-causing fats. But Eleanor N. still had difficulties in doing all she wanted to accomplish. There were mornings when she remained in bed until noontime, and only then did she emerge because of obligations, but she still felt tired.

Then she happened to attend a demonstration of juice extractors at a local health store. The nutritionist explained how a glass or two of freshly prepared juices could work "instantly" in providing energy, especially for those who felt they needed a "quick lift." Was this what she needed? Eleanor N. purchased one juice extractor, then prepared several morning tonics which she sipped and swallowed upon awakening. No delays. It was astonishing. Eleanor N. experienced a surge of vitality. Almost from the first juice. She realized she needed a swift burst and the instant assimilation of juices would do the trick. She has juices daily, calling them "miracle workers" of energy. Delicious, too!

Which Juices Are Compatible?

Dr. M. C. Alfred Vogel, of Basel, Switzerland, and author of *The Nature Doctor*, explains, "Some people assume that it is permissible to combine fruit and vegetable juices, such as orange with carrot juice. This, of course, is no better than eating fruit and vegetables at the same time, which is apt to cause fermentation and flatulence, especially in sensitive people.

"Generally speaking, one juice can be mixed with another of the same kind, so that the best way is to take, for example, carrot with beetroot juices at one time and orange and another fruit juice some other time. This way your digestion will not suffer.

"As a rule, it is better to drink only one juice, not a mixture. What is more, sipping is much better than gulping it down, because little sips, properly insalivated, will avoid digestive disturbance. The energizing effect will be greater, too.

"Insalivating well helps to warm ice-cold juice in the mouth and so avoid chilling the stomach. A bite of crisp bread or rusk with each sip of fruit juice will help to neutralize the acidity somewhat and protect the stomach lining.

"If, in spite of all their goodness, you simply cannot tolerate fruit juices, mix them with muesli. Vegetable juices are best added to soups and stews, after these have been cooked."

While some people will experience more energy from only one juice, others find that a mixture of different juices will do the trick. Whatever works for you should be a part of your program.

Drink Your Way to Superenergy

All energy on our planet derives from the sun, and growing plants— fruits and vegetables—are the most available form of that energy. Make use of fresh juices for direct energy . . . and better health, too.

HIGHLIGHTS

1. Raw juices are tasty ways to supercharge your body with speedy energy.
2. Raw juices containing specific nutrients not found in cooked foods that help give you amazing energy.
3. Select a juicer at your health store that suits your personal needs.
4. Be cautious with packaged juices that are devoid of important energy-boosting nutrients available only in nonprocessed juices.
5. Eleanor N. was revitalized quickly with juices she called "miracle workers" of energy.
6. A Swiss doctor explains how juices can be compatible . . . or not.

····*Twenty-one*

Look younger, live longer, boost energy with easy exercise

How much would you pay to look younger, live longer, and enjoy more energy? What do you think it would cost to be able to gain control over your life and energies, recharge your batteries, improve your health, happiness, and outlook on life?

Such benefits are priceless—and you can have them for free, as a gift. All you have to do is get up and walk! That's right, just walk!

Simple WALKING BOOSTS YOUR ENERGY

Daily walking will help burn up excess fats and calories (the main cause of fatigue) and revitalize your entire body. Walking balances your blood pressure, helps lower uric acid levels, and makes your arteries more elastic and your body more flexible and youthful. Walking is an exercise that will increase your blood's oxygen-carrying capacity. This means you get more energy-boosting oxygen where you need it, faster and more efficiently. Because of that efficiency, your cardiovascular system learns how to work less. You experience a feeling of vitality and energy.

Exercise is good for mental energy. By making your heart more efficient, it improves brain circulation and functioning. A 60-minute exercise session—whether walking, cycling, playing tennis, jogging, swimming, or skiing—will sweep away the fatigue-causing cobwebs from your brain and give you a fresher perspective on your surroundings. You know you surely do "think better" after a brisk walk!

Exercise Daily—Feel Energetic

Basically, fitness is considered to be a level of physical attainment that allows you to endure vigorous exercise for long periods with good energy. *Note:* The energy needed to sustain this intense activity is dependent upon your body's ability to transport oxygen through your bloodstream—and the capacity of your heart, lungs, and muscles to take in and use this oxygen. When this happens, it means that your heart, lungs, and circulatory system (cardiovascular and cardiorespiratory systems) are well-conditioned.

How can you achieve energy through physical fitness? By setting up a schedule that includes daily exercise. You can begin with walking. Need an incentive? Here it is—*easy weight loss*.

While strengthening your heart and lungs, as a walker you will also burn calories, which is the key to weight loss. Few forms of exercise can promise such benefits at the low-risk rate that walking offers. It's easy to walk your way to a slimmer body and more youthful vigor and energy!

Getting Started

It's easy to walk your way to more youthful health and energy. After consulting with your health practitioner, map out a fitness walking plan on paper, taking into consideration your age and current fitness levels. Here are a few pointers.

Mental Preparation

Even if you haven't exercised in a long time, remember that walking is natural and easy. You need not "gear up" mentally. Most important is to try to walk every day, even if it is not far, or at least three times a week. Just get out there and move, whether you have a serious goal or not.

Physical Preparation

Warm up by doing gentle, nonbouncing stretches for your arms, legs, and back. Walking uses many muscle groups; warming up will make your workout comfortable from the start.

Wear clothing that is right for your climate. Layering is always helpful to prevent chills and heat loss in cold weather; net jerseys and loose shorts allow for ventilation in warmer weather.

PHYSICAL ACTIVITY/CALORIE COUNT

Calories Used per Hour	Activities	
120–150	Strolling 1 mph	Light housework
150–240	Typing, manual	Golf, using power cart
	Riding lawn mower	
240–300	Cleaning windows	Cycling 6 mph
	Mopping floors	Golf, pulling cart
	Vacuuming	Horseback (sitting to trot)
	Walking 3 mph	Pushing light power mower
	Bowling	
300–360	Scrubbing floors	Golf, carrying clubs
	Walking 3.5 mph	Tennis, doubles
	Cycling 8 mph	Calisthenics (many)
	Table tennis	Ballet exercises
	Badminton	Dancing (foxtrot)
	Volleyball	
360–420	Walking 4 mph	Roller skating
	Cycling 10 mph	Horseback
	Ice skating	("posting" to trot)
420–480	Hand lawn-mowing	Tennis, singles
	Walking 5 mph	Water skiing
	Cycling 11 mph	Folk (square) dancing
480–600	Sawing hardwood	Paddleball
	Jogging 5 mph	Horseback (gallop)
	Cycling 12 mph	Basketball
	Downhill skiing	Mountain climbing
600–660	Running 5.5 mph	Cycling 13 mph
Above 660	Running 6 or more mph	Squash
	Handball	Ski touring (5+ mph)

Shoes can be the most single important factor in your comfort and success in any activity. Don't wear running shoes for walking—they're meant for the high impact of running. Walking shoes help your feet roll along in a heel-toe motion and have more flexible soles for faster walking.

Start Your Personal Program . . . Easily

Think of scenic routes in your area (if walks are too far from your home or office, you may be tempted not to go). Attractive scenery makes walking more pleasant.

Speed and length of time at an increased heart rate are most important, distance is least important, especially when first starting out. Set a time goal you think is reasonable for your fitness levels, 20 minutes, for instance. Keep a chart of how far you went on the same 20-minute walk for a week or two, using familiar landmarks as reference points.

Slow but Sure Is Energizing

Work on improving speed gradually before lengthening the time of your workout. When you've been able to increase your speed significantly (a 17-minute-mile pace is a good goal), then you're ready to go out for longer periods of time, gradually stretching your original 20 minutes to 25, 30, 40 minutes, or more. Remember, for maximum energy potential, the trick is to maintain your best speed. Charting your progress can be confidence-boosting and motivating.

When you have a well-established program, vary your walks by climbing hills or stairs, extras that work your buttocks, thighs, and calves, as well as your heart.

A walking partner can add a personal dimension to the time you spend on the road or track. Strengthen ties with friends or family by walking together; pretty soon, walking will be a part of your energy-boosting life-style.

How do you pace yourself?

Build up slowly. No matter where you begin, you will be able to build up your exercise time or pace as your body becomes more fit. You can find out how hard to exercise by keeping track of your heart rate.

(See chart.) Your maximum heart rate is the fastest your heart can beat. The best activity level is 60 to 75 percent of this maximum rate. This 60–75 percent range is called your heart rate target zone.

When you begin your exercise program, aim for the lower part of your heart rate target zone (60 percent) during the first few months. As you get into better shape, gradually build up to the higher part of your target zone (75 percent). After six months or more of regular exercise, you can exercise at up to 85 percent of your maximum heart rate—if you wish. However, you do not have to exercise that hard to stay in good condition.

To find your heart rate target zone, look for the age category closest to your age, and read the line across. For example, if you are 43, the closest age on the chart is 45; your heart rate target zone is 105–131 beats per minute.

Note: Your maximum heart rate is usually 220 minus your age. The figures are average and should be used as general guidelines.

Take Your Pulse

To see if you are within your heart rate target zone, take your pulse immediately after you stop exercising. Follow the instructions included with the chart and you will then be able to monitor your progress very easily.

How to Take Your Pulse

1. Place the first two fingers of your hand at either side of your neck just under your jaw. You should feel your pulse easily at your carotid artery. Do not use your thumb; it has a pulse of its own.
2. Using your watch or the clock, count for 10 seconds.
3. Multiply by 6. This is your heart rate per minute.

To gain aerobic benefits, you need to elevate and maintain your heart rate for the duration of your workout within a safe but effective range, or "target zone," of 60–75 percent of the maximum predicted heart rate for your age. When you begin an exercise program, you should keep your heart rate at the lower (60%) end of your target zone. As you get in better shape, gradually build up to the higher (75%) level.

After 6 months, you can exercise at 85% of your maximum heart rate if you wish. But you do *not* have to exercise that hard if you don't want to.

To find your target zone, look for the age category closest to your age and read the line across.

Age	Target 60–75%	Average Maximum Heart Rate 100%
20 years	120–150 beats per minute	200
25 years	117–146 beats per minute	195
30 years	114–142 beats per minute	190
35 years	111–138 beats per minute	185
40 years	103–135 beats per minute	180
45 years	105–131 beats per minute	175
50 years	102–127 beats per minute	170
55 years	99–123 beats per minute	165
60 years	96–120 beats per minute	160
65 years	93–116 beats per minute	155
70 years	90–113 beats per minute	150

To see if you are within your target heart zone, take your pulse *immediately* after you stop exercising. If your pulse is below your target zone, exercise a little harder next time. If it's above your target zone, exercise a little easier.

Be sure to warm up

Before any activity, remember to warm up. This prepares your muscles for work and allows your oxygen supply to ready itself for what is to come. Muscles perform best when they're warmer (100°F.) than normal body temperatures (98.6°F.). Warm-up exercises include jumping jacks, skipping rope, jogging in place, and stretching. You can also warm up with a less intense version of your main activity—for example, walking or jogging before running. An adequate warm-up is 10 to 15 minutes.

Be SURE TO COOL DOWN

After an activity, the cool-down enables your body's cardiovascular system to return to normal *gradually,* preferably over a 10- to 15-minute period. *Careful:* Bringing your activity to an abrupt halt can cause light-headedness or nausea. The cool-down could be described as a "warm-up in reverse" because it consists of the same types of exercises as your warm-up. It's when you do the exercises that determines whether they are your warm up or your cool down. Resistance exercises and flexibility exercises, for example, are both effective before and after your vigorous aerobic activity. Always remember that warm-up and cool-down are just as important as the activity phase. Both can prevent many common injuries from occurring.

Three STEPS TO ENERGY-BOOSTING WALKING

You can walk your way to maximum energy with these three basic steps:

1. You should be able to hold a conversation with someone beside you as you walk. Walking alone? Talk to yourself out loud. Do you feel breathless? You're walking too fast. Always take the "talk test" to determine whether you are overdoing it.

2. Your walk should be comfortable and free of any pain. If you have discomfort in your jaw, neck, or chest, slow down. Never allow yourself to have any pain! You'll only defeat the purpose.

3. After your brisk walk, if you seem unusually tired, or if the fatigue lasts for more than an hour, the walk was too strenuous. Next time, walk slower and not as far. Your walk should be

energizing, not fatiguing. *Careful:* If you have a dizzy or light-headed feeling, or if your heart beats too fast while you walk, ease up! If you feel unpleasant, or if you develop insomnia or if your nerves are frayed, you've been pushing too hard. Be sure to "listen to your body." It will let you know when to slow down or speed up.

CASE HISTORY—
"Why Am I Losing My Grip? I'm Always Worn Out!"

It was only 2:00 P.M., but Brian U.J. felt as if he had already put in a full day. Work was piling up on his desk. The phone kept on ringing. He tried to push himself, but his body and mind seemed stuck in first gear. He had back trouble, felt a stress headache coming on.

Brian U.J. was tempted to reach for another cup of black coffee . . . or a candy bar. He needed more energy. He had been careful with his eating plan, included much less fat and more complex carbohydrates with moderate protein. Then why was he so exhausted? His nerves were frayed. What was wrong? Was he losing his grip?

The company fitness trainer listened to Brian U.J. and said, "You're letting your oxygen levels become depleted; I've asked you so many times to spend 30 to 60 minutes in an exercise session but you never followed through. Your energy-boosting plan works with better nutrition *plus* exercise. You can't have energy with only nutrition; you need to revitalize your oxygenation system with fitness. Even if it is only 60 minutes of brisk walking, it makes a world of difference."

Brian U.J. was told to devote this time to daily walking. It turned out to be a dynamic energy booster. The daily walk became a gentle and youthfully stimulating movement that generated high energy by increasing blood circulation, pumping fresh oxygen into his body, and relieving muscle strain brought on by stress.

It was astonishing. Within three weeks, Brian U.J. became supercharged with energy. He was "getting started" at 2:00 P.M., with so much vitality, he could even work overtime, if need be. His secret?

Energy-boosting nutrition *plus* 60 minutes of daily walking. A terrific combination that helped him feel younger than ever.

Aerobic Exercise Is an Energy Booster

Aerobic exercise is an energy enhancer because it boosts the level of oxygen in the bloodstream. "Increasing the amount of oxygen in your system is the key to increasing your energy," says David Gardner and Grace Joely Beatty, management consultants in Rancho LaCosta, California, and authors of *Never Be Tired Again*. "The glucose from your food combines with oxygen in your cells and produces the high-energy molecule adenosine triphosphate, or ATP for short.

"If there is insufficient oxygen in your cells, the glucose produces only 2 molecules of ATP. But with enough oxygen in your body for all the glucose to continue with it, 36 ATP molecules are produced."

Oxygenate your system for more energy with aerobic exercises—doctor-approved jogging, swimming, cross-country skiing, aerobic dancing (yes, ballroom dancing is energizing and fun, too), and brisk walking. You'll feel all the more alert in body and mind with the energy boosting of an oxygen revitalization.

Stress, Fitness, Energy

"The ability to handle stress is as important as, if not more important than, native managerial ability in rising to the top and functioning effectively once there," says James Rippe, M.D., director of the Exercise Physiology and Nutritional Laboratory at the University of Massachusetts Medical School, author of *Fit for Success*.

According to his findings, exercise is effective against stress because it produces beta-endorphins, the powerful, morphinelike substances that are linked to feelings of well-being. Dr. Rippe notes that being fit is helpful in boosting energy. He tells us that conditioned bodies adapt more efficiently than others to stress, pumping out less adrenaline and thereby limiting the degree to which the heartbeat increases. Furthermore, when you're in good shape, your body will release endorphins at stressful times—just when you need them most.

CASE HISTORY—
Husband and Wife Recharge Themselves with Exercise

Falling asleep after dinner made Walter K. appear much older than his 62 years. His wife, Helga K., was also complaining of constant tiredness. The couple operated a small dry goods store that took up much of their time, but there was no need for them to feel all that exhausted.

The couple made some nutritional changes. Less fat eased their fatigue. But they needed another energizer—exercise. Walter K. shuddered at the idea of lifting weights (not a healthy exercise and could be dangerous) and disliked workouts in a gym. Helga K. felt she could exercise only with her husband. She was willing to go jogging or participate in gymnasium workouts, but decided to follow a plan her husband would accept.

The exercise? *Walking!* Together, they worked out a simple routine. They set up a schedule. Every evening, at a specified time, when they closed their store, they would go for a brisk 60-minute walk. This would continue every single day. In so doing, they helped supercharge their bodies with energy-boosting oxygen and soon were able to banish so-called "aging fatigue."

Which Activity to Choose?

Whatever is comfortable for your personal needs. Pick what is most fun for you. Don't punish yourself. Don't overdo it. Don't hate exercise. Devise a program that you enjoy, feel comfortable with and are likely to stay with throughout your life.

How Long to Exercise?

The minimum amount of exercise involves walking two miles in less than 30 minutes at least three days a week or two miles in 30 to 40 minutes five days a week. *Important:* For high levels of energy boosting, the minimum amount is walking two miles in less than 30 minutes five to seven days a week, or running two miles in 20 to 24 minutes five days a week.

Any exercise, including walking, is an energy booster as long as your get your heart rate up consistently for 20 to 60 minutes. In practice, the best aerobic exercises use large muscle groups for at least 30 minutes. These exercises include jogging, walking, swimming, cycling (stationary or bicycle), rowing, cross-country skiing, and aerobic dance . . . the fun conditioner. It is the *continuous* activity that is most energizing, *not* the stop-stand-start that you have in tennis, for example. It's important to set your schedule and stick to it if you want energy boosting (and who doesn't?).

Walking Energizes and Rejuvenates Your Brain

Research shows that brisk walking can stimulate thought by increasing your brain's supply of oxygen; walking can boost your emotional energy through the release of natural, mood-elevating brain chemicals called endorphins. Regular walking can:

- Reduce discomfort of headaches by stimulating circulation to both your brain and scalp.
- Reduce risk of stroke by keeping blood free-flowing, by keeping your brain arteries more youthfully elastic.
- Reduce or eliminate risk of senility by keeping your brain's blood vessels free of plaque.

And, remember, exercise has an energizing benefit on your emotional health, too. Exercise increases your energy levels substantially. You'll be able to sweep away the blues, feel less stress, ease anxiety, and have a youthful feeling of creativity and confidence.

How much do you have to pay to gain all these rewards? Nothing—only your personal incentive. So get up right now—and take a walk!

HIGHLIGHTS

1. Exercise is the second half of your energy-boosting program (nutrition is the first half) that helps you look younger and live longer.

2. Walking is an easy and energizing exercise . . . although you can try other aerobic programs to help burn fatigue-causing fat and excessive calories.

3. Follow the guidelines for getting started; remember to warm up, cool down . . . and exercise every single day for energy boosting.

4. Brian U.J. feared losing his grip because of chronic fatigue—until he discovered a simple energy booster—daily walking! He soon became revitalized and youthfully alert.

5. Aerobic exercise helps send energizing exercise through your body and mind. Think youthfully with exercise.

6. Walter K. and Helga K. became an "exercise couple." Their brisk walking gave them dynamic energy in a short while.

7. Keep your brain young with energizing walking or any other oxygenation exercise you enjoy. Whatever, stick to it!

•••Twenty-two

Your lifetime program for vibrant living

• • • • • • • •

The very word "fatigue" is enough to make you feel tired. Why does it happen? How can you stimulate a tired body and mind and enjoy a more youthful life span? You need to identify the type of fatigue that is dragging you down, and then you need to follow a simple but dynamic set of steps to supercharge your batteries for more youthful energy.

For some of you, only a few simple changes will help beat fatigue. For others, more adjustments are needed. But fatigue, for whatever reason, can be overcome with the use of energy boosters.

Are You a Victim of Stubborn Fatigue?

You do not get tired once in a while. You stay tired, week after week, month after month. You may have some relief with rest, recreation, or even medication, but the stubborn fatigue returns to make you more worn out than before.

Stubborn or chronic fatigue is that feeling of an absence of energy. If you go through your daily activities, it is due to an enormous effort of your will. You force yourself through the day or night. But the truth is, you feel like a dead weight. Much willpower has to be gathered to do anything more than your necessities. And even routine activities can be a drain on what little energy you have.

You Are Tired Before You Begin

You can beat this fatigue once you identify the cause and take advantage of the many energy boosters available. Why are you so tired? Which of the following fit your personal picture?

Physical Fatigue

It can be hereditary but you still can reach your optimum level of performance when you get yourself in better shape. Conditions such as obesity, hypoglycemia, high blood pressure, and arteriosclerosis could bring on fatigue. But when you improve your fitness level, your physical problems are soothed and you enjoy more energy.

Mental Tiredness

Symptoms are yawning, drowsiness, and an inability to focus on activities. You may have pushed your thinking and creative abilities to the limit. You have mental tiredness when you perform the same task over and over again. In most situations, rest, a change of scenery, and some recreation, will help solve mental tiredness.

Emotional Fatigue

This type of tiredness is seen in those who hurry and worry. Are you caught up in a fast-paced society? Do you work against the clock? Are you trying to reach difficult or impossible goals? Do you face endless obstacles? You run down your body and mind and develop emotional fatigue. Even if you have a full night of sleep, you awaken exhausted. You cannot stop running! The key here is to lighten up on obligations, delegate responsibilities; tell yourself you can only accomplish a certain amount and no more. You are not going to run . . . run . . . run. You will stop when you have reached your limit. You'll ease emotional fatigue by putting the brakes on your activities.

Are You Bored?

A monotonous lifestyle, whether working on the assembly line or following a rigid routine every single day, can cause fatigue. The problem here is called "sameness," a routine that does not vary. You are fatigued because boredom means a decline of hormones in the brain; this lack of stimulation makes you sleepy. The remedy here is to start making changes throughout the day. Take frequent "breaks" wherever and whenever possible, and do something completely different. You'll feel the stimulation to your brain, nervous, and hormonal systems when you try different sparks to break up boredom of any sort.

Do You Feel Depressed?

It could be a vicious cycle. You are tired and then you feel depressed, and vice versa. Something is wrong. You have a bad case of the blues. You may try to escape reality with sleep but this means less activity and less energy and more glooms when you awaken. By easing your depression, by improving your nutritional picture, by becoming more involved in activities you enjoy, you should help improve your emotions and experience more energy. Above all, never let your spirits sink into self-pity. If you feel sorry for yourself, you become all the more fatigued!

Anger Can Bring On Fatigue

If you feel angry, if you lose your temper, you become drained because of the enormous emotional-physical strain placed on your body. Of course, you should not repress your anger; if you do, your muscles become tense, your blood sugar zooms, hormones pour into your bloodstream. These reactions become "bottled up" as you swallow your anger. You become exhausted. You are all drained out. You have a restless sleep because of this bottled up hostility. You need not start to shout and scream to "get it out of your system." But you can use reason instead of a temper, and you can become physically active to "work off" your accumulated steam. You'll then feel all the more energetic and happier, too.

Anxiety Can Bring On Fatigue

You're filled with tension. You are extremely sensitive to any situation that seems challenging. You are stressful and you worry. Apprehension causes hormone levels to zoom upward. Your body rebels and tries to protect you by "slowing" your activities. You could then feel gloomy and depressed. Your hormonal-nervous system balance has been upset, and you are caught up in an overload. The penalty is reduced energy and recurring fatigue. You need to cope. Roll with the punches. The strongest tree in the forest is the one that bends to the violent storm while others are broken under the impact. Become more flexible. You'll ease anxiety and the symptoms of fatigue.

QUICK-ACTING ENERGY BOOSTERS TO PUT SIZZLE INTO YOUR DAILY LIFESTYLE

How can you enjoy full-throttle living? It could be through using one or two amazing energy boosters. Your goal is to try to build as many of these remedies into your lifestyle to enjoy speedy or "instant" energy boosters. Is being pooped your problem? Then try these remedies to help you get recharged speedily:

1. *Breathe deeply.* Regular sustained breathing helps overcome oxygen-starved fatigue. Take frequent "oxygen breaks." Refresh your lungs and brain with more oxygen. Relax and breathe deeply for four or five minutes. Whenever you feel fatigued, wash away exhaustion with sustained breathing.

2. *Rehydrate yourself.* Since your brain is about 75 percent water, dehydration affects its efficiency very quickly. Too little water brings on fatigue as well as headaches and problems with concentration. Thirst is not always an adequate guide to your drinking needs. Fatigue often precedes thirst as a warning that your body's supply of water is running low. A good rule of thumb: drink at least six 8-ounce glasses of water a day.

3. *Keep yourself physically active.* Any exercise you do regularly will help stimulate your energy. Even if it as simple as walking or more vigorous as jogging or cross-country skiing, it should be done on a daily basis. Exercise helps elevate brain chemicals that improve your mood and give you a healthy energy boost.

4. *Prepare high-energy drinks.* Herbal teas—they are caffeine-free—are always helpful in lifting your spirits and giving you a good feeling. A bit of honey offers better taste and a touch of glucose to make you feel energetic.

5. *Try a nap.* This could be a personal remedy. But for many, a 15-or 30-minute catnap will improve your alertness, efficiency, and general mood. You need not drive yourself to the breaking point. Instead, plan to take an occasional daily catnap . . . and you should be able to supercharge your body and mind with an energy boost.

6. *Eat for energy.* Plan meals around energy-boosting, low-fat, nutrient-rich foods—it's easy! Enjoy whole grains, legumes, moderate amounts of lean meats and fish, and a variety of fresh fruits and vegetables. Remember, minimize intake of animal fats since they are to blame for your fatigue! A low-fat eating program does not mean eating like a monk! You can occasionally indulge in some rich food, but keep it to a minimum and eat only a few spoonfuls! *Careful:* Beware of labels that blazingly declare "no cholesterol" on foods such as oils, peanut butter, margarine, which are actually high in fat. Any type of fat should be limited if you want to enjoy more energy.

CASE HISTORY—
Feels Gloomy, Always Tired, Constantly Yawning

His family and coworkers thought Alex Q. was being rude. In the midst of a conversation, he would start yawning without control. He would nod his head and doze off. Sometimes, right at the luncheon or dinner table, he would be unable to keep his eyes open.

When Alex Q. fell asleep at the reception of his daughter's wedding, his wife decided something had to be done to give him more energy. An endocrinologist said he appeared to be in good health but needed to follow some simple energy boosters—more rhythmic breathing, adequate liquids, a bit more activity (he was a sedentary payroll administrator at a local lumber mill), and if overcome by an urge to sleep, to go off and nap for 20 minutes or so. Alex Q. did respond with more energy, but he still kept dozing off and yawning . . . although with less frequency. What was wrong?

His endocrinologist had him take various tests and the results showed he was still "cheating" with a high-fat diet. The animal fat was clogging his circulatory system, blocking free transfer of nutrients, making him overburdened with fatigue. The remedy? Much less fat. In three days, Alex Q. experienced such energy, he felt as young as a bridegroom. And that was good, because his other daughter was soon to wed and he was not going to sleep at the reception!

YOUR HANDY GUIDE TO GET YOUR ENERGY SIZZLING

You need to revive your sagging spirit, and your body along with it. If you have the feeling of weary-down-to-your bones fatigue, if you cannot take the dog out for a walk, if you cannot pick up your socks, then it's time to get your energy sizzling.

You can banish fatigue and boost your energy with one or more of these sizzlers. It's important to see what works for you and then to stick with it. Perhaps one energy booster gives you a more vibrant feeling. Or you may need several of them. You'll know what works when you experience the joy of daily living.

1. *Get enough sleep.* If you toss and turn the night before, you'll feel tired the next day. If you have trouble sleeping, follow these tips. Avoid any caffeinated drinks, especially after sunset. Go to bed at the same time every night. Avoid alcohol which interferes with sound sleep. Plan to ease worries or stress after sunset and condition yourself for refreshing sleep.

2. *Beware of diet-caused fatigue.* If you are on any unwise "crash" diet, you're vulnerable to fatigue. Depriving yourself of foods, denying yourself necessities, causes inefficient calcium metabolism and exhausted muscle tissues. This brings on tiredness. A sound diet includes a variety of foods, about 1,200 to 1,500 calories a day, gradual weight loss of about 1 pound a week. Avoid eating big meals late at night. Your body cannot burn off calories as efficiently at bedtime as earlier in the day. And, remember, *never* skip meals. You'll only play havoc with your blood sugar—and bring on severe hunger. Complex carbohy-

drates are filling and low in calories. Make them the mainstay of your dieting plan.

3. *Be sure to keep active.* Regular exercise prompts your body to efficiently deliver oxygen to your muscles, increasing your energy. Exercise seems to nourish your brain, makes you feel better and able to cope with everyday stress.

4. *Are drugs zapping your energy?* Various drugs such as diuretics, antihistamines, pain relievers, antihypertensives, oral contraceptives, and anticonvulsants, to name a few, may well bring on fatigue. Are your taking a drug? Does it make you feel drowsy? Call your health practitioner and/or pharmacist. Ask for a complete drug history to determine if this medication is to blame for your fatigue. Perhaps two drugs are zapping your energy. Whatever you do, *never* discontinue any prescription drug without consulting your physician first.

5. *Stress may drain away your energy.* Energy is needed to cope with the responsibilities of daily life. If you use up your supply of energy, you become overwhelmingly fatigued. You may be victimized by stress if, for example, you find yourself in a dead-end situation. You lose control. You feel trapped. To help minimize stress, try relaxation techniques. Take frequent 30-minute "vacations" from your tasks whether at home or at your job (or both). "Escape" for a while and come back feeling more refreshed.

6. *Do you have tired blood?* Take the iron out of a bridge and it collapses. Run low on iron in your blood and you may collapse, too. Women lose iron because of their monthly period and need to replace the supply. The U.S. Recommended Daily Allowance for adults is 18 milligrams of iron. It is also found in such foods as beef liver, dark meat turkey, and lean ground beef (but these are also high in fat, so easy does it!). You may also obtain iron from lima beans, sunflower seeds, apricots, prunes, broccoli, blackstrap molasses, sun-dried fruits, cherry juice, almonds, and raisins.

7. *Escape the sugar trap.* Sugar will give you a jolt, but you'll pay for it later. A sugar burst flooding your bloodstream prompts your body to release insulin, which rounds up the sugar for storage. Soon, your sugar "high" becomes a sugar "low." Instead, reach for a complex carbohydrate that is released into the bloodstream at a slower rate. You'll have a longer-lasting energy booster.

8. *Shed those excess calories.* Carrying 10 or 20 extra pounds can be an exhausting burden. Obesity wears you out emotionally, too. Get rid of those unwanted pounds, and you'll feel lighter and more energetic.

9. *A brisk shower is revitalizing . . . in minutes.* It may be cold, warm, or hot, whatever is comfortable. The trick here is to stand under *falling water*. It creates a set of negative ions—molecules with an extra electron that tends to revitalize your system. Ever notice how much better you feel after a big storm? Or how energized you become when near a waterfall? The falling water sends negative ions in the air to lower certain brain chemicals and allow you to enjoy newly released energy boosters. Try a 15-minute brisk shower for a supercharge of vitality.

10. *Wake up with an energizing breakfast.* You can use up to 750 calories throughout the night. Even if you don't feel hungry in the morning, your body has been depleted of nutrients that give you energy to face a brand new day. *Caution:* If you skip breakfast, you'll feel tired, achy, with the low-blood-sugar blues! Not to mention that exhausting midday slump!

11. *Have an energizing lunch.* A light but filling lunch, raw vegetables, or salads with legumes will keep you energetic. If you eat a heavy lunch, your work efficiency slows and you feel tired.

12. *Improve your social life.* Mix with happy and pleasant people who will help boost your energy. A circle of family and friends with whom you can exchange common interests can make all the difference between fatigue and energy.

13. *Explore new horizons.* Take a vacation—it could be to Europe or to a local resort or even a weekend in a pleasant vacation area. It's a surefire energy booster. (You'll feel it when you return.) Getting away from it all gets you out of your routine. Put distance between yourself and your obligations. You'll feel a supercharging of vitality. You need to take your thoughts off one thing and put it on something else. When your "escape" ends and you return, you'll feel an energy boost, you'll see life in a new context, and that is most invigorating.

14. *Set your goals.* Know where you are going. Give yourself something to look forward to. When you anticipate good things to come, you experience an energy boost. You will liven up, enjoy more energy. Give yourself a target. You may need a deadline to keep moving forward. Give yourself both short and long deadlines so neither becomes too routine.

15. *The largest meal could be lunch.* This is individual; if soup and salad and a piece of fruit do not satisfy you for lunch, then make this change: eat your major meal of the day at lunch and follow it up with a 20-minute walk. *Benefit:* Eating most of your calories early in the day will fuel your body to keep you active. Be careful in selecting the fuel you use. Complex carbohydrate is a swift burner to give you swift energy. Fat, on the other hand, is a slow burner, meaning it will slow you down. *Balance:* Complex carbohydrate with a little fat as part of your larger meal.

16. *Protect yourself from noise.* Whether noise comes from airplanes roaring overhead or from noisy neighbors in your midst, it drains your energy. Noise adds to your stress load; it could permanently damage your hearing. Noise makes you annoyed, irritated, and exhausted. Keep it quiet at home. Put carpets where noise could be muffled. You might even think of using earplugs to enjoy a little energizing peace and quiet. But avoid noise—an invisible but deadly energy robber.

In the *long* run, it's doing what you really want to do that becomes an energy booster.

CASE HISTORY—
"Am I Getting Old Before My Time?"

Fatigue kept creeping up on Dora Anne A. until she lamented that she was not even 60, anxious to continue working as a part-time schoolteacher while managing a household and taking care of her husband. Yet she was always tired. Even getting up was as much work as having to get the house in order, and there was little of that to do because it was a small apartment. "Am I getting old?" She would complain, "It's way before my time!"

A school nurse who was also a nutritionist took an assessment of her daily routine. She found the clues to the tiredness that made Dora Anne A. "old" even at a youngish 58 years of age. She told the part-time schoolteacher to have a good breakfast (she always skipped it) and a high-power lunch free of fat (no more greasy hamburgers and fries) and to take frequent oxygen breaks, try meditation, take walks, mix more socially. She was told to ease up on fatty foods and concentrate on more wholesome meals. These changes reversed her tiredness. In three weeks, Dora Anne A. was a powerhouse of such energy that she boasted, "I'm getting younger with energy all the time—thanks to energy boosters!"

HOW TO EAT YOUR WAY TO SIZZLING ENERGY

Just because it is a salad doesn't mean it has to be dull. With some tasty changes, you can enjoy meals that are high in complex carbohydrates but low in sluggish fat. Energize yourself quickly with these tasty meals:

> *Energy Booster Potato Salad* (high fiber, low fat). Toss cooked potato chunks with low-fat yogurt and reduced-calorie mayonnaise. Add green pepper, carrot slices. Sprinkle on curry. Toss in fresh dill and chopped scallions.

Energy Booster Dressing (low fat). Whisk together equal amounts of honey, Dijon mustard, canola oil, and rice wine vinegar. Then toss with shredded cabbage, chopped bell pepper, and grated carrots. Great as coleslaw!

Guilt-Free Creamy Dressing. Thicken low-fat yogurt with a small amount of reduced-calorie mayonnaise. Spice it up with curry or tarragon.

Short-Order Energy Salads. Toss a can of chickpeas or beans into a salad of tuna, peppers, capers, onions, carrots, and zucchini. Dress with balsamic vinegar and a stingy dash of oil.

Middle East Favorite. Try tabbouleh—made with quick-cooking bulgur wheat, chopped parsley, tomato, olive oil, and lemon juice. To couscous, add chick peas, dried zucchini, and bits of roasted red pepper.

Fruit Energizing Tips. Perk up coleslaw with apple chunks, pineapple, and raisins. Add slices of nectarine to a green salad. Shop for nutrient-packed, dark leafy greens, such as watercress, chicory, romaine, and Boston lettuce. Bitter-tasting greens may need getting used to so begin by mixing them with mild-tasting iceberg lettuce.

Salad for a Meal. Use leftover grilled chicken or barbecued steak by slicing the meat and serving it on a bed of assorted greens, surrounded by cooked potatoes and lightly steamed vegetables tossed with reduced-calorie Italian dressing. (You don't need a lot for an energy meal; remember that three to four ounces is sufficient and satisfying for animal protein.)

ENERGY-BOOSTING FOOD TIPS

- Top your cereal with fresh or sun-dried fruit; branch out from the usual bananas and raisins and try some berries, sliced peaches, diced melon, or chopped apricots, dates, and California fresh figs.
- Use fresh fruit to top your waffles or pancakes instead of syrup (saves on calories and fat, too!)

- For lunch, have a salad on the side—either tossed with low-fat dressing or a fruit salad.
- Add lettuce, tomatoes, bean sprouts, and thinly sliced cucumber to your sandwich; add carrot or celery sticks to the lunch.
- Mix fresh fruit in a carton of low-fat yogurt.
- Keep sun-dried fruit like raisins, apricots, or California fresh figs at your desk or in the car for nibbling.
- Keep cut-up vegetables in your refrigerator—they're great energy boosters.
- Snack on fruits like a bananas, figs, or dates when you want something sweet.
- Make a quick, low-fat, energizing shake by blending fresh fruit with low-fat or nonfat yogurt and skim milk.
- Add vegetables to your main dish, such as broccoli, cauliflower, zucchini with tomatoes in pasta casseroles or baked chicken.
- Instead of having only one cooked vegetable, stir-fry a variety of vegetables, such as broccoli with sliced carrots and mushrooms.
- Add cut-up raw vegetables to your green salad. Serve fruit salad instead of tossed salad for a change.
- Puree lightly sweetened fruit and drizzle over slices of low-fat angel food cake.
- Serve baked apples stuffed with raisins.
- Sprinkle chopped dates and a little honey on a banana sliced lengthwise.

Energy—how to get it, how to keep it

You can unleash your energy potential for a richer and more productive life. Eat the foods that add, instead of deplete, energy. Keep yourself physically and mentally active. Switch on your inner source of energy with a variety of foods, tonics, and snacks. Take advantage of those foods that boost energy—and avoid those that rob your energy. You *can* regenerate your body and mind with energy boosters.

Are you sick and tired of feeling sick and tired? Get ready for a new awakening—with the powerful energy boosters waiting for you. Reach out . . . and become energized—how wonderful it is!

HIGHLIGHTS

1. You are tired for a variety of reasons, nutritional, physical, emotional. Find yourself in these causes and take steps to correct.
2. You have a set of six basic-acting energy boosters to put sizzle into your daily lifestyle. Try them right away.
3. Alex Q. was able to energize his body and halt the embarrassing chronic yawning and sleepiness he felt on the job and when mixing with family. A simple nutritional change worked energizing wonders.
4. Try any (or all) of the 16 handy energy sizzling tips—they work swiftly and make you feel alive and active.
5. Fatigue made Dora Anne A. feel she was getting old before her time and she was not even 60. A basic dietary change made so much difference, she was soon feeling younger with more vitality than ever before.
6. You can eat your way to dynamic energy with the tasty tips presented. Delicious—and dynamite in terms of energy boosting that lasts and lasts.

Index

A

Acetylcholine, 16, 211
Aerobic exercise, 27, 305, 307
  as energy booster, 4, 70-71, 77, 167, 202
  and memory improvement, 27
Alcohol, 92, 93, 168
  avoiding, 188, 228, 247
  detoxification program, 108
  as energy thief, 107-8
  and insomnia, 133
Alert Yourself (juice), 292
Alfalfa leaf, 275
Allicin, 274
Almonds, 101
Alzheimer's disease, 15, 17-18
Anemia, 214
Anger, and fatigue, 313
Animal protein, 86
Anise, 23
Antihistamines/antihypertensives/anti convulsants, and fatigue, 317
Anxiety, 93
  and fatigue, 313-14
Apples, 276
Apricots, 52, 54, 57, 276
Aromatherapy, 40-45, 203-4
  case history, 204
  energy-boosting scents, 203
Ascorbic acid, *See* Vitamin C
Asparagus, 52, 99
Aspirin, and CFS, 37

B

Bananas, 7, 28, 51, 52, 151, 273
Banana Yogurt Energizer, 171-72
Barley, 197, 273-74
Bayberry, 102
B-complex vitamins, 6, 7, 9-10, 27-28, 74, 167, 171

Beans, 273
  See also specific types
Beef liver, 52
Bee pollen, 23
Beets, 52, 272
Berberine, 102
Berries, 51
Beta-carotene, 167
Beta-endorphins, 305
Bilboa extract, 23
Biogenic amines, 211
Biological clock, resetting, 129
Bipolar depression, 212
Black beans, 151
Black cohosh, 102
Blackstrap molasses, 52, 54, 59, 120
Blood-brain barrier, 16
Blood sugar, 170, 316
  defined, 82-83
  and ketosis, 114
  seesaw, 85
Blueberries, 277
Blue cohosh, 23
Blue (color), and depression, 218, 220
Body-mind makeover, planning for, 193
Boredom, and fatigue, 312
Brain Booster (juice), 291
Brain food, 13-29
  choline, 15-18, 20
  herbal teas, 22-23
  herbs, 20-24
  Morning Brain Tonic, 20
  tryptophan, 18
  tyrosine, 18-20
Bran, 101, 187, 288
Breakfast:
  Banana Yogurt Energizer, 171-72
  Breakfast Energy Food, 90, 92
  Energy Booster Breakfast, 172-73
  energy-boosting foods for, 171
  Energy Breakfast, 194-95
  and fatigue, 6, 73, 318